THE DESPOT'S APPRENTICE

BRIAN KLAAS

The Despot's Apprentice

Donald Trump's Attack on Democracy

HOT BOOKS

Hot Books may be purchased in bulk at special discounts for sales promotion, corporate gifts, fund-raising, or educational purposes. Special editions can also be created to specifications. For details, contact the Special Sales Department, Skyhorse Publishing, 307 West 36th Street, 11th Floor, New York, NY 10018 or info@skyhorsepublishing.com.

Hot Books® and Skyhorse Publishing® are registered trademarks of Skyhorse Publishing, Inc.®, a Delaware corporation.

Visit our website at www.hotbookspress.com.

10 9 8 7 6 5 4 3 2 1

Library of Congress Cataloging-in-Publication Data has been applied for.

Cover design by David Gee

Print ISBN: 978-1-5107-3585-9
Ebook ISBN: 978-1-5107-3593-4

Printed in Canada

To Ellie,
Always there,
Always right.

CONTENTS

FOREWORD

The world is burning, and yet the firelight illuminates the way out. The times are dire, even catastrophic. Nonetheless we can sense a grand awakening, a growing realization all around the globe that "people have the power, to dream, to rule, to wrestle the world from fools" in the prophetic words of Patti Smith.

But in order to rouse ourselves from the nightmares that hold us in their grip, we need to know more about the forces that bedevil us, the structures of power that profit from humanity's exploitation and from that of the earth. That's the impetus behind Hot Books, a series that seeks to expose the dark operations of power and to light the way forward.

Skyhorse publisher Tony Lyons and I started Hot Books in 2015 because we believe that books can make a difference. Since then the Hot Books series has shined a light on the cruel reign of racism and police violence in Baltimore (D. Watkins' "The Beast Side"); the poisoning of U.S. soldiers by their own environmentally reckless commanding officers (Joseph Hickman's "The Burn Pits"); the urgent need to hold U.S. officials accountable for their criminal actions during the war on terror (Rachel Gordon's "American Nuremberg"); the covert manipulation of the media by intelligence agencies (Nicholas Schou's "Spooked"); the rise of a rape culture on campus (Kirby Dick and Amy Ziering's "The

Hunting Ground"); the insidious demonizing of Muslims in the media and Washington (Arsalan Iftikhar's "Scapegoats"); the crackdown on whistleblowers who know the government's dirty secrets (Mark Hertsgaard's "Bravehearts"); the disastrous policies of the liberal elite that led to the triumph of Trump (Chris Hedges' "Unspeakable"); the American wastelands that gave rise to this dark reign (Alexander Zaitchik's "The Gilded Rage"); the energy titans and their political servants who are threatening human survival (Dick Russell's "Horsemen of the Apocalypse.") And the series continues, going where few publishers dare.

Hot Books are more condensed than standard-length books. They're packed with provocative information and points of view that mainstream publishers usually shy from. Hot Books are meant not just to stir readers' thinking, but to stir trouble.

Hot Books authors follow the blazing path of such legendary muckrakers and troublemakers as Upton Sinclair, Lincoln Steffens, Rachel Carson, Jane Jacobs, Jessica Mitford, I.F. Stone and Seymour Hersh. The magazines and newspapers that once provided a forum for this deep and dangerous journalism have shrunk in number and available resources. Hot Books aims to fill this crucial gap.

American journalism has become increasingly digitized and commodified. If the news isn't fake, it's usually shallow. But there's a growing hunger for information that is both credible and undiluted by corporate filters.

A publishing series with this intensity cannot keep burning in a vacuum. Hot Books needs a culture of equally passionate readers. Please spread the word about these titles – encourage your bookstores to carry them, post comments about them in online stores and forums, persuade your book clubs, schools, political groups and community organizations to read them and invite the authors to speak.

We're engaged in a war of ideas, a war for the hearts and minds of the American people. For too long, this war has been dominated by Fox News, right-wing talk radio and the bestsellers that they manufacture. And by the corporate-sponsored discourse of the liberal media -- including the New York Times and NPR-blessed authors and pundits who keep their social commentary within acceptable boundaries.

It's time to go beyond this packaged news and propaganda. It's time for Hot Books...journalism without borders.

David Talbot, 2017

INTRODUCTION

AMERICAN AUTHORITARIANISM?

It could never happen in America. Right?

Two years ago, in Minsk, I met with Mikalai Statkevich, a presidential candidate in Belarus—a country often called the "last dictatorship in Europe." During his campaign, Statkevich had spoken out in favor of democracy and had organized a peaceful protest against the dictator, Alexander Lukashenko. For those "crimes," Statkevich was beaten, then abducted. Thugs from the ruling regime grabbed him, put a bag over his head, and forced him into a van. For an hour, they drove around without telling Statkevich where they were heading. His mind was racing. Was he being taken to a secluded forest to be shot? A dirt road to be beaten to death? Would he ever see his family again? As it turned out, Statkevich was tossed into a cold, dark, bare jail cell and left to rot. The regime allowed him to speak to his family for only one hour per year. Other dissidents from the opposition were tortured, handcuffed onto a medieval-style rack, and stretched until their bones cracked and they "confessed." In that horrifying environment, Statkevich watched five years of his life slip by, day after bleak day.

When Statkevich finished his story, both of us were shaken by what he had just told me. Then, Statkevich looked me straight in the eye and said: "You don't know how lucky you are. Never take your democracy for granted. You won't realize what it's worth until it's too late."[1]

I study despots. The president of Belarus is one; Donald Trump, the current US president, is not. But Trump is acting like a despot's apprentice—an understudy in authoritarian tactics—who threatens to corrupt democracy beyond repair. A year since his election in November 2016, he has already done serious damage—and it could get much worse.

Trump is no Mussolini or Hitler, no Stalin or Castro. Anyone who makes those comparisons is an alarmist, belittling the suffering of millions at the hands of those tyrants. Trump is hardly an evil mastermind. Instead, he is a democratically elected leader, operating within the confines of one of the world's most stable and robust democracies. His behavior is constrained by democratic institutions, and his decisions are scrutinized by a robust and free press. Even if he wishes it were otherwise, Trump cannot rule by decree. In fact, during his campaign, Trump promised to enact ten major pieces of legislation within his first 100 days. He has, so far, enacted none of them. How can a man who has struggled even to change the health care laws or build a wall be authoritarian?

Over the years, I have learned that most despots are not only twisted, but also incompetent. They are often bumbling, tragicomically unready characters who are defined not by their disciplined efficiency or effectiveness but by their reckless authoritarian instincts and impulses. Sometimes, those instincts are married to a destructive ideology, such as Nazism or Communism. But much of the time, despots are driven by narcissism, an unquenchable ego that yearns for fame, public adoration, and stardom. For many authoritarian leaders throughout history, their greatest fear was that they would be nobodies—once gone, soon forgotten.

INTRODUCTION

Despots dread being, as Trump often says in his most stinging insults, someone "that you've never heard of."

Take Paraguay's longtime dictator, Alfredo Stroessner. He ruled the South American nation for thirty-five years, until a military coup in 1989 forced him into exile. During his reign, Stroessner wanted to make sure that everyone was constantly thinking of him. He erected a giant flashing neon sign with his name on it overlooking Asunción, the capital city. Photos of Stroessner were everywhere. His name was everywhere. He even renamed a city after himself: Puerto Stroessner. But he also wanted to make sure that you knew he was the best despot—like you'd never seen before. To make sure his subjects knew he was getting things done, bigly, he referred to himself as "El Excelentísimo."

Stroessner's ego was deadly. Challenging his cult of personality was dangerous. One senator who dared, Carlos Levi Rufinelli, was tortured six separate times. The regime used torture to enforce its narrative of what was true and what was false. "When they put the needles under your fingernails," Rufinelli later recalled, "you tell them anything, you denounce everybody, and then they say, 'See, you were lying to us all the time.'" In one particularly barbaric episode, Stroessner's regime recorded the screams of a schoolteacher, Martin Almada, as he was being tortured for the "crime" of advocating for higher teacher pay. Thugs from the regime then called Almada's wife and played the recording for her. Next, they delivered his blood-soaked clothes to her house. An attached note instructed her to come and collect his corpse. Her husband wasn't actually dead, but she died of a heart attack at the shock.[2]

Stroessner's impulses grew more destructive because he was operating in a system that indulged rather than blocked them.

When people could have stood up to him, they backed down. Over time, Stroessner got away with worse and worse abuses.

When someone with authoritarian instincts and autocratic impulses enters any political scene, there are three major ways to stop them becoming a despot.

First, there's preventing them from getting into power. Demagogues are a dime a dozen. They are harmless if nobody listens to them. Most would-be demagogues and despots just scream into the wind, because their dangerous fantasies are never married to real power. Stroessner or Stalin would have been "nobodies" had they remained an irrelevance on the fringe.

Second, the political system can block a would-be demagogue in power from becoming a despot. When a dictator seizes power in a place like Turkmenistan or Equatorial Guinea, there aren't any serious checks and balances in place to stop them from becoming a tyrant. However, in many countries, such as the United States, robust institutions exist that were conceived and established to divide power rather than consolidate it. Those institutions are helpful at blocking the rise of a despot, but they are not failsafe.

If those institutions fail, the final roadblock to despots is the people. American-style checks and balances are not imbued with magical powers—they are only as strong as those who deploy them when democracy is under duress. Physically, the US Constitution is no more than ink on a piece of parchment. People, not institutions or documents, protect democracy. If the citizenry allows democracy to wane, it will.

Donald Trump has authoritarian instincts and reckless autocratic impulses that have already been boosted since he acquired presidential power. Still, American democracy is resilient. The democratic institutions and democratic values of the people are a serious bulwark against any effort to advance authoritarianism. For example, when Trump repeatedly said during the campaign that the United States should bring back torture because "it works,"[3] politicians, journalists, activists, ordinary citizens, and even the military pushed back. He has dropped it—for now. Democracy in the United States will not fade easily. But it could still fade, ebbing away day after bleak day, until it's too late. Well-established democracies like the United States don't usually die with a bang. If authoritarianism is going to establish a beachhead on America's shores, it will creep up on us, and democracy will go out with a whimper.

Democracy is fragile. Like a sandcastle, it takes a long time to build and even longer to perfect, but can be washed away with a single powerful wave—like a military coup d'état or a revolution. Thankfully, those powerful waves are unlikely in the United States. But democracy can also be eroded gradually, as each wave takes a few grains of sand with it, year after year. The Trump waves are the most serious threat to American democracy in modern history. Most of the main pillars upon which democracy stands firm—the press, rule of law, ethics guidelines, voting rights, election integrity, respect for independent institutions, and even a shared sense of what is true and what is false—are under attack. Trump is the one behind these attacks, using tried and true authoritarian tactics that are familiar to those who live under despots and dictators but not to citizens of the United States. Unfortunately, to those in the know, Trump's practices seem chillingly familiar.

For the last six years, I've interviewed hundreds of people on the frontlines of the global battle for democracy—in sub-Saharan Africa, the Middle East, Southeast Asia, and beyond the Iron Curtain of the former Soviet Union. I've met with former despots and dictators and the (surviving) candidates who challenged them; with torture victims and those who oversaw their torture; with journalists and government spin doctors; with top-level ministers and the rebels who sought to depose them; and with coup plotters and the generals who stopped them. From the Sovietized streets of Belarus to Thailand's military dictatorship, and from the dysfunction of Madagascar to the toppled dictatorship of Tunisia, I've sought to understand how authoritarianism spreads and democracy dies.

Living in these countries for extended periods was a crash course in the tactics and methods of despots. I saw how they manipulate the truth, using lies as tools of control. I saw how despots abuse or destroy the press, silencing any independent sources of information that could undercut their lies. I saw how despots jail their opponents and pardon their allies. I saw how despots scheme to rig elections to ensure their own victories. I saw how despots scapegoat unpopular minorities, deflecting blame for their own failures. I saw how despots make a mockery of government ethics and indulge in kleptocracy, a regime of corrupt thieves who use political power to line their own pockets. I saw how despots reward their families, hiring based on bloodlines rather than résumé lines. I saw how despots politicize institutions that dare challenge them, turning popular anger toward the increasingly rare voices of dissent from within their regime. And I saw how despots whip their supporters into a rally-around-the-flag frenzy of misplaced patriotism, wrongly equating people who oppose the government with people who oppose the nation.

There are now rumblings of these tactics in America. They are distant—for now. The horrors I've seen first hand—of dissidents with spinal injuries and emaciated children scrounging for food in garbage piles—are the real and ugly face of authoritarian despotism. The United States, for all its problems, is nowhere near these human catastrophes or government failures. Claiming otherwise is hyperbole that minimizes far worse atrocities and abuses. But the death of democracy and the rise of authoritarianism start with complacency. In places where democracy has recently been destroyed, such as Thailand or Turkey or the Philippines, or where democracy is fading fast, as in Hungary, would-be despots have chipped away at the limits placed on their power. Left unchallenged, aspiring strongmen grow bolder. Citizens often don't realize what is happening—until it's too late.

In the United States, we have not yet reached that tipping-point. Americans are some of the luckiest people on Earth. We are born into a society of riches and freedoms. There's poverty and inequality and injustice, but we are blessed with democratic avenues to redress those grievances. People can protest openly. We have a meaningful say in decisions made about our lives. When we speak out, we are protected, not tortured. Sadly, though, what we take for granted can be taken away.

The Founding Fathers of the United States anticipated that this moment would arrive. They designed a system built to withstand a divisive demagogue. They put checks and balances in place. They carved out a separation of powers that makes it difficult to consolidate power in a single person. But their enduring genius is being tested in ways they could not have anticipated. Americans are split, and despots are most likely to emerge when the political or economic system—or both—fractures. As a nation fractures, it creates an opening that an opportunistic, self-interested demagogue can exploit. That opening now exists in the United States, and Donald Trump is starting to exploit it.

So, how did we get here? Abraham Lincoln famously said that "a house divided against itself cannot stand." He was right.

Political polarization has spun out of control, as centrifugal forces push Red (Republican) and Blue (Democratic) America further and further apart. Partisanship has become more about tribal identity than about disagreements on how to govern American society. For many Americans, being a Democrat or a Republican is a fundamental character trait, not a flexible opinion.

Today, that's more problematic than ever before, because the gulf between Democrats and Republicans is wider than at any previous point in modern history. For both parties, the extremes have become more extreme—and there are more people who consistently express far-left or far-right views than at any point in recent history. Perhaps most damaging is the rising perception that those from the rival party are not just disagreeing compatriots but disagreeable enemies. In the late 1950s, a poll asked Americans whether they hoped their daughter would marry a Democrat or a Republican. The majority said they didn't care either way; it was an unimportant characteristic of a potential partner. In 2016, nearly two-thirds of respondents said they wanted their child to marry someone from their own political party.[4] In such an environment, where acceptable love is defined by party affiliation, how can a democratic system—built on shared values and hard-fought compromise—thrive?

Several drivers are accelerating this American polarization. The menu of media options has lengthened considerably in the last few decades, so Americans can now self-select into partisan echo chambers that affirm their beliefs while demonizing their political rivals as enemies. Depending on which item you choose from the menu, you could think that the world is all blue skies or that the sky is falling. In a vicious feedback loop, our pre-existing biases shape the news we choose, and the news we choose reinforces our pre-existing biases.

That feedback loop is compounded by the rise of uncompetitive elections across the country. In the 2016 elections for the House of Representatives, the average margin of victory was a huge 37.1 per cent—a figure you'd expect to see in the sham elections of North Korea, not in the United States.[5] Only eight incumbent members of the US House of Representatives lost their re-election bids—in a body of 435 elected officials—even though polls consistently show that Congress is about as popular as cockroaches.[6] Some blame can be put on gerrymandering, the cynical drawing of inkblot-like district lines to distort the will of voters. Some blame should be put on ourselves, too, as most of us move to places where people think like us—it is hard to imagine a competitive election between Republicans and Democrats in either downtown San Francisco or rural Alabama. And, of course, there's plenty of blame due to the absurd pile of money being injected into American politics, where it's hard to win without millions to spend. For a system that is supposed to be built on fairness and competition, these developments are damning.

As our elections become less and less competitive, politicians become more and more extreme. After all, if you were a politician running to get elected in a district that was 85 per cent Republican or 85 per cent Democratic, why would you ever compromise? You'd know that you could never lose, except following a primary challenge from within your own party. The smart and rational move is to vote rigidly along party lines and work against "the other side," and these days that's precisely what most politicians do. Their constituents become more extreme in turn. Many voters in solidly red or solidly blue districts stop voting. Why bother? They already know who is going to win. They disengage. Another powerful negative feedback loop.

Furthermore, there is a rising and justifiable backlash against the United States government for its failures to deliver economic prosperity to all citizens. Between 1935 and 1960, the average voter's standard of living roughly doubled. Like clockwork, it doubled again over the next quarter century, from 1960 to 1985. But then, from 1985 to 2010, it stagnated.[7] Since then, the average American hasn't seen much improvement. At the same time, incomes for the richest Americans have soared. Economic growth has boomed, but wages have flat-lined. Economic inequality is now at historically high levels.[8] Decades of steady GDP growth mask the hidden reality of a skewed economy. The rich are thriving; the rest are surviving. Parts of rural America are dying.

I witnessed those changes firsthand when I was co-managing a campaign for governor in my home state of Minnesota during 2009–10. Our campaign crisscrossed the state, visiting all eighty-seven counties in eighty-seven days. In the wake of the Great Recession of 2008–9, it was clear that the urban areas of Minneapolis and Saint Paul were booming again. The suburbs were rejuvenating. But the financial collapse on Wall Street decimated some of Main Street Minnesota beyond repair. Places like Aurora, Minnesota were once mining boom towns; now, all that's left are shuttered windows, antique shops, and bars. Three decades ago, the iron ore mining industry directly employed 15,000 people in the state; now it's down to 4,000.[9] The median age in rural Minnesota has risen steadily, with young people leaving as soon as they move out of their parental home. These changes are real. They are devastating to the people who experience them.

Finally, there's demographic change. As a result of immigration and natural demographic shifts, the United States is getting less white. That has elicited a cultural backlash from many Americans who see a more equal society as a threat to their privileged white place within it, or who just want things to go back "to the way they used to be." Barack Obama's election victory was a signal of how far the nation had come in making strides toward racial justice. But the racially-tinged backlash to his presidency underscored how far we still have to go.

The combination of these factors—tribal partisanship, media polarization, uncompetitive elections, the death of bipartisan compromise, political disengagement, economic decline, rising inequality, and demographic change—has created a perfect storm. As it swirls around American politics, authoritarianism finally has a chance to make landfall too. Angry citizens who think the other side is an enemy don't have the patience for thoughtful compromise and reasoned debate about policy ideas. They want quick solutions—the "I alone can fix it" candidate, not the "incremental change" candidate. And, over time, millions of Americans have gravitated toward authoritarian attitudes. When the problems are this bad, they feel, screw checks and balances if they are a roadblock to the solutions.

In 2009, two political scientists even predicted the rise of someone like Trump by demonstrating that a new divide had emerged in American politics: not between right and left, but between classic liberals on the one hand (in the European sense of being in favor of liberal democracy, with all its rights and protections for minority viewpoints) and authoritarians on the other.[10] Citizens with authoritarian attitudes are far less concerned with democratic procedure and far more concerned with getting their way. Voters with such attitudes exist on the right and on the left, but most of them have self-sorted into the Republican Party. In the process, they have created an ideological rift within the party—between authoritarian populists and more traditional conservatives.

The full extent of this rift was unclear before 2016. That's because, as researchers noted, many people have what are called "latent" authoritarian attitudes.[11] In other words, they will be more easily seduced by a candidate who plays up an authoritarian angle, even if they may not seek out that person themselves. If a candidate shatters accepted political norms and behaves like a strongman, they will flock to him like moths to an orange and yellow flame. Enter Donald Trump.

In 2016, political scientists began studying what caused people to back Trump's surprising candidacy. Sure enough, they found that authoritarian personalities—most of whom were in the authoritarian populist wing of the Republican Party—were overwhelmingly drawn to Trump.[12] Candidates from the more traditional wing of the party, like Jeb Bush, never really caught fire. Among diverse demographic factors—age, race, income, region, religion—having an authoritarian personality emerged as the most consistent predictor of support for Trump. He had captured the authoritarian vote and activated millions of "latent" authoritarian voters in the process.

Authoritarian voters imperil democracy. They are more likely to follow a leader than an agenda; they are more dogmatic and less persuadable than their classically liberal counterparts; and they are more likely to cheer as democratic norms are shattered. Of course, Trump's base is not fully authoritarian; there are many people who voted for him to vote against Hillary Clinton, or because they believed in his pledges to "drain the swamp" or crack down on illegal immigration. Some liked Trump's "fresh" brand of politics. Some liked the show. Some believed he was their only hope to resurrect rural America. Some just wanted to stick it to the Democrats. And some were, let's face it, racists. But Trump's base is nevertheless home to a disproportionate number of authoritarian voters, and they reward him for abusing and attacking the democratic system. If deporting illegal immigrants or punishing Hillary Clinton means cutting corners and disregarding the Constitution, so be it.

Although Trump has proved incompetent at governing so far, he has proved masterful at galvanizing authoritarian voters behind him. Furthermore, he has discovered one of the biggest vulnerabilities in America's democratic system: how little of it is based on law. The Founding Fathers couldn't have anticipated every future threat to democracy. They couldn't imagine something like Facebook, let alone how foreign adversaries could use it to weaponize disinformation. They couldn't anticipate reality television or the rise of a celebrity-obsessed culture, where people might know the names of Beyoncé's three kids, but can't name the three branches of government.[13] But the Founding Fathers did realize that some unpredictable threats would emerge. That's why they tried to create a system that would produce political norms—the expectations of politically acceptable behavior—to prevent catastrophic damage. Most aspects of American democracy are protected by these norms—the "soft guardrails" of democracy. There's no law, for example, requiring presidents to release their tax returns, but convention says they must release them, so they do.

Until now. Trump is careening through the soft guardrails of American democracy, shattering them without a second thought. They aren't constraining him. Instead, Trump is corrupting political norms, as Americans gradually come to accept previously unacceptable behavior. The Republican Party was complicit in this corrupting of American politics by allowing Trump to get so far without being denounced, and the Republican-controlled Congress is complicit today for allowing Trump's authoritarian behavior to continue without consequences. Republicans seem to have a pre-ordained rotation of words that they use to respond to

Trump. Some are "disappointed." Others are "concerned." And when things really get out of hand, they're "troubled." But for most in the party, their actions end with words. As a result, Trump keeps at it. In the process, authoritarian behavior is entering the political mainstream and becoming normalized.

Think about the first time you heard the term "fake news," the first time you can remember Trump recommending that his election opponent be locked up, or the last time you read about Trump continuing to spread a lie even after being corrected. All of it was once, recently, shocking. Now it's routine. After all, many people say, "that's just Trump being Trump." As crazy behavior becomes routine, it makes it easier for politicians to get away with previously out-of-bounds actions. Citizens become numb to the violation. It shatters longstanding political standards and the mores that hold our political system together.

When Trump first issued a travel ban to seven Muslim-majority countries, a little more than a year after calling to ban all Muslims from entering America during the campaign, there were spontaneous mass protests at airports across the country.[14] When he reissued a slightly modified travel ban a few months later, there was no such immediate response, and no protests were sparked at airports.[15] Americans had just accepted it. Similarly, when Trump drew false moral equivalence between neo-Nazis and those who were protesting them in Charlottesville during the summer of 2017, there was mass outrage—but when he said almost the exact same thing about Charlottesville a month later,[16] it barely made headlines.

This is one of the most insidious features of authoritarianism: it beats people into submission because you can't fight 100 battles all at once. Citizens are forced to pick and choose. Authoritarian leaders are aware of this fact and they exploit it to their own cynical ends. But as the normalization of unacceptably authoritarian behavior proceeds, the threat to American democracy grows. Normalization is like fertilizer to despotism. As people accept previously unacceptable behaviors as a new normal, creeping authoritarianism slowly but surely uproots democratic traditions.

Such gradualism is why creeping authoritarianism poses the greatest threat to democracy in the United States. If someone tried a blatant power grab, as with a military coup d'état, it would be repelled immediately. And if someone who was obviously a dictator tried to become an American despot, Speaker of the House Paul Ryan and Senate Majority Leader Mitch McConnell would grow a spine. They would block such a power grab, because it would be obvious. But with creeping authoritarianism, things aren't so clear-cut. For political leaders and citizens alike, the change occurs so incrementally that it's harder to stand up to it—particularly while Trump's showmanship dazzles and distracts. Authoritarian abuses that would dominate weeks of news cycles in normal times seem like blips instead. A day later, it's onto the next Trump outrage. We can't keep up, and we get tired of trying to keep up. Trump is counting on that and exploiting it for political gain.

He is also exploiting the fact that the United States is a divided country. But we should at least be able to agree on the importance of democracy. That's why I focus here on the nonpartisan value of democracy itself, rather than making partisan critiques. This book is not about tax policy or health care or the legitimate debates that should, in a healthy democratic society, be the source of divisions between citizens. Instead, I use what I call the Romney/McCain test. If Mitt Romney (the losing Republican candidate in 2012) or John McCain (the losing Republican candidate in 2008) would likely have taken the same tack as Donald

Trump on an issue, then it's probably just part of the ebb and flow of democratic politics. Both men probably would try to lower corporate taxes. Neither of them, however, would call to ban Muslims from entering the country. Neither of them refused to release their tax returns, because they both believe in the democratic value of transparency. Neither of them would be more vocal in their criticism of Hillary Clinton than of Vladimir Putin. Neither of them would struggle to forcefully and unequivocally condemn neo-Nazis or the Ku Klux Klan—nor did they, after Charlottesville.[17] Trump fails the Romney/McCain test on almost a daily basis.

Meanwhile, he is excelling in his apprenticeship to despots. Trump has blurred the line between fact and falsehood, subverting the truth for his own opportunistic ends. He has attacked the press relentlessly, demonizing journalists who form a key pillar of democratic government. He has politicized the rule of law, calling for his defeated election opponent to be locked up while pardoning political allies who have been convicted of crimes. He has acted as Vladimir Putin's apologist-in-chief after his campaign sought to collude with the Russian government to win the election. He is seeking to distort future elections by suppressing votes. His administration has flooded "the swamp" with ethics violations rather than draining it of them. He has politicized nonpartisan institutions, labeling them as part of a sinister deep state plot against him. And he has engaged in nepotism, putting his unqualified daughter and son-in-law at the highest echelons of the federal government. He even hired his son's wedding planner to oversee federal housing in New York and New Jersey—cronyism at its worst.[18]

These authoritarian machinations have prompted not just Democrats but also Republicans such as John McCain, Mitt

Romney, Jeff Flake, and Meg Whitman to worry about the threat that Trump poses to self-government in the United States. During the 2016 primary campaign, Romney even went so far as to invoke the wisdom of John Adams's warning against the threat posed by demagogues and despots: "There has never been a democracy yet that did not commit suicide." In case there was any doubt who he was talking about, he ended his speech by saying, "[Trump] has neither the temperament nor the judgment to be president and his personal qualities would mean that America would cease to be a shining city on a hill."[19]

Finally, Trump doesn't stop at attacking democracy on home soil; he's also undermining it abroad. Trump has had adoring things to say about strongmen across the globe, from Turkey to the Philippines. His foreign policy has tried to scrub democracy from the mission statement of the US State Department.[20] But what can you expect from a man who has tweeted about "ratings" more than 300 times, but human rights only once—to mock them?

The threat that Donald Trump poses to democracy is real. Ronald Reagan was right when he said that "Freedom is never more than one generation away from extinction. We didn't pass it on to our children in the bloodstream. It must be fought for, protected, and handed on for them to do the same, or one day we will spend our sunset years telling our children and our children's children what it was once like in the United States where men were free."[21] Recent research from Yascha Mounk at Harvard and Roberto Stefan Foa from the University of Melbourne has shown that young people take democracy for granted in the United States. Three in four Americans born in the 1930s—the generation that witnessed the horrors of totalitarianism—believe that it is "essential" to live in a democracy. Fewer than one in three Americans born in the 1980s agree.[22]

Americans mistakenly tend to think that we are immune from authoritarianism. It could never happen here. But in the run-up to World War II, 20,000 Americans packed Madison Square Garden for a pro-Nazi rally.[23] Swastikas were raised alongside portraits of George Washington,[24] and the pre-war isolationist movement pledged to put "America First."[25] While the US didn't ban Japanese people from entering the United States "until we figure out what the hell is going on," as Trump has suggested for Muslims of all nationalities, America's government did round up Japanese-Americans and shut them in internment camps. People involved in those black marks on our history are still alive. It's not as distant as we sometimes think.

Where do we go from here? If he makes it to the end of his term, there is still a lot of Trump left. Can our democratic sand castle survive years more of these authoritarian waves? And if it doesn't, what are the most likely scenarios for where we'll end up by 2020 when Trump is supposed to be up for re-election?

As I see it, there are four plausible scenarios, ranging in order from the optimistic to the cataclysmic. First, the Trump Vaccine. If the backlash against Trump is robust enough, he could end up acting like a vaccine for American democracy. Perhaps he will galvanize enough opposition that more political norms are enshrined into law and civic engagement becomes resurgent. In this hopeful scenario, citizens deploy to the ramparts and defend democracy.

Second, Democratic Decay. This is the most likely scenario. America's democratic sand castle doesn't get washed away, but it is severely damaged as wave after wave hits its walls. The damage will be gradual, but it will add up. Even if Trump's presidency is a failure, he can still poison the minds of millions of people to hold authoritarian views. That damage will take decades to repair—if it is possible at all.

Third, the Forerunner. In this scenario, Trump paves the way for an even more dangerous successor. This person, a Trump 2.0, will have the authoritarian instincts of Donald Trump but the polished smoothness of Barack Obama and the people skills of Ronald Reagan. With Trump normalizing authoritarian behavior, Trump 2.0 can do even more damage.

Finally, there *is* the prospect of American Authoritarianism. If a person like Donald Trump is in office in the aftermath of a mass casualty terror attack, a widespread war, or a nuclear nightmare, it is plausible that American democracy could die with a bang. This is, thankfully, the least likely scenario. But it is not impossible.

Democracy is worth defending. It's time we all heed the words of Mikalai Statkevich: "You don't know how lucky you are. Never take your democracy for granted. You won't realize what it's worth until it's too late."

1

DOUBLETHINK

"For, after all, how do we know that two and two make four? Or that the force of gravity works? Or that the past is unchangeable? If both the past and the external world exist only in the mind, and if the mind itself is controllable—what then?"

George Orwell, *1984*

In *1984*, George Orwell's hauntingly prophetic dystopian novel, the authoritarian government led by Big Brother wields an unspeakably powerful weapon: the ability to change what is true and what is false. "The past was alterable. The past never had been altered. Oceania was at war with Eastasia. Oceania had always been at war with Eastasia." But Winston, the novel's protagonist, grapples with these "alternative facts" that he knows to be untrue. "Oceania was at war with Eurasia ... The Party said that Oceania had never been in alliance with Eurasia. He, Winston Smith, knew that Oceania had been in alliance with Eurasia as short a time as four years ago. But where did that knowledge exist? Only in his own consciousness, which in any case must soon be annihilated."[1]

Throughout *1984*, Winston experiences the disorienting feeling of being unmoored from any fixed truths. His lived experiences are at odds with Big Brother's narrative. His senses tell him one thing; the party tells him the opposite. Orwell refers to this experience as "doublethink"—"the power of holding two contradictory beliefs in one's mind simultaneously, and accepting both of them." Or, as Orwell also put it, "it means also the ability to *believe* that black is white, and more, to *know* that black is white, and to forget that one has ever believed the contrary." Everyone in this dystopian world is spoon-fed statistics and facts; they must relentlessly repeat carefully scripted slogans and accept the regime's narratives—even if those narratives continue to shift. Slowly, Winston's ability to discern the difference between fact and falsehood is eroded. At the end of the story, he is tortured until he finally accepts something he knows to be untrue: that two plus two equals five. That, Orwell suggests, is the point where a despotic regime achieves total control—when the line between the truth and lies becomes unrecognizably blurred.

I've seen this firsthand across the globe, because in every authoritarian state I've lived in, there has always been a cult of personality around the leader. Sometimes it was religious or spiritual; other times, there were embellishments or myths that became popular legend. Questioning them was akin to questioning the nation. It was an area of dissent that became off limits. And that was made possible because truth itself came under attack.

In Zambia, for example, I interviewed the family of the late Captain Steven Lungu, alias Captain Solo, who tried to overthrow the government of Frederick Chiluba in 1997. When the coup plot failed, the government told the public that Captain Solo had plotted against the government on a whim, as part of an alcohol-induced fantasy. According to them, he was a drunken fool who had developed delusions of grandeur—a catastrophically misguided night out, so to speak. But when I interviewed Marian Chibwedele, the radio announcer whom Solo held at gunpoint while announcing the coup, she told me that "he was sober and asked me for a cup of tea."[2] The Zambian government's official narrative was simply more politically convenient; a drunken fool is easier to dismiss than a disgruntled army officer. The official narrative stuck. It became the only truth. Only a small group of people knew what had really happened.

Dictators throughout history have blurred the line between fact and falsehood for three main reasons. First, it allows the ruling regime to get away with poor performance. If the economy is faring badly or the government is not delivering on its promises, that doesn't really matter so long as the people believe otherwise. Second, bombarding the public with lies undercuts the power of independent sources of facts that try to correct the record. If there is one report that says the economy is strong and another that says the economy is weak, many people will end up with at least a muddied view of the situation. Even if the economy is in fact in freefall, the competing narratives confuse people, prompting them to question which "reality" is real, and which is false. That is a powerful weapon in political battles, when control of information so often determines support for the regime. Third, and finally, telling untruths about a ruler allows the regime to construct a cult of personality around the despot. In some cases, the popular mythology around a ruler is so absurd that it's hard to believe that anyone is seduced by it; but even in those cases, the ritual of repeating blatant lies ends up having an impact. Over time, the dictator morphs into a larger-than-life figure, occasionally elevated to the status of a demi-god in the minds of his followers.

The cult of personality surrounding North Korean dictator Kim Jong-un is perhaps the most insane of all. Of course, North Korea's cult of personality was not built recently. Instead, it began with the hagiography of the modern regime's founding father,

Kim Il-sung. Statues of the latter began cropping up as early as 1949. His son, Kim Jong-il, who would later take over as North Korea's dictator, was tasked with building up an impenetrable mythology around his father—one that would rival Orwell's dystopia in its absurdity. Soon, President Kim was known as the "Great Leader." According to popular mythology, he had descended from heaven in godlike fashion. The building of Kim Il-sung statues then went into overdrive. They appeared everywhere. Today, there are an estimated 34,000 dotting the landscape—one statue every 2 miles on average.[3]

When Kim Il-sung died in 1994 and his son took over, the absurdity of the Kim dynasty's cult of personality only accelerated. North Koreans were taught that Kim Jong-il invented the hamburger, supposedly an original Korean delicacy that he eloquently dubbed "double bread with meat."[4] Somehow, that name didn't catch on. But Kim wasn't just a culinary trendsetter. According to state media, Kim Jong-il's bizarre yet iconic gray button-down uniform took the fashion world by storm; the government told the country's citizens that a French expert in *haute couture* had remarked, "Kim Jong-il mode, which is now spreading expeditiously worldwide, is something unprecedented in the world's history."[5] Fashion designers couldn't get enough of mimicking Kim's style, and stores across the globe were selling out of anything that even closely resembled the wardrobe of the hamburger-inventing dictator. But just in case anyone doubted his greatness, during his reign Kim Jong-il also assumed the following titles (in no particular order): Wise Leader, Unique Leader, Brilliant Leader, Beloved Father, Guiding Star of the 21st Century, Sun of the Communist Future, Mastermind of the Revolution, Ever-Victorious Iron Willed Commander, Glorious General Who Descended from Heaven, Great Man Who is a Man of Deeds, Highest Incarnation of Revolutionary Comradely Love, and the somewhat more modest Superior Person.[6] To be fair, these seem like well-deserved titles for a man who—according to state mythology—wrote 1,500 books and composed six operas.[7] His supernatural powers, it was said, meant that he never had to go to the bathroom.[8]

When Kim Jong-un took over from his father in 2011, he was not to be outdone when it came to telling his people outlandish lies. According to the state narrative, Kim Jong-un learned how to drive when he was three years old.[9] He is also apparently a gifted musical composer and a skilled artist.[10] And, of course, while it's technically permissible to try out one of the other twenty-seven state-approved haircuts, why would a self-respecting North Korean man opt for anything other than Kim's iconic do, nicknamed the "youth" or "ambition" cut?[11]

Quirkiness aside, Kim is a ruthless, brutal despot who terrorizes his people, takes joy in murdering opponents in gruesome ways, and is overseeing the full-scale destruction of his country. Various reports have suggested that Kim has murdered at least 340 dissidents during his short time in office, including officials who had the audacity to commit crimes such as slouching in a meeting or having a "bad attitude."[12] In May 2015, Kim Jong-un summoned an elite crowd to a military school in Pyongyang, where Defense Minister Hyon Yong-chol was murdered at short range with an anti-aircraft gun—a weapon that could shoot down a jet.[13] Kim had another minister burned alive with a flamethrower while he watched.[14] He has also executed at least one family member, via a firing squad of fully automatic machine guns.[15] In short, Kim Jong-un is a murderous tyrant with a sick affinity for killing his enemies in creatively depraved ways.

Crucially, though, North Korea has mastered what few regimes can—it has blocked the flow of information to the population and undercut all alternative sources of truth and fact. As a result, it is understandable that some North Koreans believe the absurd myths that they are spoon-fed; after all, Internet access is restricted to senior officials and all news sources are state propaganda.[16] The line between fact and fiction is blurred to such an extent that, like Winston in *1984*, people are unsure whether to trust their senses, or the government's narrative.

Donald Trump is nothing close to *1984*'s Big Brother, Kim Jong-un, or North Korean brutality. Kim is an autocratic monster, one of the world's worst rulers. Donald Trump is a democratically elected president, operating within the confines of the world's most powerful democratic state. But there are certainly ways in which the Trump administration is engaged in a far less extreme, but still worrying, effort to blur the line between fact and falsehood in American politics. In modern American history, no president has ever told so many easily debunked lies in such a short period of time. No president in modern American history has made so many demonstrably false statements with no regard for the truth. And no president in modern American history has ever told an obvious lie—one that we can plainly see is false—with the aim of bolstering his personality cult.

Until Donald Trump. On the day after Donald Trump was inaugurated as the 45th President of the United States, he sent Press Secretary Sean Spicer not just to tell the world a lie, but to tell them a lie that they could see was a lie with their own eyes. Spicer aggressively accosted the world's media for "unfair" coverage of the previous day's inauguration ceremony. He looked into the cameras and said that the crowds at Trump's inauguration had been "the largest audience ever to witness an inauguration, period."[17] They were not. Subway ridership figures in DC on the day of Trump's inauguration weren't even close to those for

President Obama's first inauguration in 2008. Police estimates of crowd size weren't even close.[18] Most of all, there were side-by-side photographs of the inauguration—and anybody could see that Obama's inaugural crowd was massive compared with Trump's, which was half empty on the Washington Mall. Of course, all of this information about crowd size is petty and meaningless—or it was, until the White House decided to lie about it, blatantly, in order to stroke Trump's ego and begin fostering a larger-than-life personality cult around Donald Trump. This shouldn't be surprising—Trump has tweeted about "crowds" more than 250 times; by comparison, he's tweeted about Afghanistan forty times, and poverty twelve times.[19] Of all the problems facing the country, in his first statement to the nation and the world President Trump's narcissism prompted him to focus on lying about inauguration turnout. At the time, we couldn't know how well this was to foreshadow his presidency, but it would soon become clear that this was only the first step. Trump began to lie more or less every day, relentlessly promoting easily debunked falsehoods from the most powerful office on Earth.

During the 2016 election campaign, the independent, nonpartisan website PolitiFact fact-checked an array of statements made by Trump in his speeches. 70 per cent of his statements were false. Only 4 per cent of his statements—one in twenty-five—were fully and undeniably true.[20] At the time of writing, Trump has made 1,145 false or misleading claims since he took office in January 2017.[21] Not all of these are necessarily "lies" in the sense that a lie typically implies intent to deceive. But Trump no longer deserves the benefit of the doubt. When normal people make a mistake and say something that is untrue, they apologize. They correct the record. They stop repeating the same falsehood. Donald Trump does none of those things. He knows he's misleading, deceiving, or fabricating outright falsehoods. But he doesn't care. And that is why it is absolutely clear that Donald Trump is a serial liar. This is not an opinion, or a malicious interpretation of facts. There is no other way to put it, when a man so deliberately uses untruths as a political weapon.

Why does Trump lie so much? It's hard to know for sure. At times, it's almost as if he's lying just for the sake of it, or as if he can't help it. For the most part, though, there are two overarching characteristics that explain most of Trump's untruths. First, there are the deliberate lies used to advance a specific part of his political agenda. These are the most insidious, as they will certainly be believed by tens of millions of people. Unfortunately, such beliefs will be hard to reverse, meaning that Trump's assault on the truth will have damaging effects even after he leaves office. We'll call these the Big Brother lies. Second, there are the lies aimed simply at stroking his ego. He lies to cover up his shortcomings, deflecting criticism and downplaying any perception that he may have made a mistake. These lies are the brainchild of a psyche so fragile that it must say things that are simply untrue in an effort to protect the ego. We'll call these the Little Man lies. Regardless of the reasoning behind it, and even if the lies' content seems trivial, the consequences remain serious: enshrining a culture of deliberate dishonesty in the White House.

Of course, many critical and engaged citizens recognize Trump's relentless streams of lies, half-truths, and falsehoods for what they are. But there's a problem. Our brains are hard-wired to accept the premise of lies before we reject them. Neurological and psychological research has shown that, when presented with a purported fact, humans go through two main stages of cognition. First, in order to understand a statement, we must at least try to accept the premise that it's correct. If Donald Trump says that he didn't support the Iraq War, we start by contemplating the premise that this is possibly true. Then, in the second stage of cognition (which often happens a split second later if we have the relevant information), we are critical of that premise.[22] If we have already heard audiotape of Trump saying he was in favor of the Iraq War (which he was), then it's easier to correctly classify that statement as a lie. The problem is that Trump exploits our neurological vulnerabilities—even among the most vigilant citizens—to deliver not one lie, but a relentless barrage of lies. It's hard to keep up.

Psychologists call this unfortunate phenomenon "illusory truth." When asked to identify statements as true or false over a series of repeated exercises, people started to identify truth at higher rates for the statements that appeared most frequently over time—regardless of whether they were true or not.[23] In other words, among an armada of lies, some will slip through the blockade of facts that engaged citizens use to determine what is true and what is false. The more lies that come our way, the more vulnerable we are to believing some things that are untrue.

Even worse, fact checks don't necessarily help. When lies are political, they are particularly prone to what is called "motivated reasoning"—we accept or discount the believability of a given statement based on who is saying it.[24] So, if you're someone who believes firmly that Barack Obama was a wonderful president, you may be more prone to believing things he says even if there is evidence to suggest that it is only a half-truth or a misleading statement. Political psychology researchers like Brendan Nyhan of Dartmouth College have shown that the combination of partisanship and lies is a potent one, in which supporters of a given candidate are resistant to being told that the person they support is lying.[25] Trump has weaponized this phenomenon; as he pumps lie after lie out into the world, many among his political base eat it up as though it were true. Correcting the record may take years, if it is possible at all.

What's more, Trump may be the instigator of this new political culture of normalized dishonesty, but it is likely to have a corrosive effect on American political discourse more broadly. Research suggests that people who are exposed to untruthful statements are more likely to be loose with the truth themselves. It's easy to imagine how this proceeds: when people who oppose Trump get into debates with people who support him, Trump's opponents could succumb to the temptation to be equally dishonest with the facts. After all, they are doing it—why shouldn't I too? Over time, this will likely degrade the quality of American political discourse in ways that are difficult to rectify.

Beyond the outright lies, Trump also uses other tactics that are frequently the hallmark of authoritarian governments: whataboutism and gaslighting. These can be even more effective at creating a *1984*-style haze in citizens' minds as they wonder: is that really true?

Let's start with whataboutism. This term was most recently popularized by the British journalist Edward Lucas, but it references a tactic that authoritarian governments—particularly the Soviet Union—perfected long ago.[26] The concept is simple: when an accusation is levied against you, simply deflect that criticism by saying "Well, what about..." and then naming something that an opponent may have done, thereby simultaneously drawing a false equivalence while failing to answer the criticism. For example, when the Soviet government was accused of its horrifying human rights abuses that left millions dead, it might point to race relations in the United States as evidence that America was just as bad. Russia's modern-day despot, Vladimir Putin, does the same thing, pointing to botched Western interventions in Libya or Afghanistan when he's asked about Russia's unilateral annexation of Crimea or incursions into eastern Ukraine.[27] Whataboutism provides powerful deflections for supporters of a given side, who parrot the same retorts over and over. For the Trump administration's first year in office, there has been no shortage of such linguistically challenged parrots eager to engage in whataboutism. Take Trump spokeswoman Kellyanne Conway, for example. The only words in her whataboutism repertoire seem to be "Hillary Clinton" and "Benghazi," as though returning to past allegations against a defeated election opponent is some sort of magical elixir that absolves all future wrongdoing.[28]

Donald Trump himself has repeatedly engaged in whataboutism, endlessly bringing up Hillary Clinton whenever he is accused of a new scandal or caught in a fresh lie. But perhaps Trump's most striking use of whataboutism was his response when an American journalist asked him about his inability to criticize Vladimir Putin, a man who is known to have murdered journalists and dissidents who opposed his regime. "There are a lot of killers," Trump replied. "We've got a lot of killers. What do you think—our country's so innocent?"[29] In horrifyingly casual terms, Trump equated his own country—one governed by rule of law, where extrajudicial killings of journalists and opposition figures do not happen—with one of the world's most ruthless despots, Vladimir Putin. Worst of all, he employed Putin's own tactic—whataboutism—to defend him, while drawing an absurd false equivalence with America.

Whataboutism is insidious as an authoritarian tactic because it allows political figures to get away with wrongdoing and lies by exploiting popular anger against a perceived enemy. For years, Trump used Barack Obama as that common enemy. During his election campaign, it was Hillary Clinton. Now that he's president—it's still Hillary Clinton. As the months tick by, Trump's whataboutism is going to need a new bogeyman. But unless his own party begins to call him out on these deflections, it is likely to persist as a powerful tool to draw attention away from Trump's unacceptable behaviors or lies.

Then, there's Trump's gaslighting. This term is named after the 1938 play *Gas Light*, in which a husband attempts to convince his wife that she is insane—by making small changes and manipulating her environment, but then insisting she must have imagined them whenever she brings them up.[30] One of these changes is the husband's dimming of the gas lighting in the house, hence the term. Gaslighting is also a term frequently used in the context of abusive relationships, as abusive partners may gaslight their victims to convince them that they are insane or being completely unreasonable. In authoritarian governments, the abuse is no less insidious, as it aims to force citizens to question their own sanity, rather than the government's narrative. Winston's experience in *1984* was an example of systematic gaslighting.

During the campaign, Trump gaslighted America repeatedly. On stage, on live television, he told supporters at a rally that he would "pay [their] legal fees" if they "knock[ed] the crap out of" anti-Trump protesters in the audience.[31] When later confronted with those statements, without flinching Trump responded, "I didn't say that."[32] Tens of millions of people have seen the video of candidate Trump mocking a physically disabled reporter from *The New York Times*, yet as president-elect Trump tweeted "I would NEVER mock disabled" after Meryl Streep spoke about the incident at the Golden Globes in early 2017.[33] In office, he continues to deny saying things—even if there is a video or Twitter record of him saying them. For example, in one tweet, Trump likened the US intelligence agencies to the practices of Nazi Germany.[34] Ten days later, he blamed the "dishonest media" for suggesting that he had any feud with the intelligence agencies. Of course, Sean Spicer's untrue boast about the inauguration crowd size was the most obvious form of gaslighting; on that occasion, we could see the images side-by-side to know he was lying. But for most of Trump's lies, whether about voter fraud or the Russia investigation, there is no visual aid to debunk the story, and tens of millions of people fall for it. Over time, that weakens democracy, because democracy relies on citizens accepting a shared set of facts before they can truly start debating policy ideas or values; if Republicans and Democrats inhabit fundamentally different realities, it will be impossible to forge democratic consensus.

Whataboutism and gaslighting both have the same purpose: to try to excuse the inexcusable, while muddying the waters of truth. When done effectively, this can be a huge gift to authoritarian leaders, from Kim Jong-un, to the Soviet Politburo, to Vladimir Putin. But it can also be a horrifying masterstroke for democratically elected leaders with authoritarian impulses, like President Trump. But how, precisely, is Trump weaponizing misinformation as a means of blurring the line between fact and falsehood?

Let's start with the worst type of Trump's dishonesty: the Big Brother lies. These serve a specific political purpose—they lead people to believe untruths so that Trump can advance particular parts of his agenda. Trump rose to prominence in the modern Republican Party by promoting the racist and completely fabricated lie that President Barack Obama was born in Kenya. In dozens of interviews and twenty-three separate tweets over nearly five years, Trump repeatedly peddled this lie as fact. The purpose of spreading it was to discredit America's first and only African-American president as African rather than American. Even when

President Obama produced his birth certificate, showing that he was, in fact, born in Hawaii, Trump did not relent. In fact, he went so far as to congratulate himself in the 2016 election campaign for finally getting to the bottom of the conspiracy theory. It was as if someone had peddled the myth that the American government faked the moon landing, then had seen moon rocks, but continued to spread the lie, before eventually congratulating themselves on arriving at a truth that was already apparent to anyone with half a brain. Trump's "birtherism" should have made it clear that he is a man willing to spread demonstrably false stories so long as they confirm his narrative or advance his own political standing. But this was just the test run for Trump's presidency.

On 27 November 2016, just a few weeks after winning the Electoral College but losing the popular vote (the raw national total of votes), Trump tweeted, "In addition to winning the Electoral College in a landslide, I won the popular vote if you deduct the millions of people who voted illegally." Since that tweet, Trump has repeatedly suggested that 3 to 5 million people voted even though they were ineligible to do so. I will return to this lie in much greater detail in Chapter 6, but suffice it to say that it is absolutely untrue. In making this bogus claim, however, Trump is the first winning candidate in world history to question the integrity of a process that he won. After all, it's a secret ballot, so if mass illegal voting had taken place (it didn't), there would be no way of knowing the breakdown of those illegal votes. At first glance, then, it seems perplexing that Trump would suggest he benefitted from a compromised electoral process.

But Trump always has his reasons. In this case, he had two. First, he could stroke his fragile ego by falsely claiming that he had actually won the popular vote. Second, he could lay the groundwork for a voter suppression campaign that would disenfranchise minority voters who will likely oppose his re-election (this is already underway, and will be discussed in detail in subsequent chapters). As with most of Trump's lies, it served its purpose. According to a poll taken in August 2017, 47% of Republicans believe he won the popular vote—even though he lost it to Hillary Clinton by nearly 3 million votes. Even more horrifying, 68% of Republicans mistakenly believe that millions of illegal immigrants voted in the 2016 contest. And here's the authoritarian kicker for good measure: 52% of Republicans surveyed said that they would support postponing the 2020 presidential election if President Trump suggested that doing so was necessary to ensure that only legal citizens could vote.[35] Democracies die when presidents can postpone elections based on the mythology of a pernicious lie. While it remains unlikely in this case, Trump has tilted the needle further toward that sad prospect than any other president in modern American history. If, in future, he wants to exploit the false realities that he's created for his own political advantage, the possibilities are endless.

Trump also unleashes his Big Brother lies when he's feeling defensive. Needing to deflect attention from the growing media cacophony about the FBI's investigation into his campaign's contacts with Russians and the Russian government, he let loose a flurry of unhinged tweets just after 6am on 4 March 2017: "Terrible! Just found out that Obama had my 'wires tapped' in Trump Tower just before the victory. Nothing found. This is McCarthyism!" This was completely untrue. As subsequent inquiries showed, Obama had done no such thing. What's more, McCarthyism is defined as "the practice of making accusations of subversion or treason without proper regard for evidence." In other words, by making accusations of illegal phone tapping without any evidence that this had taken place, Trump engaged in the very practice of which he was baselessly accusing Obama, absurdly discarding reality in true Orwellian style. The many lies related to the Russia investigation are discussed in detail in Chapter 4 (on Trump's disdain for the rule of law).

Other lies in the Big Brother category include his false claims that President Obama's signature health care law, Obamacare, "covers very few people" when it in fact extended insurance coverage to roughly 20 million Americans; that "122 vicious prisoners released by the Obama administration from Gitmo [Guantanamo Bay] have returned to the battlefield," when in fact 113 of them (93 per cent) were released by George W. Bush's administration;[36] that "We have a lot of plants going up now in Michigan that were never going to be there if I—if I didn't win this election, those plants would never even think about going back. They were gone" (those investments were already planned well before the election); that "the story that there was collusion between the Russians & Trump campaign was fabricated by Dems as an excuse for losing the election" (even though the FBI began its investigation in the summer of 2016,[37] months before the election took place); that CNN's critical coverage had meant that their "Ratings [were] way down!" (even though CNN's ratings at the time had hit five-year highs).[38] Finally, Trump claimed that his own proposed health care bill—which would have cut Medicaid spending for the poor and disabled by nearly a trillion dollars over a decade[39]—actually increased funding for Medicaid. Big Brother would have been proud: "War is Peace. Freedom is Slavery. Ignorance is Strength."

Beyond the Big Brother lies, there are the Little Man lies. These are the ones that don't particularly serve Trump's political agenda, and are unlikely even to make much of a difference in his ability to govern—their only purpose is to further boost his already hyper-inflated ego. For confirmation that Trump requires this constant reassurance, look no further than to the fact that he reportedly receives a booklet of exclusively favorable news stories, twice per day. During their time in office, Trump's former chief of staff Reince Priebus and his former communications director, Sean Spicer, would reportedly bicker over who could give Trump the good news that he so clearly craved.[40]

Trump has been bruised by the fact that he didn't win the popular vote, so he continually invokes his Electoral College victory. He has repeatedly claimed it was a "landslide." In fact, forty-five of America's fifty-eight past presidential elections had wider margins than Trump's victory—in historic terms, his Electoral College victory over Hillary Clinton was extremely close. Furthermore, he boasted about his mythical landslide by claiming "I guess it was the biggest Electoral College win since Ronald Reagan." Trump received 306 Electoral College votes. Since Reagan, George H.W. Bush received 426 in 1988; Bill Clinton received 370 in 1992 and 379 in 1996; and Barack Obama received 365 in 2008 and 332 in 2012.[41] In other words, besides George W. Bush's razor-thin wins in 2000 and 2004, Trump won the Electoral College by a smaller margin than every president since Reagan. His statement to the contrary was completely wrong, and pointless—except to stroke his ego.

Then, of course, there is Trump's claim that he's had more legislation signed than any president since Harry Truman. First off, that's not true. When Trump made this claim in July 2017, he had signed fewer bills than Presidents Clinton, Carter, Truman, and FDR. More to the point, Trump's claim is so obviously misleading as to be absurd. The reality is that he has attempted to pass off a flurry of largely meaningless bills as signs of his "substantive" achievements. Three bills appoint people to the Board of Regents of the Smithsonian Institution; one deals with the national crisis of what to do if the Merit Systems Protection Board lacks a quorum; and, perhaps Trump's crowning jewel—HR 1362—renames an outpatient clinic in Pago Pago, American Samoa.[42] Of the thirty-eight bills he had signed when he made his boast, twelve of them renamed buildings or memorials, made low-level appointments, or were procedural tweaks. In other words, in his first half-year as president, Trump had signed no major bills. To conceal this, he came up with a convenient lie that was also extraordinarily and deliberately misleading—and a particularly audacious boast, given that candidate Trump had promised to sign ten major bills in his first 100 days in office, as part of his "Contract with the American Voter." At the time of writing, he has signed none of them, even as he approaches a year in office.

If you're already inclined to disregard the importance of truth, then claims about your electoral or lawmaking record might easily seem worth lying about. But Trump also lies, seemingly pathologically, to boost his ego, even over trivial details. In late July 2017, for example, Trump gave a bizarre address to the Boy Scouts of America, in which he thanked the children attending for voting for him (they can't vote) and then proceeded to boast about his attendance at a "hot cocktail party" in New York, before hinting at one of his friend's raunchy parties on a yacht. It was a strikingly surreal moment in a surreal presidency. Afterward, Trump claimed that the head of the Boy Scouts had called him to say that "it was the greatest speech that was ever made to them." This was untrue. The Trump administration later acknowledged that no such call had happened.[43]

Trump simultaneously boasted to reporters that "Even the president of Mexico [Enrique Pena Nieto] called me" to talk about how border crossings between Mexico and the United States had fallen (since Trump's rise to power, presumably). This was also untrue— no such call took place. The White House later argued that Trump was referencing remarks that Pena Nieto had made to Trump at the G-20 summit in Hamburg (also in July). In that case, it appears that Trump's need to control the "truth" to reflect him in the best possible light is so great that he must even adjust reality into a partial truth, through the addition of small, false details. Pena Nieto taking the time to call up his American counterpart makes Trump sound more important than if they had just discussed the issue on the sidelines of a summit. In any case, it is clear that Trump simply doesn't hold the truth in high regard, and casually discards it whenever the impulse strikes him.

Just as horrifying, Trump has amplified and elevated fringe media sources that peddle absurd, racist conspiracy theories. He has appeared on InfoWars, a program that has suggested that the massacre of children at Sandy Hook elementary school was a "false flag" operation that didn't really take place.[44] Try to imagine that: the president of the United States legitimized an outlet claiming that the parents of twenty young schoolchildren who were murdered made the entire thing up as part of a government conspiracy. InfoWars has also claimed that September 11 was orchestrated by both the American and Israeli governments;[45] that the FBI was involved in the 2013 Boston Marathon bombing;[46] and that NASA is running a child slave colony on Mars.[47] Its legitimization by figures like Trump has been to such an extent that NASA actually had to issue a public statement assuring people that this last myth was not true (to which InfoWars would of course reply: "That's what they want you to think").

Trump has also re-tweeted people who peddle bogus conspiracy theories like the now infamous Pizzagate hoax, which falsely claimed that Hillary Clinton was running a child sex ring out of a Washington DC pizzeria. That hoax produced real-life scares, as a man took it upon himself to walk into the pizza joint and shoot his rifle into the ceiling, demanding an end to the fictional sex ring. It goes without saying that the president should never be even remotely tainted by such people. Yet Donald Trump enables and amplifies their voices, imbuing their dangerous and blatantly false ideas with the legitimacy that comes from the office of the American presidency.

Lie, after lie, after lie. And these lies are important because they have serious consequences. Americans and the world must be able to trust the president of the United States during an international crisis. But why would anyone take him at his word when he has already made hundreds of demonstrably untrue statements since taking office in January 2017?

Beyond the risks of the White House losing credibility, democracy itself is at stake. The scaffolding of the democratic process rests upon a foundation of informed consent of the governed—one that relies on citizens being able to agree upon basic facts. If partisan divides also mean reality divides, in which Trump opponents believe (correctly) that voter fraud is an extremely small problem in the United States and Trump supporters believe (incorrectly) that it is widespread, then how can we have a reasoned debate about electoral laws and voter registration procedures? Moreover, elections lose their potency as a tool to hold politicians accountable if political figures can simply construct their own realities, puffed up by an absurd cult of personality. Trump has not fooled everyone, of course, but he has fooled tens of millions—so much so that the line between fact and falsehood has blurred. As Trump chips away at the value of truth in American politics, he simultaneously chips away at the foundations of democratic rule. As historian Timothy Snyder put it, "If we don't have access to facts, we can't trust each other. Without trust, there's no law. Without law, there's no democracy." In other words, to erode democracy, you must first erode truth—and this is precisely what Donald Trump is doing in America.

In September 2017, former Trump spokesperson Sean Spicer appeared in a lighthearted cameo on the Emmy television awards show: "This will be the largest audience to witness an Emmys, period, both in person and around the world!" This "joke" was a tacit acknowledgement that Spicer had lied on behalf of the president of the United States. Most people already knew that. But the Emmy cameo was another process that I've seen firsthand while living in authoritarian states with governments who treat the truth as disposable when inconvenient: normalization through humor. When you live under the cloud of an incompetent government that routinely lies, jokes are a common coping mechanism. But as Americans find themselves laughing with Spicer as a new political celebrity, it's yet another breakdown of political norms. If the punchline is that our government is filled with liars, rewarding and laughing along with its (former) representatives will lead more of them to lie. Why wouldn't they, if the only consequence is a newfound cultural popularity? And so slowly, joke by joke—lie by lie—the truth starts to fade.

To assert power over people, you must assert power over truth. Even if Trump's lies are occasionally so obvious as to be clearly false, they still infiltrate the minds of tens of millions of Americans. Worse, it would be impossibly time-consuming to fact-check every statement being made in politics, so the sheer volume of Trump's barrage of lies further fosters uncertainty about the truth. Even if you can't get your people to believe you, if you can get them to question things they should know to be true, then you've already won.

As autocrats from Kim Jong-un to Vladimir Putin have learned, and as Orwell so presciently warned, sowing doubt in citizens' minds over what is true and what is false is a powerful instrument of control: "If both the past and the external world exist only in the mind, and if the mind itself is controllable—what then?" In Trump's America, we may unfortunately have an answer to that impossible question sooner than we think.

2

FAKE NEWS!

In an era of unprecedented political dishonesty, the independent voice of the media is more essential than ever. A free press is as fundamental to democracy as oxygen is to people; without it, citizens cannot make informed choices—and so cannot govern themselves effectively. Democracy dies in the shadows; a free press shines a light into those dark corners, to make sure that government of the people, by the people, and for the people stays alive. But all too often, Americans take this fundamental freedom for granted. I've seen for myself what happens when freedom of the press is obliterated. It's not pretty.

On the morning of 22 May 2014, the residents of Bangkok, Thailand awoke to yet another noisy day of street protests. The country had ground to a halt, as tens of thousands of demonstrators clogged downtown Bangkok in opposition to a court's decision on 7 May to remove the democratically elected Prime Minister Yingluck Shinawatra. Thailand's military brass, which projected itself as an honest broker in negotiations aimed at defusing the situation, had begun 22 May in discussions with leaders of the protesters and counter-protesters who had been clashing for weeks,[1] but talks quickly broke down. The military decided to take advantage of the impasse. Soldiers flooded the streets in full camouflage, wielding assault rifles and clearing protest camps. The military suspended the constitution, shut down all radio and television stations, imposed a mandatory curfew nationwide, and took control of Thailand. They quickly criminalized any speech or statements that criticized the army. Thailand had just experienced another military coup d'état. The country is still under the rule of a military dictatorship today, led by General-turned-Prime-Minister Prayuth Chan-ocha.

I arrived in Bangkok a few months after the coup, hoping to better understand its transition to authoritarian rule. Since 2014, I've been back several times to interview more than a hundred elite political figures in Thailand's volatile political sphere—including generals, prime ministers, diplomats, soldiers, activists, and journalists. No interview has stuck with me more than my discussions with Thai journalist Pravit Rojanaphruk, an Oxford-educated reporter who covers the politics beat for English-language Thai newspapers. In late 2014, I met him at a Starbucks at Bangkok's upscale Siam Paragon mall, a place so luxurious that it has Rolls Royce and Ferrari showrooms in the shopping center. In a country that still faces the challenge of extreme poverty, the mall was a testimony to Thailand's inequality, forged by failed political leadership and countless military coups. But of all the intrigue offered by Thailand's broken political system, what I'll never forget is Pravit's story of how his ability to report the truth has been suppressed since the fall of Thai democracy.

After the coup, the junta began to round up and arrest "undesirables." As they did so, Pravit was surprised to see his name flashed across television screens nationwide. "I was number six, the sixth 'undesirable,'" he told me while sipping on an iced coffee. "My fear was only slightly dampened by the pride that being sixth brought me. I guess I was edged out from making the top five." His pride notwithstanding, Pravit was kidnapped and taken, against his will, to a military camp to the west of Bangkok, for a bit of what the military called, in positively Orwellian terms, "attitude adjustment." The aim, he told me, was "part intimidation and part Stockholm Syndrome. We didn't have a choice in going, but once we were there, they treated us extremely well. We got to choose between steak and lobster for dinner each night. The wine was $100 a bottle. And we even played a friendly football match against our military captors."[2] But the subtext of Pravit's kidnapping was not lost on him. If he played ball and acted as a regime propagandist rather than an independent journalist, he could expect to be treated well. If he didn't—well, he probably wouldn't want to find out what would happen.

Pravit did find out. As a journalist who believes deeply in the necessary power of a free press to inform the citizenry, he continued to write articles that were critical of the military government for its poor human rights record and failure to hold elections (as of late 2017, no elections have been held in over three and a half years since the coup). When I met with him again in the same Starbucks in March 2016, he was somewhat more discouraged—and the military was no longer courting him. Instead, they were bullying and intimidating him. He described how he had recently been arrested again, but this time without the wine, steaks and football. Instead, he was tossed into a "4 meter by 4 meter cell, with no air conditioning" in Thailand's scorching heat. As he literally sweated his future, the message from the military was, once again, crystal clear: continue trying to speak truth to military power and it will land you back in this cell immediately. Eventually, he was released.[3]

"There's a saying in Thai we have," Pravit told me during my most recent meeting with him in Bangkok, "that eventually a pig no longer fears being slaughtered. Well, I'm now that pig, and I'm not going anywhere, and I'm not going to stop speaking up either."[4] That's the last time I saw Pravit, and it may be the last time I see him for a while. In August 2017, he was charged with two counts of sedition for criticizing the military junta for failing to respect democracy.[5] At the time of writing, his case is pending. Shortly after attending his court dates, when he was told that he faced up to fourteen years in jail for suggesting that the military government was (obviously) undemocratic, Pravit was brave enough to publish a stirring defense of press freedom titled "Why Sedition Charges Won't Silence Me." In direct language, he explained how the outcome of his case was much bigger than his own fate: "The grey area where no one really knows what constitutes sedition under military rule makes this a chilling effect and ensures greater self-censorship of anything critical of the junta ... The hazier the boundaries of what constitutes sedition, the more effective they become in instilling fear." Pravit is absolutely right—to destroy press freedom, you don't need to shut down every newspaper; you just need to make journalists fear the consequences of speaking truth to power. He nonetheless remains undaunted: "I know that many, many years from now, when I and dictator General Prayuth Chan-ocha are no longer alive," he wrote, "history will judge me more kindly."[6]

Pravit's bravery showcases that a free press is worth fighting for—even when journalists must place themselves at personal risk to preserve it. When democracy is under attack, citizens can only fight back to protect self-government if they are informed—and informed consent of the governed starts with courageous journalists like Pravit Rojanaphruk. Despots all over the world fear above all else an independent press that cannot be bent to their will. Authoritarian rulers know that they will be foiled so long as a free press survives. But once the media is cowed or destroyed, it's open season for dictators. They can prey on democratic institutions with impunity, because nobody will know about it—and even if they did, there would be no public forum to criticize it.

Thailand is only one of many countries that is in the midst of an all-out assault on press freedom. Turkey is also currently engaged in one of the most systematic attacks on a free press in recent history. Authoritarian strongman Recep Tayyip Erdogan has jailed journalists on a mass scale and demonized the media at every opportunity. A decade ago, a smear campaign by the government against journalist Hrant Dink ended with a government supporter assassinating him in cold blood.[7] It was the logical conclusion of a system that scapegoated journalists relentlessly from the president downward. Since then, Erdogan has branded journalists as enemies of the nation. He has also suggested that they are subversive elements of a "deep state" plot against his regime. Sound familiar?

In recent years, thousands of Turks have been jailed for insulting the president. Journalists have been slandered as terrorists. And it all got a lot worse in the summer of 2016, when a failed coup plot against Erdogan's regime provided a convenient pretext for him to crack down even further, decimating what was left of Turkey's free press. In October 2016, an inquiry into Turkey's treatment of its press "found cases of physical attacks on journalists, raids on media outlets, threatening rhetoric, increasing use of slander and anti-terrorism laws to target the media, ongoing imprisonment of journalists and deportations of foreign correspondents."[8]

But Erdogan's truly sinister masterstroke has been his crafty reliance on "softer" crackdown methods to beat journalists into submission. He doesn't have to jail everyone to get them to do his bidding. Instead, he has used financial leverage to silence vocal critics. When someone writes a critical piece against his regime, he might order a tax audit of the journalist or the journalist's family. Other times, he might send cronies to inspect the building where the press outlet is located and "discover" code violations. In at least one instance, the fines imposed were equal to the market capital of the publication.[9]

Vladimir Putin has long taken the same approach in Russia.[10] To get rid of NTV, a private TV station that was known for critical coverage of the government, he could simply have shut it down. But that could have been seen as too heavy-handed and may have prompted pushback from Russian civil society. Instead, Putin sent in the tax enforcers, who managed to find some trumped up charges against the station's ownership.[11] Later, NTV's owner was indicted on fraud charges that were almost certainly politically motivated. Then, once the owner caved and the station was sold to the government, the fraud charges were dropped. Under state control, NTV morphed from a government critic into a vocal cheerleader. This "soft" destruction of the press can sometimes be accomplished with authoritarian capitalism, by going after the media's wallet rather than kidnapping or jailing journalists. Thailand's military government has also engaged in this tactic by threatening journalists with defamation lawsuits, trying to make the prospect of exorbitant legal fees serve as a deterrent against critical press coverage.[12]

I've seen the same types of tactics deployed by despots and undemocratic governments across the world, from sub-Saharan Africa to Southeast Asia. Unfortunately, it's nothing new. It's tried and true. Throughout history, destroying a free press or bending it to the regime's narrative has been one of the first and essential steps in dismantling democracy. But aspiring despots and democratically elected leaders with authoritarian impulses may not always be able to destroy a free press completely—particularly in places where media institutions are firmly embedded and have a long-established history of holding the government to account. When you can't bend the press to your will, the next best thing is to bend public opinion against the press itself.

Hitler sought to do precisely that. When media outlets criticized his regime as he consolidated power under the Third Reich, Hitler referred to them disparagingly as the *Lügenpresse*, or Lying Press. Even beyond defaming journalists as liars, autocrats throughout history have also decided to label their outspoken opponents as "enemies of the people." Goebbels did it under Hitler. Lenin and Stalin did it in the Soviet Union. Chairman Mao called his detractors the enemy of the people. And Hugo Chavez of Venezuela referred to his critics as "enemies of the homeland."

While Trump is not even close to inhabiting the same moral universe as these dictators, he has certainly joined the club of leaders who demonize the press. He is echoing their language and borrowing their tactics, attacking the press with incendiary, divisive language. On 17 February 2017, he tweeted: "The FAKE NEWS media (failing @nytimes, @NBCNews, @ABC, @CBS, @CNN) is not my enemy, it is the enemy of the American People!" He followed that outburst with a speech at the Conservative Political Action Conference later the same month, repeating that phrase: "they are the enemy of the people." In the world's most powerful democracy, this is an astonishingly authoritarian accusation.

It's also completely unjustifiable. Trump denounces the press because they are doing their jobs: holding powerful people to account on behalf of citizens. When Trump lies, they report it. When Trump's staff is in turmoil, they cover it. And when Trump does something that is incredibly out of step with American democratic values, like calling to ban an entire religious group from entering the country (as he did in December 2015), some members of the press are critical of him for that. This is how democracy is supposed to function. But journalists expose Trump's failures, and he hates them for it, relentlessly attacking them in retaliation. In the process, he has co-opted the term "FAKE NEWS" (he always writes it like that, as though full capitalization would somehow make his childish and baseless outburst seem more authoritative).

Thankfully, American media institutions are stronger than those in Russia, Thailand, or Turkey. Donald Trump can send all the tweets that he wants and it won't cause journalists at *The New York Times* to stop writing. In fact, press coverage of his administration's shady dealings has caused the departure of many key administration staff, from Michael Flynn to Anthony Scaramucci. The press has held up well to the barrage of ridiculous accusations from the blowhard-in-chief. However, Trump still poses three key threats to the role of the press in American democracy.

First, by weaponizing popular distrust of the media, he is creating a culture that will outlive his time in office. By the end of the Trump presidency, tens of millions will wrongly believe his claim that every word printed in two of America's most respected newspapers, *The Washington Post* and *The New York Times*, is just "FAKE NEWS." Tens of millions will believe the same of CNN, ABC, CBS, and NBC—networks that have brought Americans reliable news coverage for decades. It will take an enormous amount of time to repair that damage. Second, Trump has already hinted that he might use some of the "softer" forms of authoritarian crackdowns on the press—as seen in Thailand, Turkey, and Russia—in an attempt to cow media outlets into more favorable coverage. Third, Trump is encouraging violence against journalists, creating an atmosphere in which it would be horrifying but, sadly, not surprising if a reporter were attacked or even killed by someone who falsely believed that members of the media are the "enemy of the American people."

But let's start with what has already happened. In a matter of months, President Trump has convinced a sizeable minority of the American public that most news organizations cannot be trusted. Several polls have asked citizens to identify the more trustworthy source of information, choosing between President Trump and an array of news outlets. Given Chapter 2's documentation of Trump's pathological inability to tell the truth, you'd expect that he wouldn't fare well in that match-up—and you'd be right, if you were sampling Americans from across the political spectrum. But when we only look at Republicans, the story changes. Amongst self-identified Republican voters, 71% of people trust Trump rather than *The Washington Post* (13%). The numbers are similar for CNN and *The New York Times*. Surprisingly, though, Trump's war on the media appears also to have made Republicans distrust news sources that are deliberately conservative in their editorial stance. Take *The Weekly Standard* magazine and the semi-monthly *National Review*, which cater to Republicans and conservatives. Republicans trust Trump over these publications by wide margins, too—70% to 10% for *The Weekly Standard* and 68% to 12% for *National Review*. Perhaps most shocking, however, is that only 23% of Republicans trust Fox News over Trump, while 54% would trust information from the president over information from the network—despite its unwavering support of him in its opinion coverage.[13] All told, when asked whether they trust the press generally, only 9% of Republicans responded yes.[14]

What we are seeing, then, is Trump's ability to politicize public interpretations of independent sources of information that are not directly tied to the White House. It's incredibly dangerous for democracy. How can public debate and policy compromise be found if a full half of the political spectrum distrusts not just left-wing and centrist media outlets, but also right-wing ones? Trump's inability to corral his legislative agenda into place—and its exposure by independent media—has not halted his assault on those sources, and, sadly, it's working. A core institution protected by the First Amendment is under attack.

But Trump's attacks on the press go beyond creating a sense of distrust. They also seem to be sharpening authoritarian attitudes toward press freedom more generally. That isn't terribly surprising, given that Trump is labeling journalists as "enemies of the American people." But it is still shocking to see that, according to one poll conducted in the summer of 2017, 45 per cent of Republicans—against just 18 per cent of Democrats—indicated that they would support shutting down media outlets that had produced biased or inaccurate reporting. Just 20 per cent of Republicans (half the number of Democrats) said they would be opposed to such an authoritarian crackdown on the press.[15] Any such attempt would be straight out of the playbook used in places like Turkey or Russia—one that should be totally alien and unacceptable in the United States. There is, of course, some evidence that this acceptance of autocratic government intervention in the media sphere has been a hallmark of Republican views for some time.[16] But now, Trump is exploiting this public acceptance of despotic abuse of the press, paving the way for a further erosion of journalism's critical role in American democracy.

Even if Trump doesn't "go full autocrat" in his dealings with the press, he has hinted at using authoritarian capitalism to induce less critical coverage of him. Drawing on Thailand's record in threatening defamation lawsuits for those who criticize the government, Trump has threatened to "open up" libel laws so that media outlets would face the threat of huge legal fees for their reporting. At a campaign rally in Texas in February 2016, Trump pledged to his supporters that he would make legal changes to try to stop critical reporting. "One of the things I'm going to do if I win ... I'm going to open up our libel laws so when they write purposely negative and horrible and false articles, we can sue them and win lots of money. We're going to open up those libel laws."[17] Purposely false articles are already libelous under existing law; the only change Trump was really proposing was to allow litigation against media organizations for publishing "purposely negative and horrible" articles, which would be a violation of the freedom of the press. After all, what good is a press that can only write fawning stories of the president and his entourage?

Trump didn't back away from this threat once he became president. In March 2017, he tweeted, "The failing @nytimes has disgraced the media world. Gotten me wrong for two solid years. Change libel laws?" Again, his threat was in response to what he perceived as "wrong" analysis or interpretations of him—not to maliciously untrue reporting that deliberately aimed to deceive readers. Of course, when outlets like *The New York Times* do make mistakes, they issue corrections—as is standard practice for all legitimate news organizations. Trump knew what he was doing: trying to threaten an industry that has suffered financially in recent years by suggesting that he would bring costly lawsuits against those that dared challenge the White House narrative, just as the Erdogan regime has put financial pressure on troublesome media organizations in Turkey.

Beyond his suggestion that he could sue journalists over negative reporting, Trump has also taken a leaf directly out of Putin's authoritarian book: he is trying to bully the media with threats of tax changes affecting the owners of critical press outlets. In particular, Trump has done this repeatedly in reference to *The Washington Post*, which has published some of the most damaging information about the dubious ties between Trump's 2016 campaign and the Russian government. Its reporting has been accurate and certainly not libelous.

The Washington Post is owned by Jeff Bezos, founder of Amazon.com. Otherwise, the two organizations are completely separate. Donald Trump is trying to exploit their common ownership in a bizarre threat to Bezos's Amazon wallet, in the hopes of pressuring *The Washington Post* to reduce its critical coverage of the Trump administration. In June 2017, Trump tweeted: "The #AmazonWashingtonPost, sometimes referred to as the guardian of Amazon not paying internet taxes (which they should) is FAKE NEWS!" This absurd outburst is problematic not just because it displays an authoritarian impulse aimed at inspiring self-censorship due to a threatened change in government tax policy, but also because it's threatening something that already exists. Amazon.com collects sales taxes in each one of the forty-five states that charge sales tax, along with Washington DC. Vladimir Putin was smart enough to threaten press outlets with something other than a tax they already pay.[18] To be fair, though, Trump is new to this. He may get savvier in his bullying.

Beyond empty threats, the Trump administration does have one real opportunity to try and force more positive press coverage. CNN, which Trump attacks regularly and which he has called "very fake news," is owned by a parent company, Time Warner. A proposed merger between Time Warner and AT&T is currently under review by the US government. A senior Trump administration official told *The New York Times* that "White House advisers have discussed a potential point of leverage over their adversary [CNN]."[19] In other words, they are openly acknowledging a terrible conflict of interest—even embracing it, contemplating an egregious abuse of power—in order to threaten CNN into submission. In any other presidential administration, this would warrant serious investigation; in the world of Trump, it's about five hundredth on the list of improper behavior.

A vow to "open up" libel laws, a threat of higher taxes for newspapers that criticize the president, and the specter of using mergers as leverage over press outlets that dare to do likewise—these are the hallmarks of despots who seek to avoid jailing journalists, but still hope to achieve a simple goal: undermining the free press and forcing journalists to think twice before speaking truth to power. It likely won't work. Thankfully, Congress hasn't shown any particular inclination to play ball with the authoritarian impulse to change libel laws, and even if they did, most US media outlets are sufficiently resilient not to be intimidated by an American strongman. But remember: all of this has happened in less than a year of the Trump presidency. It may be a disturbing foreshadowing of something much worse to come. Anyone who somehow still thinks that Trump believes in the freedom of the press as a bedrock principle of democracy is simply delusional.

In addition to the systematic efforts to erode public trust in journalism and to use "soft" authoritarian capitalism to bully media outlets into submission, Trump is also creating an anti-press culture that uses explicitly violent imagery to scapegoat reporters. In this atmosphere, there have already been several violent attacks on the media. It may only be a matter of time before a Trump supporter, following the president's word that journalists are "enemies of the American people", decides to kill someone.

In March 2016, Corey Lewandowski, Trump's upstart campaign manager, was arrested in Florida and charged with assault. The charges stemmed from an altercation with Michelle Fields, a reporter with the pro-Trump website Breitbart. Fields said that she had tried to ask Trump a question, only to have Lewandowski grab her and nearly knock her to the ground. She filed a police report. There is a standard operating procedure in Trump world when a story like this breaks: deny, deny, and deny—until caught red-handed. Lewandowski called Fields delusional. Then incontrovertible video evidence emerged, and other reporters backed up Fields's version of events. It was clear that Trump's campaign manager had improperly grabbed and forcefully shoved a reporter. If only this were an isolated incident; instead, it was a warning of what was to come once Trump became president.

In late May 2017, two attacks on the press occurred within days of each other. In Montana, a state that Trump won by more than twenty points, Congressional candidate Greg Gianforte bodyslammed Ben Jacobs, a reporter for the British newspaper *The Guardian* who was simply trying to ask him a reasonable question about his position on Trump's proposed health care legislation. Gianforte then issued a statement riddled with inconsistencies that, as in Lewandowski's case, denied that the event had taken place. However, several witnesses and audiotape of the event confirmed that Gianforte was lying. Jacobs had him caught red-handed on tape—his broken glasses, and the minor injuries of others, were further evidence of the assault. Gianforte eventually released a "revised" statement that essentially admitted everything Jacobs had alleged. In response, Trump said nothing—he simply continued to tweet praise of Gianforte and called on Montanan voters to elect him in the special election (by-election) being held the following day. The electorate obliged, sending a man to represent them in Washington who pled guilty to assault shortly after his election. Before Trump, a candidate who physically assaulted a journalist would have been pressured to resign in disgrace, to avoid tarnishing the party or the president—and certainly wouldn't do well if they did make it to the polls.[20] In the Trump era, Gianforte has been welcomed with open arms by both Trump and the Republican leadership in Congress. What kind of message does that send if a Congressman can beat up reporters without any political consequences?

A few days later, it became apparent that the awful message of the Gianforte incident had been received loud and clear in Kentucky, a state that Trump carried by a wide margin of 63 per cent to Clinton's 33 per cent. Somebody (it's still not clear exactly who) took it upon themselves to shoot up the *Lexington Herald-Leader* newspaper, riddling its offices with small-caliber bullets and leaving shattered glass on the street below. The windows of the press room, where most reporters sit, were also hit by gunfire. Thankfully, nobody was hurt. But this was a harrowing episode and is unlikely to be the last incident of its kind; if you ask any reporter from a mainstream news organization what their e-mail inbox or Twitter feed looks like in 2017, it's ugly—routine death threats and incredibly vile abuse have become a disgusting price to pay for covering politics in the era of Trump.

Just in case anyone doubted how Trump felt about violence toward the press, he took it upon himself to make clear that he thought physical attacks on journalists are a laughing matter, even to be encouraged. In early July, President Trump tweeted a modified GIF video of himself appearing on the fake wrestling television program WWE. At the time of Trump's appearance on that show a decade earlier, he was shown repeatedly punching a man on the ground, in a way that made Congressman Gianforte's bodyslam look like a bear hug. But in the version of the GIF that Trump spread to his 35 million Twitter followers in July 2017, the man's head had been replaced by the CNN logo. The message, invoking authoritarian imagery, was unmistakable. It was a tacit endorsement of violence against journalists. Worse still, the image he tweeted had been modified by a user on the social media site Reddit. This user, the elegantly named HanAssholeSolo, had posted the modified video along with dozens of extremely racist comments, repeatedly using the N-word and joking about killing African-Americans. In resharing the image, Trump gave its despicable author a platform—the most powerful one on Earth. He amplified the voice of a racist who joked about murder while endorsing a culture permissive of violence against media representatives—a disgusting display and an authoritarian attack on press freedom, from the man charged with protecting and defending the fundamental freedom of the press as enshrined in the United States Constitution.

But Trump always likes to push the boundaries of what he can shock us with. Just over a month after tweeting the modified CNN image, he re-tweeted a cartoon image of a train hitting a person with a CNN logo for a head.[21] This was particularly insensitive because it came just days after a young woman, Heather Heyer, had been hit by a car and killed while protesting a rally of white supremacists, neo-Nazis and members of the KKK. In response to that tragedy, Trump said that "many sides" were to blame and that there were "very fine people" attending the Klan rally.[22] The cartoon image of a train hitting a journalist, days after a woman died after being hit by a white supremacist's car, was neither subtle nor amusing—and the parallel only served to showcase how real the threat is in Trump's America. Trump later deleted his re-tweet, but the message was already out there.

Trump's assault on the press has already involved weaponizing public distrust, using authoritarian capitalism to try to influence media coverage, and creating a permissive culture of violence against journalists. But his subversion of the press doesn't end with these offensives; he's also taking a page straight out of the despots' playbook by trying to limit the flow of information to the press with unprecedented levels of opaqueness in government—while simultaneously facilitating a media apparatus that echoes state-controlled media outlets in authoritarian regimes across the globe.

In May 2017, Trump threatened to cancel all future White House press briefings "for the sake of accuracy."[23] He did have a point; his press briefings are routinely filled with lies, misleading statements, or half-truths, whether it was Sean Spicer, Sarah Huckabee Sanders, or the short-lived Anthony Scaramucci on the podium. (The latter lasted only a few days before he was fired after suggesting to a reporter, on the record, that Trump's former Chief Strategist Steve Bannon auto-fellates on a regular basis.)[24]

In seriousness, though, Trump's suggestion was truly Orwellian. A more reasonable individual would have dealt with inaccuracies being spread from the White House podium by, for instance, trying to insist that staff be more accurate. Trump's take on the matter was to scrap the briefings completely, or to hold them every two weeks, rather than daily as was previously the norm. He never followed through on this threat, but the idea has now been voiced—he may yet curtail press briefings in the future.

Furthermore, for months in 2017, the White House began to ban video recording during press briefings. Reporters were allowed to report what was said, but couldn't tape it or broadcast it live, as had been standard practice since the end of the Cold War. The video is important, because it allows us to see clips of the Trump administration explaining their behavior to the American people, without hiding in the shadows of audio recordings or newspaper text.

Furthermore, US presidents are expected to hold solo press conferences semi-regularly, to answer questions directly from reporters. These exercises are important because press secretaries have "plausible deniability"—they can deflect journalists' questions by saying that they aren't aware of the president's position on a given issue, or haven't spoken to him about it. When the president himself is in front of reporters, he can't dodge their questions nearly so easily. In the spirit of transparency, President Obama held eleven solo press conferences in his first year of office. That was slightly more than George W. Bush's five in his first year as president, but not quite as many as Bill Clinton's twelve in 1993. George H.W. Bush went furthest in recent history, holding twenty-eight in 1989. As of September 2017, Trump has so far held just two, putting him on track to have given the fewest solo press conferences for a president's first year in office since detailed records began with Richard Nixon.[25]

Moreover, the Trump administration has banned American journalists from covering the Trump White House—even at times when it has allowed foreign reporters access. On 10 May 2017, in a now infamous meeting with Russian Ambassador Sergey Kislyak and Russian Foreign Minister Sergey Lavrov, the American press was denied access, whereas the Russians were allowed an official photographer, from the state-owned TASS news agency. Shortly after the meeting, a series of embarrassing photos emerged of President Trump smiling and laughing with the two Russians (who had almost certainly played a role in meddling in America's 2016 elections).[26] The only reason the American public has seen those photos is because of foreign—Kremlin-owned—press. Trump is hardly a champion of transparency in government.

A few weeks later, Secretary of State Rex Tillerson held a press conference with Saudi Arabian Foreign Minister Adel bin Ahmed Al-Jubeir. Foreign media were invited but American journalists were not. Again, domestic media were eventually able to cover the event after the fact, but only because they were provided with a transcript from Saudi state television. In this absurdist twist, the world's most powerful democracy had to rely on journalists from one of the world's most brutal autocracies—one that lacks a free press—in order to report on a press conference featuring a US secretary of state.

Finally, beyond these worrying trends against press access, Trump is facilitating the creation of a media apparatus that rivals state media propaganda in other, more despotic countries, operating to boost authoritarian government narratives. This has partly been made possible by an extremely friendly outlet in Fox News, which often uses indefensible editorial decisions to obscure negative news about Trump while covering bogus and discredited stories against his opponents. But it also relates to Trump TV, a new venture that looks and feels like state propaganda.

Trump is an avid consumer of the early morning Fox News program "Fox and Friends." The anchors of the show, who have previously included people selling fawning pro-Trump books,[27] offer only overwhelmingly positive coverage of his administration, even in the midst of its most egregious scandals. In return, Trump has tweeted about the show on more than 400 occasions. As president, he has retweeted its account an astonishing seventy-four times—something that he virtually never does with any other media outlets. Trump's wholesale endorsement of Fox News has also been shown in the exclusive interview access he gives the station, shutting out other major networks that might ask more than softball questions.

Take Pete Hegseth's questions for Trump in an interview that aired on 25 June 2017. "Who's been your biggest opponent?" he asked. "Has it been Democrats resisting? Has it been fake news media? Has it been deep state leaks?" For a member of the press to co-opt Trump's inappropriate use of "fake news media" in referring to mainstream outlets who abide by the common professional ethics required of American journalists was extraordinary. Similarly, endorsing Trump's use of the term "deep state" in reference to government civil servants and the US intelligence community was beyond the pale; the term was originally coined to refer to shadowy assassination plots in Turkey and Egypt. This interview was sycophantic journalism at its worst. It wasn't holding a democratically elected leader accountable. It was cheerleading for him. There wasn't a single question that challenged Trump's narrative in the entire lengthy interview—even though the president was being investigated at the time for possible criminal activity, and had historically low approval ratings.

Other Fox News coverage of the Trump administration has been, at times, completely indefensible. Of course, it is wholly acceptable for a cable news channel to favor a particular narrative. That's part of freedom of the press and free speech within it. But when stories that clearly shone a negative light on Trump were breaking, Fox News acted as an active apologist for him instead— and occasionally even spread genuinely fake stories that had been repeatedly debunked. In so doing, the network gravitated away from its role as a news outlet, and moved toward serving as a propaganda outlet, attempting damage control for the president and willfully ignoring facts rather than reporting news. In late July 2017, Fox News host Jesse Watters said, on air, that "many people wish President Trump was a dictator, maybe [then] we could repeal Obamacare."[28] That same month, Lou Dobbs called criticism of Trump an attempt to "carry out a coup d'état against" him, dangerously and inappropriately equating democratic dissent with the military overthrow of a democratically elected leader. Having seen firsthand how military coups can destroy countries from Madagascar to Côte d'Ivoire to Thailand,[29] I did not find the comparison remotely amusing.

As the Russia investigation continued to break with new and increasingly damaging information for the president's campaign team, Eric Bolling of Fox News suggested on air that "Maybe the Russians were colluding with Hillary Clinton." There was no evidence to suggest this was the case, and mountains of evidence to suggest it was not. After all, I'm pretty certain that Hillary Clinton didn't work with the Russian government to hack the Democrats' servers and her campaign chairman's e-mail to ensure that she would lose the election. But when it comes to pushing a misleading narrative favorable to the president, Fox News always steps up to the plate.

The network's onscreen reporting has been absurd too. In one graphic, it put Trump's face alongside text that read "The First 100 days!" Below, the graphic listed "health savings accounts; US-Mexico border wall; Congressional term limits; and 25 million jobs."[30] Of course, none of these things were achieved in Trump's first 100 days in office—not even close. That dishonest reporting went on air to millions of people and was then tweeted out to millions more as though it were fact. Individual on-air personalities like Sean Hannity have gone even further. Hannity has spent countless hours of programming devoted to the totally debunked Seth Rich conspiracy theory. This fabricated story suggests that a former DNC staffer, Seth Rich, was murdered by Hillary Clinton's campaign because he was involved in the WikiLeaks e-mail leaks that damaged Clinton's election prospects.[31] The US intelligence community has unanimously concluded that Russia hacked the servers and John Podesta's e-mail accounts without the help of any staff. The news side of Fox News has completely retracted earlier reporting that breathed life into

this baseless, disgusting conspiracy theory. But Hannity continues to run with the story, drumming up a public embrace of this
false narrative. For Trump, it's a dream come true, because this
"coverage" simultaneously slanders his favorite political punching
bag, Hillary Clinton, while providing some false political cover for
his campaign's own scandals.

On top of this complimentary coverage from Fox News, we
have Trump's attempt at his own state TV outlet. Trump TV
debuted in July 2017 with a program called "Real News of the
Week," yet another insinuation that credible, well-sourced, accurate reporting from mainstream media outlets is "fake news." The
inaugural clip starts off with this propaganda-style gem: "Overall,
since the president took office, President Trump has created more
than 1 million new jobs." First off, no, he didn't—presidents can
influence the economy but they certainly don't create jobs unless
they authorize the hiring of new government workers, soldiers,
and the like. Secondly, the newscaster, Kayleigh McEnany, failed
to mention that the 1 million jobs added under Trump between
February and August 2017 represents the lowest rate of job
growth for this six-month period in the last five years.[32] The rest
of the clip is riddled with errors and inaccuracies. In strikingly
Orwellian fashion, the "real news" is filled with false and misleading stories, while the "fake news" is far more accurate—and cor-
rects errors on the rare occasions when they do occur.

As media scholar Tom Rosenstiel puts it, "the risk of losing an
independent press, even if that press is very heterogeneous, is that
you lose an institution that is dedicated to getting the facts right.
Whether they're partisan or not, they're at least dedicated to getting the facts right. If we lose that, we're in a very dangerous
place."[33] If millions of people start getting their news from Trump
TV, we will already have started to enter that very dangerous place.

FAKE NEWS!

Past American presidents have loathed the media. An aggressive watchdog media makes it harder for presidents to act without public scrutiny. Of course, that's the point of a free and independent press. And that's why most past American presidents, while criticizing the press, have still acknowledged its role as a lynchpin of democratic society. George W. Bush, who had his share of spats with reporters, reminded us of this simple fact in an interview about a month after Trump took office. "I consider the media to be indispensable to democracy," he said. "I mean, power can be very addictive and it can be corrosive and it's important for the media to call to account people who abuse their power, whether it be here or elsewhere."[34] He's absolutely right about that. It's worrying that such a reminder was necessary.

Democracy is based on informed consent of the governed. For people to consent to their government, they have to know what is going on, with access to well-sourced, credible reporting that is not constantly being unfairly maligned as "fake news." Without that, democracy is nothing more than a hollow shell for authoritarian rule. Donald Trump is bringing us closer to that undemocratic precipice. Between weaponizing distrust toward the press, threatening them with financial costs for negative reporting, encouraging violence against journalists, and accelerating the creation of a parallel state media apparatus, Trump would like us to believe that anyone who criticizes his administration is "fake news" and an "enemy of the American people." He's wrong. And most Americans know he's wrong. Those that he calls the "fake news media" are accurately reporting facts. Those facts are undermining his administration not because they are conspiring against him, but because the facts themselves are not popular with most Americans. Yet the damage is still being done. For tens of millions of Americans, Trump has fostered tremendous distrust of independent sources of truth. That damage will be difficult to repair. His assault on the press and the undemocratic fallout may be one of his longest-lasting legacies. That is, unless we—like Pravit Rojanaphruk of Thailand—are brave enough to defend democracy by protecting press freedom while it's under attack.

3

LOCK HER UP!

I arrived in Minsk, the capital of Belarus, in early December 2015. As an American, I was led out of the main passenger line at border control and shuffled off to the side. When the woman behind the desk saw my American passport, she pulled out a special magnifying glass, like the ones diamond jewelers use to investigate a precious stone. She inspected each page carefully, and finally, reluctantly, waved me through without a word. A little while later, my phone started buzzing with security alerts. Someone in Minsk had gained access to my Skype account. Someone was trying, and thankfully failing, to access my Facebook and e-mail. It had taken the government less than an hour to hack me.

They probably had advance warning that I was coming. I had been corresponding with several high-profile dissidents, activists, and presidential candidates who were certainly being monitored by the KGB, the Belarusian spy service that still uses the Soviet-era acronym. I shouldn't have been surprised. What can you expect from the country that many refer to as "the last dictatorship in Europe"?

Rule of law does not exist in Belarus, at least not for anyone connected to the regime. I quickly began to understand what that meant in practice. I interviewed opposition politicians, journalists, activists, and even artists who had been harassed, jailed, or assaulted for their political views. One of my interviewees, presidential candidate Uladzimir Nyaklyayew, had been beaten almost to death in the street on election day in 2010, by regime thugs wielding iron rods. His wounds were so severe that he was put in an intensive care unit at the hospital. Then, when it became clear that Nyaklyayew would survive, he was abducted from the hospital and tossed into a dark prison cell. His crime? He dared to defy the dictator, Alexander Lukashenko.[1] Somehow, those who stand up to the dictator always end up on the wrong side of the law—or an iron rod—while those wielding the rods never seem to be caught or brought to justice.

It was on a dark winter afternoon that I found Mikalai Statkevich, whom we already met in the Introduction, in a café in the center of Minsk, a city that looks and feels like a living museum of the Soviet Union. It was about 4:30pm, so the café was mostly empty. I walked over to the corner table where the ex-candidate was sitting, we shook hands, and sat down. About a minute later, a young woman walked in. Rather than choosing to sit at any of the dozens of empty tables, she made a beeline for us. She sat down in the booth behind us, took out her phone, and pretended to read the news. Statkevich, seeming amused, explained in a low voice that he had deliberately picked an establishment that he knew wasn't bugged—clearly forcing the KGB to come and eavesdrop in person. He told me the story of his arrest in 2010, right after Uladzimir Nyaklyayew was beaten nearly to death. There were no chants of "Lock him up!" but Statkevich was tossed in a jail cell and left to rot, sentenced to six years in prison for simply trying to hold a peaceful rally in support of his candidacy.[2]

LOCK HER UP!

In 2015, as part of a negotiation with the European Union, the dictator, Alexander Lukashenko, pardoned Statkevich. The pardon was used as a political bargaining chip, giving a peaceful candidate his freedom in exchange for a loosening of Western sanctions on Belarus. When I met Statkevich in Minsk, he had only just been freed. The whole fiasco exposed a terrifying truth about rule of law in Belarus: it is what the dictator makes it. If he says you're guilty, you are. If he says you're innocent, you are. Those that are loyal get promoted. Those that are disloyal end up fired or in jail. Despots control the law. It is their weapon, a tool to keep people in line by scaring them off standing up to the regime. A person's freedom can become a political bargaining chip, to be traded in exchange for political concessions or favors. Pardons are politicized. Those who defend the regime's preferred values or parrot its narrative don't have to rot in jail. Those who don't, might.

The power of dictatorship is also the power to prosecute the innocent and protect the guilty. In other field research across the world, from sub-Saharan Africa to the Middle East and Southeast Asia, I've seen how societies become dysfunctional and drift toward dictatorship when rule of law becomes politicized. I've interviewed former presidents and prime ministers in authoritarian countries, and off the record they'll admit it: politicizing rule of law was an essential part of their consolidation of power—or keeping in line those who dared stand up to them. Toss a political rival in jail. Pardon a political ally. To forge an iron fist, you first must melt down rule of law until it can be welded to the despot's whims.

In functioning democracies, rule of law prevents such abuses. Politicians are subject to laws, not whims. Political loyalty has nothing to do with whether someone is convicted or acquitted of a crime. It doesn't matter if you agree with the president. It doesn't matter if the president's political supporters love you or loathe you. Justice is not to be served or withheld based on politics. On this count, the United States is lurching toward total dysfunction. Since the summer of 2016, rule of law has become highly politicized. It's the culmination of decades of dangerous political polarization. As American politics becomes increasingly tribal, it opens the door to improper politicization by Democrats and Republicans.

At the time of writing, for example, there is currently a bipartisan investigation underway into whether President Obama's Attorney General, Loretta Lynch, behaved inappropriately in overseeing the 2016 federal investigation into the then candidate Hillary Clinton's use of a private e-mail server during her time as secretary of state (2009–13). Lynch met with Bill Clinton on an airport tarmac in Phoenix, Arizona in June 2016—a move that was highly unusual and likely improper. It never should have happened, because even if it was innocuous, it gave a clear impression of partiality on behalf of the top law enforcement official in the Department of Justice. FBI Director James Comey also testified that Lynch had told him to refer to the Clinton investigation by the word "matter" rather than "investigation."[3] If that is true, it was also improper; political appointees should never try to downplay the seriousness of an investigation into their political allies.

But there is, so far, no evidence that the FBI investigation was quashed by any sort of political interference. In fact, FBI Director James Comey was aware of the sensitivities of the case and wanted to ensure that Americans could retain faith in the independence of the bureau's investigations.[4] So, in early July 2016, he opened his statement on the case by saying: "I have not coordinated or reviewed this statement in any way with the Department of Justice or any other part of the government. They do not know what I am about to say." Then, he explained that the FBI had concluded that Clinton was "extremely careless" in handling classified information. That's true. She was. But he also explained that "no reasonable prosecutor" would bring charges against Clinton, so the investigation had run its course. In the FBI's judgment, there was no criminal wrongdoing.[5]

That judgment might turn out to be good news for the Trump administration, as reporting has now uncovered that several senior Trump administration officials, including senior adviser and presidential son-in-law Jared Kushner, have been using private e-mail for public business—an internal investigation has been launched.[6] But, more importantly, rule of law can become improperly politicized when, regardless of what the law or the evidence show, a politician is deemed guilty in the court of public opinion. Even after the FBI deemed that Hillary Clinton had done nothing illegal, Trump aimed to convict her in people's minds.

On 19 July 2016—two weeks after Comey's announcement clearing Clinton of criminal wrongdoing—New Jersey Governor Chris Christie took to the stage at the Republican National Convention. He invoked his experience as a former federal prosecutor to put on a mock show trial of Hillary Clinton. He used legal terms—guilty or not guilty—to refer to political decisions taken during her time as secretary of state. "We're going to present the facts to you, as a jury of her peers, both in this hall and in living rooms around our nation," Christie said. In referencing Libya's collapse after a NATO-led intervention, Christie placed the blame at Clinton's feet before demanding, "Answer me now, is she guilty or not guilty?" The crowd roared: "Guilty!" Then Christie slammed Clinton for praising the Chinese government's purchase of American debt. "Is she guilty or not guilty?" Over and over, the crowd cried, "Guilty!"[7]

Certainly, it's fair game to criticize decisions that a secretary of state made while in office. But to invoke language of guilt and innocence for political stances or decisions wasn't an outlier, it was a strategy. During this mock trial, Christie was interrupted repeatedly by crowd chants of "Lock her up! Lock her up!" as he cataloged a litany of legal and legitimate political decisions. Rather than rebuking the crowd, he embraced it. "All right, all right," he said, smiling. "We're getting there. Give ya a few more minutes. We'll get there." (It is no small irony that Chris Christie and his entourage have long been under criminal investigation for their role in the so-called "Bridgegate" scandal, in which traffic jams were deliberately created as a means of political retribution against a Democratic mayor who was one of Christie's rivals. Two of Christie's top aides have already been convicted and he faces an ongoing investigation.)[8]

"Lock her up!" became the most memorable catchphrase of the Republican National Convention. Former Director of National Intelligence Michael Flynn, who is himself now the target of several federal criminal investigations, also led chants of "lock her up!" from the stage.[9] Throughout July, when the angry mob chanted to jail a political candidate from a rival party, speaker after speaker encouraged them by replying, "That's right!" All around the arena, enthusiastic Trump supporters could buy a wide array of "Hillary for Prison!" merchandise, including stickers showing the candidate in an orange prison jumpsuit. It was a scene straight out of a banana republic.

Then, in the second presidential debate on 9 October 2016, Trump specifically told Hillary Clinton that "you'd be in jail" if he became president. When I heard that, I gasped. I have interviewed presidential candidates who have been tossed in jail or put under house arrest in Madagascar, Zambia, Belarus, and Tunisia. Now, that threat had been made in the United States of America. Nor was it an isolated incident. At rallies Trump told the crowd that "she has to go to jail." On Twitter he repeated these insistences that Clinton "should be in jail."

In making those statements, Trump violated a fundamental principle in democratic politics. But you don't have to take my word for it. During Senator Jeff Sessions's confirmation hearing as Trump's attorney general, he said, "We can never have a political dispute turn into a criminal dispute ... This country does not punish its political enemies."[10] And yet, Sessions was one of Trump's staunchest defenders, even as the candidate was calling for his political opponent to be jailed.

Despots and dictators have the power to jail their opponents, even if they are innocent. When the rule of law becomes a weapon wielded against political opponents, democracy is dead. Thankfully, Trump's calls for Clinton to be jailed have not been answered. But the damage has been done. In polls conducted after the presidential debate wherein Trump threatened to jail his political rival, 64% of Republicans approved of the comment; only 24% thought it was inappropriate.[11] The line between rule of law and politics has been blurred.

Furthermore, despots and dictators wield the law arbitrarily not just as a weapon to attack their opponents but also as a shield for their political allies. In robust democracies, presidents aren't able to protect the guilty—but, unfortunately, the United States doesn't fully live up to that measure. Specifically, it suffers from a pretty big loophole that allows presidents to protect the guilty: presidential pardons. This power has long been abused by presidents, sometimes egregiously. For example, hours before leaving office, President Bill Clinton pardoned Marc Rich, who had been convicted of sixty-five criminal counts including racketeering, tax evasion, and doing business with Iran's rogue regime—even while the Iranian regime was holding American hostages in the early 1980s. Rich, as his name suggests, was a wealthy man. His wife funneled more than $1 million to the Democratic Party, $100,000 to Hillary Clinton's Senate campaign, and $450,000 to the Clinton Presidential Library.[12] As presidential pardons go, this was about the clearest example you could get of a quid pro quo. It was a disgrace to the rule of law.

(For what it's worth, though it's enshrined in the Constitution, I believe that the power of presidential pardon should be removed via constitutional amendment. If laws aren't working, they can be changed. If the system isn't working, it can be reformed. But the piecemeal, Caesar-like approach of thumbs-up-or-down justice is neither fair nor democratic.)

Though the Bill Clinton example demonstrates the problem with presidential pardons, most past presidents have taken the power seriously and exercised it responsibly. They consider pardon applications carefully. For the overwhelming majority of pardons, years of scrutiny are put into ensuring that the pardon serves justice rather than undermining it. President Obama, for example, commuted the sentences of hundreds of nonviolent drug offenders. Many of them had been sentenced to decades behind bars for selling a small amount of marijuana or cocaine. These were not pardons that depended on personal political loyalty; they were initiated because Obama believed that these mandatory sentences were excessively harsh. It is an important distinction. Presidents George W. Bush, Bill Clinton, Ronald Reagan, and other Republicans and Democrats throughout history have also delivered excellent pardons that advanced American justice.

President Trump, on the other hand, has gotten off to an atrocious start. As of October 2017, he has issued one pardon so far—to Sheriff Joe Arpaio. This decision was unprecedented for a few reasons. First, it was made early on in Trump's first term, rather than at the last minute, which means that the pardon could be used as a signal to others that they should stay loyal to the president, as he could pardon them too. Clinton's pardon of Rich was appalling, but at least it was done on Clinton's way out the door, which meant that Clinton would no longer have legal authority, and it wasn't possible to interpret the act as an investment in his future influence as president. Second, Trump's pardon of Arpaio didn't follow proper procedure. There was no review by the Office of the Pardon Authority to determine the merits of the pardon; it was simply announced on a whim by Trump himself. Third, and most importantly, it was the first pardon given to someone who had used state authority to pursue racist ends—since the Civil War. That sends a terrible signal about rule of law to law enforcement officers, as it tacitly endorses racially motivated tactics in policing. So, let's take a look at what Arpaio did to warrant the honor of being President Trump's first pardon.

In 1993, Maricopa County Sheriff Joe Arpaio opened "Tent City" in Arizona. It was an outdoor section of surplus tents from the Korean War housed within a larger prison complex. It was brutal by design because it was outdoors; Arpaio himself often boasted that the prisoners in Tent City would be exposed to temperatures up to 142 degrees Fahrenheit (61.1 degrees Celsius).[13] On cold days, inmates were trapped outdoors as temperatures plunged to 41 Fahrenheit (5 Celsius). Holes in the tents meant that some beds would get soaked whenever it rained. Everything about Tent City was intended to degrade as well as punish. Male inmates were forced to wear pink underwear, pink sandals, and use pink towels. Arpaio invited television cameras to film the humiliated prisoners. They were forced to work on chain gangs— a practice that mostly ended throughout the rest of the United States in 1955.[14]

Lawsuits mounted. Over and over, Arpaio lost in court, as judges ruled that treatment of prisoners was abusive or inhumane or unconstitutional. Twice, a federal judge ruled that the lack of medical care in Tent City was so awful that it was an unconstitutional violation of prisoners' basic rights. In an environment of extreme brutality and suffering, prisoners hanged themselves four times more frequently than those in Chicago or Miami jails.[15] Many of the deaths took place under mysterious circumstances with no explanation given in the paperwork. In one particularly grisly case, Felix Torres complained to prison staff that he had severe pain in his abdomen. He had told them about his ulcers. The medical staff ignored him, while he vomited over and over, screaming in agony. Finally, they gave Torres a drug that is specifically banned for people who have ulcers. The drug killed him. Yet the file simply states that he died in the hospital. Nothing more. If an investigative reporter from the *Phoenix New Times* hadn't gone through the legwork of investigating the case, we wouldn't know the full gruesome history. How many of the other 156 deaths that occurred in Arpaio's jails were due to such negligence?[16] We may never know.

While lawsuits swirled around Tent City, Arpaio became increasingly politically active. He started aggressively pushing two stances: a crackdown on illegal immigration and the bogus racist lie that President Obama was born in Kenya.[17] At one point, Arpaio segregated prisoners by race, splitting Hispanics off into a separate and more desolate part of the jail. Again, he invited television crews to film it.[18] He gave officers orders to start patrolling in search of illegal immigrants, even if they had committed no other crime. That was a violation of guidelines which left such investigations and arrests up to the federal immigration authorities. In 2011, a federal judge ruled that Arpaio's patrols were engaging in racial profiling, as they were exclusively harassing people who looked Latino. The case couldn't have been more clear-cut, given that his officers were pulling over cars and questioning people based on the color of their skin.[19] Arpaio was ordered to stop. But, despite the ruling, Arpaio insisted that the patrols would continue. He defied the court order.

At the same time, Arpaio's star rose further amongst the political right as he started to vocally push "birtherism." For those on the right, like Donald Trump, who believed that racist lie about President Obama, Arpaio became a sort of folk hero. He even went so far as to send a deputy to Hawaii to search for Obama's birth certificate[20]—unlike Trump himself, whose claims to have done so have been questioned.[21] Arpaio was a man after Trump's heart, while Trump's abusive language toward Mexicans had won him Arpaio's heart in return. In March 2016, Arpaio endorsed candidate Trump. Rather than distance himself from a man who had overseen one of America's most deliberately brutal and inhumane jails, Trump tweeted the news in celebration. Over the years, while becoming a rising political star in the nativist wing of the Republican Party, Arpaio relished his cruelty. He referred to his jails as "a concentration camp."[22] When pressed on this by a reporter, he claimed it was "a joke" before doubling down on his earlier phrase. "But even if it was a concentration camp, what difference does it make? I still survived. I still kept getting re-elected."[23] Perhaps Arpaio does not realize that election victories do not absolve abuse.

Under Trump, Arpaio will never learn that lesson. In late July 2016, Arpaio was found guilty of criminal contempt after a federal judge ruled that he had deliberately ignored a court order to cease and desist his racial profiling.[24] This was no surprise; Arpaio had repeatedly said that he would ignore the court and continue regardless. It was flagrant disregard for rule of law, as Arpaio acted as though he were above it. However, for a time, it appeared as though the consequences were about to catch up with Sheriff Joe. He was due for sentencing in October 2017.

This is when President Trump stepped in. Shortly after taking office in January 2017, he met with Attorney General Jeff Sessions and White House Counsel Don McGahn II. He asked them if there was anything they could do to get the case against Arpaio dropped.[25] That question alone was highly improper, as presidential administrations are not supposed to actively intervene in ongoing cases working their way through the courts. After all, rule of law can't function if presidents can simply intervene for their friends. Thankfully, Trump's attorneys told him that there was nothing they could do to influence the case. But, they said, he could pardon Sheriff Joe.

In late August, Trump traveled to Arizona and gave a bizarre, rambling speech. At one point, he asked the adoring audience, "Was Sheriff Joe convicted for doing his job?" The crowd cheered. They should have booed. Joe Arpaio wasn't convicted for doing his job. He was convicted for racial profiling in law enforcement, and for refusing to stop when ordered to by a federal judge. Beyond the awful example the original offense set for law enforcement, what kind of signal does it send to judges when they witness the president pardon someone who has blatantly and openly ignored a court order? What kind of signal does it send to American minorities who worry that the law is a tool not to protect them but to oppress them?

In interviews shortly before his pardon, Arpaio argued that "if they can go after me, they can go after anyone."[26] Yes, Sheriff Joe, that is an apt description of rule of law in a democracy. If they can go after a sheriff who breaks the law, they can go after a car dealer or a personal trainer or a senator or a president. Dictators can protect the guilty, but democratically elected American presidents should not be able to do the same.

The Arpaio pardon is deeply troubling in itself. But more worrying is the fact that Trump could have been using that pardon as a signal to his cronies caught up in the Russia investigation: if you remain loyal, you could get pardoned. If you flip and cooperate with the investigation, you're on your own. Trump could have waited for Arpaio to be sentenced in October, yet instead he issued a highly unconventional pardon just as Special Prosecutor Bob Mueller's Russia investigation was gaining steam. That pardon for Arpaio followed after Trump had asked his legal team whether he, the president, could pardon himself. Then Trump made the rather unusual move of tweeting that "all agree the US president has the complete power to pardon." Clearly, pardons have been on the president's mind.

4

FROM RUSSIA WITH LOVE

Past presidents may have abused the pardon power, but by using his authority to protect the guilty for obviously political reasons, Trump has inched closer to a signature move of despots. One could hope that Sheriff Arpaio's pardon was no more than an isolated regrettable incident—but the revelations to date of the investigation into Russia's links to the Trump campaign have already shown that such optimism is not warranted.

Despots and would-be despots usually use the law as a political weapon. Sometimes, though, they get careless. To win or stay in power, they bend the rules. They get involved in behavior that is unethical, illegal, or both. Because they see themselves as above the law, they break it. But in systems where rule of law still exists, despots can find themselves on the wrong side of the law—as they themselves become the focus of a criminal investigation. A cornered despot can become desperate. To save themselves, their family, or their cronies, first they deny. Then, they mislead or lie. Finally, once caught, they fire people who are investigating them, and start a campaign to deflect blame. In those moments, despots show their true colors—that they are only committed to the rule of law if it serves their own interests. When rule of law becomes a threat to their own political survival, despots try to undermine it.

In 2013, Turkish prime minister-turned-despot Recep Tayyip Erdogan (now Turkey's president) was facing serious, career-threatening allegations of corruption within his inner circle. Officials at the highest echelon of his regime were accused of receiving "bribes in exchange for ignoring zoning rules and approving contentious development projects."[1] The allegations were credible. Erdogan denied them outright. Then, police raids on members of the ruling elite netted $17.5 million in cash, which was allegedly slated to be used for bribery.[2] Erdogan's supporters then began disseminating fabricated stories, aimed at providing political cover. But the probe continued and began to broaden, to include Erdogan's son. As his family began to be dragged into the net of suspicion, it was obvious that the prime minister himself was the next logical target.

Erdogan isn't one to be constrained by the pesky guardrails of democracy, such as the rule of law. Before the prosecutorial net started to close in around him and his goons, Erdogan simply fired the four prosecutors assigned to the investigation. He reassigned other senior judges and prosecutors. Erdogan also reassigned 470 police officers.[3] It was the largest purge in the history of Turkey's judiciary. A few months later, prosecutors dropped the case altogether. They could see the writing on the wall: pursuing the case was career suicide. Then, after trying to interfere in the investigation, Erdogan deflected blame for the scandal. It was the fault of his enemies, he claimed. The Jews were behind the allegations. The Americans were behind it.[4] It was a witch hunt by his opponents and enemies. He painted himself as the victim of an elaborate conspiracy that seemed to fly in the face of all available evidence.

Nobody seems to investigate Erdogan any more. Democracy failed. Erdogan could protect himself, his family, and his political allies with impunity. His machinations offer an important warning for America, as the Trump-Russia investigations continue to unfold. While the parallels are imperfect, Trump and his campaign have followed the same pattern as Erdogan's Turkey: engage in unethical and possibly illegal behavior; deny it; mislead or lie about it; try to fire the people involved in the investigation; and then deflect the blame onto someone or something else.

A version of that pattern has, of course, played out previously in American history. In the summer of 1972, five men broke into the Democratic National Committee's headquarters at the Watergate Complex. They tapped phones and photographed secret campaign documents. Their aim was simple: to get dirt on their Democratic opponent to help President Richard Nixon win re-election in the upcoming 1972 presidential contest. But on the night of the break-in, the five men were caught and arrested. Everything began to spiral out of control in what would become the biggest American scandal of the twentieth century.

Initially, Nixon flat-out denied any involvement in either the break-in or the subsequent cover-up. Less than a week after a special prosecutor, Archibald Cox, was named to investigate the events of the 1972 election, Nixon claimed that: "I took no part in, nor was I aware of, any subsequent efforts that may have been made to cover up Watergate."[5] This was not true. In fact, Nixon had been orchestrating an elaborate cover-up from the Oval Office. But he continued to lie and deny, before claiming that he was a victim of a political conspiracy to tarnish him. The headline of the 22 July 1973 *Washington Post* read: "Nixon sees 'Witch-Hunt,' Insiders Say."[6]

During the summer of 1973, news broke that there were tape recordings of conversations that Nixon had with a variety of figures implicated in the Watergate cover-up. Special Prosecutor Cox subpoenaed the recordings. Nixon wouldn't hand them over, citing executive privilege. Nixon then ordered Cox to drop his subpoena request, but Cox refused. On 20 October 1973, in what has since been deemed the "Saturday Night Massacre," Nixon ordered his attorney general, Elliot Richardson, to fire Cox. Richardson refused and resigned instead. Nixon then ordered Deputy Attorney General William Ruckelshaus to fire Cox. He too refused and resigned. Finally, Nixon reached Solicitor General Robert Bork, who carried out the president's order.[7]

By the summer of 1974, despite Cox's removal, the investigation had progressed considerably. Finally, on 4 August 1974, under Supreme Court order the White House released what would become known as the "smoking gun" tape, showing that President Nixon had conspired to obstruct justice by ordering the CIA to interfere in the FBI's investigation. Up until that tape was released, Nixon had falsely claimed that he was not involved in the scandal at all. Five days later, Nixon resigned the presidency and left office in disgrace.

There are striking parallels between Nixon's Watergate scandal and the ongoing investigations into the Trump/Russia scandal—with a dash of Erdogan's behavior thrown in for good measure. However, the allegations against Trump are far more serious than those against Nixon. Nixon was accused of conspiring to break into the DNC headquarters to steal documents in order to win the election. Trump's campaign team, including perhaps Trump himself, are being investigated over allegations of potential collusion with Russia, the main foreign adversary of the United States, to digitally break into the DNC servers and steal documents in order to win the election. The involvement of any foreign state—let alone Russia—makes this case an order of magnitude worse.

Furthermore, these unproven allegations extend into a social media disinformation campaign and into hacks of Hillary Clinton's campaign. Trump's campaign entourage included figures with close ties to senior Kremlin-linked oligarchs. Their Moscow connections have raised serious, credible questions as to whether Trump's campaign is beholden in any way to Vladimir Putin's government. In essence, Trump and the Trump campaign are being investigated for allegedly working with a foreign power to subvert democracy in order to illegitimately win an election. If any of those allegations turn out to be true, it would be the most serious political scandal in American history.

Finally, as with Nixon, the investigation is considering whether President Trump obstructed justice by firing the person leading the investigation—in this case, FBI Director James Comey—and whether there were any attempts from Trump or the White House to cover up or improperly downplay any damning revelations. There are therefore two components to the investigation. First, what happened during the campaign? Did Trump's campaign collude with the Russian government? Second, did Trump try to obstruct justice when those questions began being investigated? In both matters, Trump, his family, and his associates have often followed a pattern familiar to both despots like Erdogan and a former US president, Nixon: deny, mislead or lie, fire the investigator, and then deflect blame while painting yourself as the victim of a "witch hunt."

Let's start with what we know happened—with the caveat that this book went to press in early autumn 2017, when it was still unclear what the outcome of the Russia investigations would be. Many details are still unclear, and some of this information could change once the various investigations publish their official findings. However, we are already certain of three key facts.

First, the Russian government used digital tools, including hacking, in an attempt to sway the 2016 election in Trump's favor. There is clear evidence that the Russian government hacked into the Democratic National Committee servers and stole documents; hacked the e-mail account of John Podesta, Hillary Clinton's campaign chairman; organized a social media disinformation campaign; and attempted to hack into voting servers in twenty-one states.[8]

Second, top-level figures in Trump's campaign sought to collude with the Russian government to beat Hillary Clinton (whether they colluded directly or not is still the subject of ongoing investigations).[9]

Third, Trump, his campaign team, and those close to him have repeatedly misled or lied about the investigation—until they got caught. Sometimes, their stories have changed not just day to day, but hour to hour. Other times, the White House has come up with an official line, only to have President Trump contradict it moments later on Twitter.

To get to the bottom of what really happened, Special Counsel Robert (Bob) Mueller is conducting a wide-ranging investigation into Russian interference in the 2016 election and potential collusion from the Trump campaign. From what we know of the Mueller investigation so far—which is, of course, an incomplete picture—there are ten main storylines that have solid evidence behind them. Each storyline makes clear that Trump is not the victim of a witch hunt or a conspiracy but is rather at the center of a serious political scandal that is already damaging his presidency and could destroy it. Eight of the storylines relate to Trump's and his campaign's conduct during the election or the post-election transition. The final two are related to obstruction of justice allegations and whether Trump, like Erdogan and

Nixon, engaged in an authoritarian abuse of power by hindering a politically inconvenient investigation.

Storyline 1: Donald Trump's business was actively courting new commercial ventures that required Russian government approval—during the 2016 campaign.

This is important because the effort to generate new business in Russia provided Putin's government with financial leverage over Trump while Trump was discussing his plans for US foreign policy toward Russia.

On 13 October 2015, Felix Sater (a longtime Trump adviser with close ties to the Kremlin who had previously pleaded guilty to committing fraud orchestrated by the Russian mafia) sent Trump a letter of intent to build Trump Tower Moscow.[10] On or around 28 October, Trump signed the letter.[11] A few days later, on 3 November, Sater wrote to Michael Cohen, an executive vice president of the Trump Organization, boasting that he would get in touch with Putin and convince him to help ensure that Trump won the 2016 election. "I will get Putin on this program and we will get Donald elected ... Buddy our boy can become president of the USA and we can engineer it. I will get all of Putin's team to buy in on this, I will manage this process."[12]

During the 2016 campaign, Trump repeatedly denied any business deals with Russia. He made those misleading denials shortly after he had signed a letter of intent to build a major new building in Moscow. Then, when later asked questions about his ties to Felix Sater, Trump pretended that he barely knew him. "Felix Sater—boy, I have to even think about it. I'm not that familiar with him," Trump told a reporter from the Associated Press.[13] As we now know, Sater was the point person for Trump Tower

Moscow, who had worked with Trump for years and who had organized a tour of Moscow for Trump's children. The two men have been photographed together many times. Deny, mislead or lie, get caught.

Storyline 2: Two of Trump's top campaign advisers—Michael Flynn and Paul Manafort—had dubious ties to the Kremlin and became vulnerable to being blackmailed by Russia.

As Trump's business was laying the groundwork for Trump Tower Moscow, former Director of National Intelligence Michael Flynn traveled to Moscow at the request of the Russian government. He was paid $45,000 by RT, Putin's propaganda network, to give a speech in Moscow.[14] After the speech, Flynn attended an RT-hosted dinner,[15] during which he sat near Vladimir Putin. That showed alarmingly bad judgment, and a willingness to get paid to legitimize a man who had been slapped with American sanctions the previous year for annexing Crimea, part of the sovereign independent state of Ukraine. For some perspective, other "enemy" regimes subjected to US sanctions have included Cuba, Syria, North Korea and Iran. Flynn later told Congress that "I didn't take any money from Russia, if that's what you're asking me."[16] That was untrue. The Kremlin knew he had lied, and now had some leverage over him as a result.

But the real leverage came later. On 29 December 2016, just weeks before Trump took office, Flynn placed not one, but five calls to the Russian ambassador.[17] When he took office—after the calls were made, but before they became publicly known—Trump appointed Flynn as his national security adviser. Then, when news of the calls broke, Flynn initially denied that anything of substance had been discussed, stating that he had only been in touch to discuss logistics of a call between President-Elect Trump and Putin, and to wish Ambassador Sergey Kislyak a Merry Christmas (apparently ignorant that Russian Orthodox Christmas is celebrated in early January, not late December).[18] Later, Flynn flatly denied that he had discussed sanctions with the Russian ambassador. A day after that initial denial, new evidence emerged, and Flynn's story shifted—now, he couldn't be sure that sanctions didn't come up.[19] We later found out that Sally Yates, the acting attorney general, had warned Trump that Flynn was lying in public statements about the content of those calls—and that he was therefore vulnerable to Russian blackmail.[20] Despite that warning, Trump kept Flynn in his post until the media got hold of the story. Flynn then resigned on 13 February 2017.

Longtime Republican campaign adviser and lobbyist Paul Manafort also had questionable ties to the Kremlin and was vulnerable to Russian leverage. He has a laundry list of dubious former lobbying clients, including some with close ties to Putin.[21] On 28 March 2016, primary candidate Trump hired Manafort and tasked him with leading his campaign's effort to garner delegates for the Republican National Convention in the summer.[22] Within a month, Trump promoted Manafort to the post of campaign manager.

On 14 August 2016, *The New York Times* reported that Manafort had received $12.7 million in undisclosed cash payments from a pro-Russian party in Ukraine.[23] Manafort flatly denied those allegations. However, Manafort's name appeared twenty-two times in a handwritten ledger of payments. When reporters checked, they found that the other entries around his name appeared to be authentic. Three days later, news broke from the Associated Press that Manafort had secretly routed $2.2 million in payments to lobbyists in Washington.[24] Later on, in April 2017, the Associated Press confirmed that at least two of the twenty-two payments listed in the Ukrainian ledger had been made to Manafort, proof that he was lying about them being fabricated.[25]

Manafort is in serious legal trouble. In late 2017, several media outlets reported that Manafort had been the subject of several waves of government wiretaps—a development that suggests a national security court saw evidence giving them probable cause to believe that he was working with or on behalf of a foreign power.[26] Manafort and Flynn are reportedly at the center of Mueller's investigation.

Storyline 3: Did top officials in Trump's campaign intend to collude with the Russian government to get dirt on Hillary Clinton, in the aim of helping Trump win the election?

In early June 2016, Donald Trump Jr received an e-mail from British music publicist Rob Goldstone claiming that one of Goldstone's clients, Emin Agalarov, the son of Azerbaijani-Russian oligarch Aras Agalarov, had information for the Trump campaign. The elder Agalarov had previously worked with Trump in 2013 to bring the Miss Universe pageant to Moscow.[27] Agalarov, who is a close ally of Vladimir Putin, was heavily photographed with Trump flashing his trademark thumbs up in Moscow in 2013. This is important, because intelligence analysts and former intelligence officers highlight the fact that Russian spy operations usually try to make initial contact through a person known to the target.[28]

The e-mail exchange is incredibly damning. The initial message from Goldstone began: "The Crown prosecutor of Russia met with [Emin's] father Aras this morning and in their meeting offered to provide the Trump campaign with some official documents and information that would incriminate Hillary and her dealings with Russia and would be very useful to your father. This is obviously very high level and sensitive information but is part of Russia and its government's support for Mr. Trump—helped along by Aras and Emin."[29]

It couldn't have been spelled out more clearly. This was a direct offer of damaging information coming straight from the Russian government to hurt Hillary Clinton and help Donald Trump. The e-mail even made clear that this was not some rogue offer from a low-level employee, but was "high level" and "sensitive," implying that it could be related to Russia's clandestine operations. Seventeen minutes later, Trump Jr responded in an email: "If it's what you say I love it."

He was accepting an offer of political dirt on the former US secretary of state of the United States, coming from the "high level" of the Russian government—a despotic regime that works against American interests and murders dissidents and journalists. Any patriotic American would not only have turned the offer down, but immediately reported it to the FBI for urgent investigation.

On 6 June 2016, Trump Jr spoke on the phone with Emin Agalarov, a call that was supposedly about the promised information. Later, even after acknowledging the records of this call, Trump Jr told investigators that he couldn't recall it.[30] The next day, 7 June, Goldstone followed up: "Emin asked that I schedule a meeting with you and the Russian government attorney who is flying over from Moscow for this Thursday." Again, it's hard to believe how unambiguous this was. What's more, Paul Manafort and Trump Jr's brother-in-law, Jared Kushner, were looped into the conversation, with the entire thread of the conversation visible to them. They didn't object to the meeting, even though they could clearly see what it was and who was offering it. Instead, at 6:14pm Trump Jr hit send on a reply confirming the meeting.

Just hours after his son had confirmed a meeting promising dirt on Hillary Clinton, Donald Trump gave a speech promising new dirt on Hillary Clinton. "I am going to give a major speech on probably Monday of next week," the candidate said. "And we're going to be discussing all of the things that have taken place with the Clintons. I think you're going to find it very informative and very, very interesting."[31]

At 4pm on 9 June, Donald Trump Jr, Paul Manafort, and Jared Kushner met with Natalia Veselnitskaya and Rinat Akhmetshin in Trump Tower. Veselnitskaya is a lawyer who has worked closely with people in Putin's inner circle and was a lawyer for the Russian secret intelligence service, the FSB, between 2005 and 2013.[32] The FSB is the post-Soviet incarnation of the KGB. Akhmetshin is a former Soviet counterintelligence military officer turned lobbyist.[33] He later told reporters that he recalled Veselnitskaya giving the Trump campaign unspecified documents at the meeting, or leaving them in the room.[34]

So, to recap: at the same time that Russia was actively conducting cyber operations and attacks aimed at manipulating the upcoming US election, three of the top figures in the Trump campaign met with a lawyer for Putin's spies and a former Russian military officer, on the promise that they would provide "high-level, sensitive" dirt, from the Russian government, on Hillary Clinton. Some campaign law experts have suggested that, if any information exchanged hands, it might be a violation of American campaign law, which prohibits receiving anything "of value" from a foreign entity.[35]

No matter what information, if any, was exchanged at that meeting, the campaign team's judgment as it was exhibited in this entire episode should have been disqualifying in itself. Anyone who accepted that meeting gleefully, or even attended it grudgingly, has no business being anywhere near the White House. And it's hard to believe that Trump—who was in Trump Tower at the time of the meeting—was unaware of a meeting taking place in the building, attended by his son, his son-in law, and his campaign manager.[36]

A series of intelligence analysts and former American spies all agreed that the e-mail offer and the initial meeting in Trump Tower were covered by the usual telltale fingerprints of a Russia spy operation.[37] They suggest that this meeting would have been the initial point of contact, trying to figure out if Trump's campaign would be interested in working together. If their speculation is correct, the Russians would certainly have received the proverbial green light. About ten minutes after the meeting ended, candidate Trump sent out a tweet about 33,000 e-mails that Hillary Clinton had allegedly deleted.[38] It was the first time that he had tweeted such a claim. The timing was another glaring coincidence.

Then, Donald Trump Jr and Paul Manafort lied repeatedly about the 9 June meeting. On 24 July 2016—just six weeks after meeting with two Russians closely linked to the Kremlin—Manafort was asked whether there were any ties between the Russian regime and the Trump campaign. "That's absurd," Manafort replied. "And, you know, there's no basis to it."[39] That same day, Trump Jr was asked about the Clinton campaign's claim that the Russians were trying to help Donald Trump get elected. Despite having responded eagerly to the offer of dirt on Clinton "as part of Russia and its government's support for Mr. Trump," Trump Jr responded: "Well it just goes to show you their exact moral compass. I mean, they'll say anything to be able to win this. I mean, this is time and time again, lie after lie."[40]

In March 2017, Trump Jr told *The New York Times*: "Did I meet with people that were Russian? I'm sure, I'm sure I did. But none that were set up. None that I can think of at the moment. And certainly none that I was representing the campaign in any way, shape or form."[41] Again, that was not true. When *The New York Times* later reported in July 2017 that Trump Jr had arranged a meeting between the campaign and Russians, he issued a statement saying that the meeting was set up to discuss adoptions.[42] That was, we now know, a lie. A day later, the same paper reported that Trump Jr knew that the meeting was set up to provide damaging information about Hillary Clinton.[43] He issued another statement, substantially revising his previous statement to incorporate the parts that *The New York Times* had reported—inching a little bit closer to the truth, out of necessity.

The next day, on 10 July, *The New York Times* reported that Trump Jr knew that the meeting was part of a larger effort by the Russian government to help his campaign win.[44] Finally, on 11 July, after he was notified that the paper was planning to publish the entire e-mail chain, Trump Jr tweeted the e-mail transcripts. He had no choice. The "Fake News" had busted him. And then, his father had the gall to praise him for his transparency—after he had lied about the meeting for over a year, got caught, changed his story, got caught again, and finally corrected the record because the country's biggest newspaper already had the transcripts proving it. This storyline is the closest thing so far to a "smoking gun." There is no longer any debate over whether elements of the Trump campaign intended to collude with the Russian government. We have the e-mail threads showing that they did.

Storyline 4: Trump advisers met frequently and privately with Russian officials during the campaign—so much so that intelligence services noticed.

In late 2015, the British eavesdropping agency GCHQ apparently intercepted "suspicious" interactions between members of Trump's campaign and known or suspected Russian agents. They reportedly passed this information to the US authorities as part of a routine exchange of information.[45]

On 21 March 2016, *Washington Post* reporters asked Trump who was advising his campaign on foreign affairs. Trump named five people. Two of the names he mentioned were people with deep ties to the Kremlin: Carter Page and George Papadopoulos.[46] Three days after that interview, Papadopoulos sent an e-mail to seven senior campaign staff with the subject line "Meeting with Russian Leadership—Including Putin." These were the first of many failed attempts by Papadopoulos to broker a direct meeting between Putin and Trump.[47]

As for Carter Page, several media outlets reported in April 2017 that his personal communications had been monitored since the previous summer by the US government.[48] As with Manafort, this type of surveillance would likely only have been possible if a judge in a national security court had seen evidence giving probable cause to believe that Page was working with or on behalf of a foreign power in some way.[49] Page traveled to Moscow in July 2016 while he was working for the Trump campaign. It is still unclear who he met with during that trip, but he gave a speech in Moscow on 7 July that denounced American foreign policy on Russia.[50] We also know that he met with Russian Ambassador Kislyak on a separate occasion that month, on 18 July at the Republican National Convention.[51]

Kislyak had been busy with the Trump campaign in 2016. In April he had met with Trump's son-in-law, Jared Kushner, and Trump campaign surrogate Senator Jeff Sessions, at the Mayflower Hotel in Washington DC.[52] Like Page, Sessions also talked with Kislyak at the Convention in July, four days after a Russian account named Guccifer 2.0—a government actor, according to US intelligence[53]—released a batch of documents hacked from the DNC servers.[54] Sessions and Kislyak met again, privately, on 8 September and discussed the campaign.[55] Sessions would later become Trump's attorney general. However, during his confirmation hearing in front of the Senate Judiciary Committee, he made a false statement regarding his contacts with Russians during the campaign. He told Minnesota Senator Al Franken, under oath, that he had had none.[56] In fact, as we've seen, there had been many. Following the standard pattern, Sessions denied—then he was caught.

During the campaign, many Republicans had taken note of the Trump campaign's dubious ties to Moscow. In the summer of 2016, Republican House Majority Leader Kevin McCarthy had been caught on tape speculating about the source of the DNC hack during remarks at a Republican House caucus meeting. "I'll guarantee you that's what it is," McCarthy said. "The Russians hacked the DNC and got the opp [opposition] research they had on Trump." He continued, "There's two people I think Putin pays: [California Republican Congressman Dana] Rohrabacher and Trump." When some members of the Republican caucus laughed, McCarthy added, "Swear to God." Speaker of the House Paul Ryan immediately shut down the conversation and warned his members: "This is an off the record ... no leaks, all right? What's said in the family stays in the family."[57]

When asked about this conversation, Paul Ryan's spokesperson said it never happened. When reporters showed Ryan and

McCarthy a transcript of the conversation, they claimed the transcript was fabricated and false. Finally, when reporters told them that they had an audio recording of the conversation, Ryan and McCarthy shifted their story and claimed it was just a joke. McCarthy's humorless "Swear to God" on the tape didn't sound that way. Deny, mislead or lie, until caught.

Storyline 5: Did the Trump campaign allegedly push the Republican Party to remove a part of the party's platform related to Ukraine that Russia opposed?

On the same day in July 2016 that Russian Ambassador Kislyak met with both Sessions and Page at the Republican National Convention, the Trump campaign started working behind the scenes at the Convention to change the party's platform in relation to Ukraine. The change removed language explicitly supporting Ukraine's resistance against Russia's 2014 intervention. The Trump campaign initially denied any involvement in that decision, but later admitted their involvement once National Public Radio reported on it.[58] This storyline remains hazy, but may prove to be an important part of the investigation.

Storyline 6: Trump directly asked the Russian government to hack Hillary Clinton on live television.

On the eve of the 2016 Democratic National Convention, WikiLeaks began dumping hacked DNC e-mails. Then, on 26 July, five days after the last batch had been posted on the site, Trump looked straight into TV cameras and invited Russia to hack Hillary Clinton. "Russia, if you're listening," he said, "I hope you're able to find the 30,000 emails that are missing. I think you will probably be rewarded mightily by our press."[59] Trump's campaign later claimed he was joking. Perhaps a more reliable source on the seriousness or light-heartedness of such remarks is the tendency of despots abroad to make similar comments "in jest"; in 2015, the Thai junta laughed off as "political satire" Prime Minister Prayuth Chan-ocha's threat to kill journalists who didn't toe the government line.[60] The FBI, at least, didn't seem to find Trump's joke funny. By the end of July, it had opened an investigation into the campaign's collusion with Russia.

Storyline 7: There is circumstantial evidence suggesting that people affiliated with Trump were aware of the Russian government's hack of Clinton's campaign chair, before it became public knowledge.

On 12 August 2016, longtime Trump confidant Roger Stone predicted that WikiLeaks would release more information related to the Clinton campaign "in the next 90 days." On 20 August, Stone, who had been privately communicating with the Russian government account of Guccifer 2.0, predicted on Twitter a downfall for Hillary Clinton's campaign chairman, John Podesta: "Trust me, it will soon [be] the Podesta's time in the barrel."[61]

Less than ninety days later, Stone was proven right on both counts. On 7 October, one month before the election, *The Washington Post* released the notorious *Access Hollywood* tape, in which Trump bragged and joked about repeatedly sexually assaulting several women.[62] In extraordinarily coincidental timing, WikiLeaks began releasing hacked e-mails from Podesta just one hour after the tape went public.[63] Roger Stone has repeatedly boasted about his "back channel communications with WikiLeaks."[64] Trump himself repeatedly praised the organization, even as it posted hacked information almost certainly obtained from a Russian cyberattack. "WikiLeaks. I love WikiLeaks!" he told a crowd as election day neared. In this final month of the campaign, he mentioned WikiLeaks at least 164 times.[65]

Storyline 8: Trump's son-in-law, Jared Kushner, admits that he sought to establish a secret backchannel to Moscow at the Russian Embassy, and that he secretly met with Putin's banker.

In public remarks, Kushner has acknowledged that he met with Russian Ambassador Kislyak in Trump Tower during the transition period. Kushner acknowledges asking in that meeting if it would be possible to use the Russian Embassy in Washington to secretly communicate with Moscow. Kushner has claimed that his proposed backchannel was intended to speak about Syria.[66]

Two weeks after his meeting with Kislyak, Kushner then met with Sergey Gorkov, a man who has been described as a "Putin crony."[67] Gorkov oversees the Russian state-owned VEB bank, which has been slapped with US sanctions. It is unclear what the two men discussed. Kushner claims they met to discuss political matters; Gorkov claims the meeting was related to Kushner's business interests only.[68] The accounts obviously contradict one another.

Kushner also failed to disclose his meeting with Kislyak on his initial security clearance form. As the full extent of his meetings came into public view, he amended the form and added 100 contacts—quite a few to have omitted unintentionally.[69] Kushner's lawyers claimed that it was an honest mistake because a member of his staff had accidentally hit the "send" button on the digital form prematurely. That's hard to believe, though, because submission of an SF-86 security clearance form requires the person submitting it to click or enter their password at twenty-eight different points before submission.[70] What's more, the revision happened months later. Not too many people who hit send too soon then wait a few months before resending the full e-mail. Finally, whether this "premature send" explanation is true or not, even the amended version of Kushner's form failed to mention the now infamous meeting in Trump Tower that promised "sensitive information" about Hillary Clinton from a "high level" of the Russian government. He had to amend the form a third time.

Storyline 9: Trump is being investigated for obstructing justice.

On 27 January 2017, just a week after his inauguration, Trump invited FBI Director James Comey over to the White House for a private dinner. Comey later testified that Trump told him behind closed doors: "I need loyalty, I expect loyalty."[71] A bit later in the dinner, according to Comey, Trump again told him, "I need loyalty." But the director of the FBI owes loyalty to the rule of law, not the president.

A few weeks later, on 14 February, Comey attended another briefing at the White House. After the meeting ended, President Trump cleared the room completely, leaving him alone with Director Comey (a fact that has been corroborated by multiple witnesses who left the room). As soon as the two were alone, says Comey, Trump told him that he wanted to talk about his former national security adviser, Michael Flynn.[72] Flynn had resigned the previous day under the cloud of his calls with Russian government officials during the campaign. According to Comey, Trump tried to push him to end the ongoing FBI investigation of Flynn. "I hope you can see your way clear to letting this go, to letting Flynn go," Trump reportedly told Comey. "He is a good guy. I hope you can let this go." Comey apparently agreed that he was a good guy but said nothing else. If Mueller believes there is evidence to suggest that Trump was pressuring Comey not to investigate Flynn, that would invite reasonable comparisons with how Nixon tried to block the FBI's Watergate investigation. It could also be grounds for an obstruction of justice case.

On 9 May 2017, Trump fired Comey. The administration defended the decision by initially claiming that the president had not personally decided to fire Comey, but was simply acting on the recommendations of a memo written by his deputy attorney general, Rod Rosenstein.[73] But then, as he often does, Trump threw his staff under the bus and contradicted them on live television. The following is a partial transcript from Trump's 11 May interview with Lester Holt on NBC News.

> TRUMP: Look he's a show boat, he's a grand stander, the FBI has been in turmoil. You know that, I know that. Everybody knows that. You take a look at the FBI a year ago, it was in virtual turmoil, less than a year ago, it hasn't recovered from that.
>
> HOLT: Monday you met with the deputy attorney general, Rod Rosen—Rosenstein.
>
> TRUMP: Right.
>
> HOLT: Did you ask for a recommendation?
>
> TRUMP: Uh what I did is I was going to fire Comey—my decision, it was not...
>
> HOLT: You had made the decision before they came in the room?
>
> TRUMP: I—I was going to fire Comey. Uh I—there's no good time to do it by the way. Uh they—they were—
>
> HOLT: Because in your letter you said I—I, I accepted their recommendation, so you had already made the decision?
>
> TRUMP: Oh, I was gonna fire regardless of recommendation.

Clearly, Trump hadn't acted on a recommendation from Deputy Attorney General Rosenstein.

Then, there was the White House's claim that Trump's firing of Comey had nothing to do with the Russia investigation. Trump's interview with Holt continued:

> TRUMP: And in fact when I decided to just do it [fire Comey], I said to myself, I said you know, this Russia thing with Trump and Russia is a made up story, it's an excuse by the Democrats for having lost an election that they should have won.[74]

In other words, Trump admitted firing Comey because of "the Russia thing with Trump." That, too, could be grounds for Mueller to argue that Trump has obstructed justice.

Finally, there is the question of whether the American people were deliberately misled by those trying to downplay or cover up damning evidence related to the Russia investigation. As mentioned previously, when news broke of the "I love it" Trump Tower meeting organized with Donald Trump Jr, the White House released an initial statement claiming that the meeting was set up to discuss adoptions. The e-mail transcript disproves that claim. But his father may also find himself in hot water, because the White House has confirmed that the president was involved in drafting that misleading statement.[75] If Trump did indeed help draft that statement while aware that the meeting was supposed to be about delivering the Russian government's "high-level, sensitive" dirt on Hillary Clinton, the president could be in serious legal jeopardy.

Storyline 10: Trump lashed out at his attorney general for properly recusing himself from the Russia investigation.

Attorney General Jeff Sessions recused himself from the Russia investigation, having met several times with Russian Ambassador Kislyak during the campaign, and having misled the Senate Judiciary Committee by claiming that he had no contacts with Russians during the campaign. Moreover, Sessions had acted as a surrogate for the campaign now under investigation. It would have been improper for him to oversee an investigation into a campaign of which he had been part. In short, Sessions' recusal decision was the reasonable course of action.[76]

Nonetheless, on 19 July 2017, Trump began attacking Sessions for stepping out. "Sessions should have never recused himself," Trump told *The New York Times*. "And if he was going to recuse himself, he should have told me before he took the job, and I would have picked somebody else."[77] Trump followed these comments with several tweets attacking Sessions. It's hard to have a charitable interpretation of this series of events. The only plausible explanation for Trump being upset over Sessions's departure from the Russia investigation lies in the fact that it limited his ability to control that investigation. Otherwise, why would he care?

As the allegations and the investigation proceeded, Trump seemed determined to invite even more comparisons with Nixon while also drawing more parallels with Erdogan. Echoing the Watergate president, Trump tweeted more than one outburst claiming that he was the victim of a "witch hunt."[78] Declaring himself the subject of a conspiracy cooked up by his opponents, in the style of Erdogan, he has called the entire investigation a "hoax" and has repeatedly claimed that the Trump/Russia allegations are an excuse fabricated by the Democrats to explain Hillary Clinton's defeat. Yet again, that claim makes no sense. The FBI investigation into the Trump campaign's dubious contacts with Russians began in July 2016, months before the election took place. Trump has also openly discussed firing Bob Mueller, a move that, if taken, could create a full-blown constitutional crisis, just as Nixon's Saturday Night Massacre had forty-three years earlier.

A troubling pattern has emerged. During the 2016 campaign, the Trump team and its surrogates engaged in behavior that they repeatedly tried to hide. They have lied or misled repeatedly until caught. This begs the obvious question: what else haven't we caught yet?

Since taking office, Trump's actions as president have showcased scorn for the rule of law: allegedly trying to get Comey to pledge loyalty; allegedly attempting to quash the FBI investigation into Michael Flynn; firing Comey; attacking Sessions because he didn't try to bury the Russia investigation, but properly recused himself; considering firing a special prosecutor tasked with investigating Trump himself. Sadly, the list is sure to grow.

The Russia investigation is not a partisan issue. In fact, there's a tremendous amount of bipartisanship surrounding it, because it's an issue that is critical for national security and the integrity of American democracy. We still don't have the full picture. We may never know exactly what happened. But Trump's instincts echo those of authoritarian rulers and the most famously corrupt president in US history. The backlash against these instincts in relation to the Russia investigation must be bipartisan too. Only then can rule of law, a foundational pillar of democracy, be preserved and protected.

Sadly, though, Russians aren't the only ones attacking the pillars of American democracy. The threat also comes from within, as Trump's own administration turns to someone who knows how to rig an election.

5

HOW TO RIG AN ELECTION

Donald Trump is the most unpopular president in modern American history. His approval ratings fell into the mid-30s after just a few months in office, a feat never accomplished so quickly in the history of American polling.[1] Moreover, those dismal ratings were caused by Trump's behavior, rather than a war-turned-quagmire or an economy in recession—the two toxins that tend to doom presidential approval ratings. In poll after poll, it seems, most Americans find Trump embarrassing rather than inspiring.

Trump's unpopularity will have electoral consequences. It could torpedo the Republicans' hopes to retain control of Congress after the 2018 midterm elections. And if his personal ratings remain this dismal, his own reelection is highly unlikely. That is, unless Trump finds a new way to mimic autocrats around the world: by unfairly tilting the election in his favor.

There are many ways to rig an election. In 2013, Azerbaijan's dictator, Ilham Aliyev, accidentally (and tragicomically) released election results on an iPhone app the day *before* voting took place.[2] In Ukraine's 2004 election, observers in opposition strongholds were astonished to see ballots marked just a few minutes earlier suddenly appear to be blank. Those voters had been given pens that used disappearing ink; their votes were invalidated when counted because they appeared to be blank protest votes, rather than votes for their preferred candidate.[3] In the 1998 St. Petersburg mayoral elections in Russia, the ruling party tried to split the vote for opposition candidate Oleg Sergeyev by finding two people—one a pensioner, the other a plumber—also named Oleg Sergeyev.[4] Because voters couldn't tell which Oleg was which, all three received votes, and the actual candidate lost.

Savvy despots and dictators are constantly coming up with innovative ways to rig an election. But the goal is always the same: to hold elections that the ruling regime cannot lose. Incumbents use rigged elections to legitimize their rule—even though in truth they only win because they stacked the deck against the opposition. But perhaps the smartest, most sophisticated and most subtle type of modern election rigging is voter suppression—dealing opposition voters out of the game altogether. If the incumbent's supporters can cast ballots but the opposition's can't, there's not as much need for heavy-handed tactics such as ballot box stuffing and assassinating opponents.

On the west coast of Central Africa lies Equatorial Guinea, a kleptocratic dictatorship ruled by Teodoro Obiang Nguema Mbasogo. He has been in power since 1979, when Jimmy Carter was in the White House—six US presidents ago. In other words, Obiang has been in power for a long time.

Obiang is brutal and cruel. But he is also a master of voter suppression. The Gabonese minority within Equatorial Guinea disproportionately opposes the government, having long been denied equal rights. They have faced constant abuse—occasionally even lynchings—simply because their skin is darker. But these days, many Gabonese are more hopeful. They now believe in the possibility, slim as it may seem, that they can secure change at the ballot box.

Obiang is not letting them achieve change easily. He is putting nearly insurmountable barriers in the way of minority voting within Equatorial Guinea. In some minority-heavy regions that are far more likely to support regime change, Obiang's cronies have instituted a poll tax, forcing ethnic minorities to pay it at least two years before the next election. Those who forget to pay, or who simply can't afford to pay, are disqualified from casting a ballot. Those who manage to make the payment are subjected on arrival at the polls to so-called "literacy tests." These tests are administered at the discretion of the voting precinct staff. While data is scant because the government does not allow it to be studied directly, it is clear that the literacy test is not applied evenly. Voters from the lighter-skinned ethnic groups, who tend to support the government, never seem to have to take these tests.

Here are a few questions from the tests (in translation). Question 20: "Spell backwards, forwards." Question 21: "Print the word 'vote' upside down, but in the correct order." And my personal favorite, Question 23: "Draw a figure that is square in shape. Divide it in half by drawing a straight line from its northeast corner to its southwest corner, and then divide it once more by drawing a broken line from the middle of its western side to the middle of its eastern side." The test was designed to make sure that most Gabonese fail it. It's a sinister masterstroke from a self-interested regime seeking to preserve its power while disempowering anyone who could oppose it. And it works.

Except, of course, none of the above is actually about Equatorial Guinea. It's about the civil rights era in the American South. Substitute the Gabonese for African-Americans; the poll taxes in West Africa for poll taxes in Mississippi; and the "literacy test" is from Louisiana as recently as 1964.[5] You don't have to travel to a corrupt African kleptocracy to take a masterclass in voter suppression; many Americans have witnessed it firsthand. (For what it's worth, Teodoro Obiang actually is a despot who has ruled Equatorial Guinea with an iron fist since 1979, but he doesn't bother with anything other than sham elections, since he does not even allow an opposition party to exist.)

Unfortunately, voter suppression is not a tactic that has been relegated to the dustbin of American history. Instead, it is alive and well, and it poses a unique threat to the fairness and integrity of elections in the United States. With Donald Trump's rise to the presidency, voter suppression efforts in America are about to get a steroid injection. And as voter suppression efforts grow more muscular, the voices of minorities in America will quickly grow weaker.

Donald Trump lost the popular vote in 2016 to Hillary Clinton by nearly 3 million votes. He would not be president if roughly 80,000 voters in three states—Wisconsin, Pennsylvania, and Michigan—had flipped their votes to Clinton, or if 80,000 more voters in those three states had shown up to cast ballots for her. In 2018, the majority of voters are likely to vote for Democrats in House races. The best way for Republicans to maintain control of the House despite winning fewer votes than the Democrats is to manipulate the rules of the game—through voter suppression and gerrymandering—in order to retain power, against the will of most Americans.

To understand the contours of the current systematic campaign to disenfranchise America's minorities, you have to understand Kris Kobach, the mastermind of voter suppression efforts. He is now Trump's point man when it comes to ensuring "voter integrity"—an Orwellian code word for changes to election procedures that represent the modern-day reincarnation of Jim Crow laws. Kobach grew up in Kansas, where he is now the secretary of state.

He excelled in school, graduating from Harvard *summa cum laude* and following that up with a masters and DPhil in politics at the University of Oxford. Upon returning to the United States, Kobach got a law degree at Yale. He's extraordinarily smart—and extraordinarily dangerous for American democracy.

Kobach's earliest intellectual influences were at Harvard, under the wing of Samuel Huntington, a professor who would become (in)famous for his controversial "Clash of Civilizations" theory that suggested certain "civilizations" are irreconcilable. But Huntington also wrote about a racist argument against what he called the risks of incorporating disenfranchised minority groups too quickly into the democratic process. "Marginal social groups, as in the case of the blacks," Huntington warned, "are now becoming full participants in the political system. Yet the danger of overloading the political system with demands which extend its functions and undermine its authority still remains."[6] He seems to have rubbed off on Kobach.

Today, Kobach is single-minded. He is obsessed with ensuring that only American citizens are able to vote. That, of course, is an unobjectionable goal—and it's the law. There are, however, two problems with Kobach's efforts. First, the number of noncitizens who vote is miniscule. Every time he is challenged to show that the problem is real, he comes up empty. Despite his relentless efforts, he hasn't found these mythical noncitizen voters who he claims are casting ballots in droves, stealing elections right under the noses of "real Americans."

For example, there's Alfred K. Brewer, Kobach's poster child for "widespread" voter fraud and the urgent need to address it. In 2010, as Kansas secretary of state, Kobach called a press conference to unveil the smoking gun—proof that his cause was righteous and justified. Kobach proclaimed to have "discovered" that 1,996 dead people were still on the voter rolls in Kansas. This proclamation turned out to be a dud: that was just the number of people who had died before government employees performed the next routine update to the database. But Kobach pressed on with his claims regardless, telling reporters that some people who had died not only remained on the voter roll, but had voted in recent elections. To prove his claim, he triumphantly told the gathered press that Alfred K. Brewer, who died in 1996, had somehow managed to cast a ballot from beyond the grave in the 2010 primary election.

Kobach was right that Alfred K. Brewer had voted in the primary. But that wasn't terribly surprising, since it turned out that Alfred K. Brewer wasn't dead. He was alive and well, raking leaves in Wichita a few days before Halloween, when a reporter from *The Wichita Eagle* tracked him down. "I don't think this is heaven," Brewer told the reporter. "Not when I'm raking leaves." Whether the afterlife involves yardwork or not, we may never know. But it didn't take the divine to figure out that Brewer's father was also an Alfred K., and died in 1996. Kobach had simply mixed them up. Instead of being Kobach's triumphant moment, it was a humiliation. Kobach had failed to find a single example of voter fraud.

Nonetheless, Kobach used dubious cases like Alfred K. Brewer's to push a draconian new voting law in Kansas. It passed the state legislature and the governor signed it into law in 2011.[8] Residents registering to vote in Kansas are now required to prove their citizenship by producing an original copy of a birth certificate, passport, or naturalization papers. Less than half of all US citizens have a valid passport, meaning that most Kansas residents must produce their birth certificate to register to vote. Many Americans, though, don't know where that document is—or they know that it's sitting in a dusty attic in their parents' old house somewhere halfway across the country. Requesting a new birth certificate costs time and money that not everybody has. As a result, the new Kansas law acts as a *de facto* poll tax on residents who don't already have a copy of their birth certificate or a valid passport; they must effectively pay to register to vote. Guess who this disenfranchises most? Minorities, who tend to vote for Democrats. This brings us to the second problem with Kobach's measures: they reduce the power of minority voters by making it more difficult for poorer and (disproportionately) nonwhite people to vote. In Kansas, where Trump beat Clinton by 20 per cent, Kobach's ideas are popular. An estimated 84 per cent of the population is white, but, in a few counties, nearly half the population is Mexican-American. Hispanic voters, therefore, are tempting targets for Kobach's drive to make it harder for everyone to vote. In other words, while claiming to reduce illegal voting, Kobach would actually reduce legal voting.

These voter registration measures in Kansas don't only keep impoverished minority voters away from the ballot box. By way of collateral damage, the "crackdown" has also prevented an elderly war hero from voting—a right that he fought to protect. 91-year-old World War II veteran Marvin Brown flew bombers over Nazi Germany, and his ancestors fought for the Union in the American Civil War. Now, he had the audacity to want to vote! Nothing gets the goat of "real Americans" as much as those pesky World War II veterans who have the nerve to show up and cast votes after risking their lives to save Americans from fascism, right? But have no fear: Kris Kobach was ready and eager to make sure that he couldn't.

In court proceedings, Kobach questioned whether Brown had standing in the judicial system, since he didn't have the proper paperwork to prove his citizenship status. Eventually the judge ruled against Kobach, stating, "The number of noncitizen registrations are minuscule compared to the number of voters that potentially will be unable to vote."[9] But the damage from Kobach's systemic attempts at voter suppression had already paid off. By 2015, at least 35,000 Kansans had been prevented from registering to vote—not because they were ineligible, but because they didn't have the right papers.[10] It is impossible to estimate precisely how many citizens didn't register because they knew it would be a waste of time without their birth certificate in hand, but it could be a much higher number.

Kobach has also championed a system called "Crosscheck," which tries to match voter names to birth dates in order to catch double voting across state lines. "Crosscheck," it turns out, is an undemocratic joke. There are many John Smiths out there, and many Susan Johnsons too. Whenever two people with the same name and the same birthday vote in different states, the Crosscheck system flags them and may purge them from their state's voter roll. In those instances, John Smith or Susan Johnson in Delaware could show up to cast a vote, only to be turned away simply because a John Smith or Susan Johnson born on the same date in Minnesota had already cast an early absentee ballot. By polling day, of course, it's too late for the disenfranchised—often ignorant until then of having been struck off—to do anything about it. According to a 2016 study, the Crosscheck system blocked roughly 200 legitimate voters from casting ballots for every genuinely improper double vote it discovered.[11] In 2016, Kansas rejected 13,717 ballots.[12] That's more than were rejected in Florida, which has a population seven times that of Kansas. In other words, Kobach's voter suppression machine is working.

Donald Trump has learned from Kobach and is hoping to replicate the Kansas strategy on a national scale. Once elected,

Trump turned to Kobach to spearhead a new panel called the "Commission on Election Integrity." The "Commission" is a charade aimed at convincing the public that widespread voter fraud exists even though it does not. What it could do is prevent citizens from registering to vote and purge millions of eligible voters from state voter rolls before either the 2018 Congressional midterms or Trump's reelection bid in 2020 (if he makes it that far).

At rallies during the campaign, when it appeared that Trump would lose, he suggested that his defeat would prove that the system was rigged against him. In his warped view, the only way he could lose would be if millions of illegal immigrants illegally voted—against him. Even after he had won the election, he returned to this voter fraud lie as an ego boost to cover for the fact that he had won the presidency but lost the popular vote. On 26 November 2016, President-Elect Trump tweeted: "I won the popular vote if you deduct the millions of people who voted illegally." This is a lie. Trump repeating it every so often doesn't make it any more true, but it does increase the risk that a larger number of uninformed people will start to believe it.

The source of Trump's lie would be comic if it weren't so tragic. A conservative former state official named Greg Phillips seems to have singlehandedly convinced the president of the United States that at least 3 million people voted illegally in 2016. When brought onto CNN to explain his claim, Phillips spluttered and came up empty, suggesting that 3 million had been an early estimate—so early, in fact, that at the time he made it, votes hadn't even been certified.[13] Also, it appears that the claim was based on Phillips's confusion of voting in more than one state (which would be illegal) versus being registered in more than one state (which is common, particularly when citizens move from one state to another). And, in a supreme irony, it transpires that

Phillips himself was registered in not one, not two, but three states in the 2016 election.[14] In other words, Phillips—Trump's source—is a confused hypocrite who spreads debunked lies.

Let's look at the facts. There is one study that suggests voter fraud is widespread. It was written by Jesse Richman and David Earnest and published by the Monkey Cage blog in 2014.[15] The methodology of that study is completely bogus—so much so that 200 political scientists have signed a letter saying that the study used immensely flawed assumptions and did not conform to the rigorous standards of basic research.[16] To put it simply: the Richman and Earnest study is bunk. There are, of course, reputable studies about voter fraud. All of them have reached the same conclusion: voter fraud in the United States occurs, but it is extremely rare.[17]

The Washington Post uncovered four cases of voter fraud in 2016.[18] An audit in North Carolina found just one case of in-person voter impersonation for the entire state—out of more than 4.5 million ballots.[19] A 2014 study examined more than 1 billion ballots cast between 2000 and 2014 and found thirty-one verified cases of voter fraud.[20] That's 0.00000031 per cent of all ballots. A study conducted by George W. Bush's administration found an even lower rate of voter fraud: 0.00000013 per cent of all ballots cast.[21] Even when Republicans look for voter fraud, they usually come up with the same conclusion as academic studies: it's vanishingly rare.

The greatest irony of Trump's false claims of voter fraud are that Trump's own lawyers have admitted that it doesn't exist. In court documents aiming to block Green Party candidate Jill Stein's request for a recount of the 2016 election in Michigan, Trump's lawyers argued (correctly) that: "All available evidence suggests that the 2016 general election was not tainted by fraud or mistake."[22] Trump's lawyers were right. Trump is not. Worse, his allegations about voter fraud are sometimes illogical. According to Trump, a huge amount of illegal voting takes place in California.[23] Hillary Clinton was the clear favorite to win in that reliably liberal state; everyone knew that Trump didn't stand a chance. It seems unlikely that an illegal immigrant living in California, whose biggest fear is being detected by the authorities, would risk his or her American life and liberty to cast a single vote in a state where Clinton was already going to win by a landslide.

Nonetheless, Trump uses this nonsensical lie to justify his effort to nationalize Kobach's Kansas model of voter suppression. His "Electoral Integrity Commission" has requested sensitive voter data (including name, birth date, social security number, party registration, and voting history) from all fifty states. As of early October 2017, almost all of the states have declined, with some state officials telling Trump to "go jump in a lake" or to launch himself in the Gulf of Mexico.[24] These refusals are far from the end of the war on voting rights in America—they are only a victory in the first battle. Furthermore, some voters who are worried about their privacy being compromised have already de-registered, voluntarily purging themselves from the voter rolls in response to Trump's Commission. Has it become necessary to compromise your privacy in order to vote? Civil and political rights activists across the board are right to be alarmed.

Moreover, Trump's lies as president have given greater political momentum to some state-led efforts to restrict voting in ways that, like Kobach's, disproportionately disenfranchise poor, minority, and young voters. By May 2017, there had already been at least ninety-nine bills introduced in thirty-one states that aim to restrict ballot access for citizens, all in an ostensible effort to prevent something from happening that was never really happening in the first place.[25] Unfortunately, much of the damage has already been done in terms of public perceptions—which is the necessary precursor to implementing new authoritarian policies like voter suppression. More than half of Trump's voters believe, incorrectly, that he actually won the popular vote,[26] and one in four American adults believes that "3 to 5 million voters voted illegally" in 2016.[27] These false perceptions will be difficult to reverse, so long as the president repeats his lie. In some Republican-dominated states, it has already taken root and it will become far easier for opportunistic Republican state officials to obstruct voting by certain people.

We should be making it easier, not harder, to vote. In 2014, just over 36 per cent of Americans voted in the Congressional midterm elections—an abysmal turnout rate that should embarrass all Americans who believe in the importance of citizen participation as a fundamental duty in a democracy. After all, people like Marvin Brown of Kansas fought in World War II so we could have the right to vote, and now most Americans are giving up that right without a fight—even before Donald Trump and Kris Kobach have found a means to try and take it away.

Even if they fail, voter suppression is only one threat to the integrity of the 2018 and 2020 elections. As we've seen, Russian meddling in the US electoral process poses a critical threat to American democracy, and Trump's actions since winning the election have invited further interference rather than taking appropriate steps to deter it. It is now a virtual certainty that the Kremlin will again attempt to tip key close elections, using dark methods including hacking. Putin is coming. We must be ready.

Though I discussed the Russia investigation in the previous chapter, it is worth highlighting one critical vulnerability that the Russians seemingly didn't fully exploit in 2016: hacking voting machines. America's voting infrastructure is outdated and vulnerable to digital tampering. In 2012, researchers from the University of Michigan identified critical gaps in the security used on voting machines. In many cases, the gap was that there was no security—at all. Some machines were connected to unencrypted, wide-open wireless networks—the equivalent of logging onto the WiFi in Starbucks. To get the government to take their concerns seriously, the Michigan researchers remotely tampered with election machinery so that every time a voter cast a vote, the machine would play the University of Michigan fight song. Another team of researchers tampered with voting machines in person—without breaking the supposedly "tamper-proof" seal on the machines. These researchers had a bit of fun too. They transformed each voting machine into a Pac-Man game, simply by changing the software.[28] The entire caper took a matter of seconds, and the government got the message: if it was that easy to tamper with voting machines, then a nefarious foreign power might try. It's a glaring electoral vulnerability and one that threatens the bedrock of our democracy.

Thirty of America's fifty states use some form of electronic voting to record and count votes. Half of those states use voting machines that do not produce any form of paper trail, meaning that it would be impossible to determine whether anyone had tampered with votes. After all, the only record is the one on the machine—there's no physical record to check against. Even for those states using machines that do produce a paper trail, the secret ballot would make it almost impossible to prove wrongdoing if an election was hacked—unless there were serious irregularities (such as a higher number of votes than registered voters in a given precinct). In other words, if the tampering were done by someone savvy (such as a foreign espionage service), it would be extremely difficult to detect, with or without a paper trail. Beyond the machines themselves, many voter rolls are stored online in databases that could be breached. If you can control that database, it's possible to disenfranchise people remotely. The convenience factor of digital voting isn't worth the glaring vulnerabilities that come with it.

Russia has already exploited those vulnerabilities. In 2016, the Russian government tried to hack into voting systems in at least thirty-nine states—and tried to delete or alter voter data in at least one instance. At the time of writing, no finding has been made public as to whether its efforts were successful, but the attempt is alarming in itself. In Illinois, for example, cybersecurity experts have documented evidence that Russia stole 15 million voter records containing "names, birthdays, genders, and partial Social Security numbers."[29] The 2016 election was likely just a test run for a future, even more aggressive Russian effort to destabilize and manipulate American democracy, using hacking and digital espionage to sow chaos and help Moscow's favored candidates win. The 2018 midterms will be the next battleground, with Trump's presumed reelection bid in 2020 looming not far off.

Any other American president would have taken a hard line with Vladimir Putin, both to punish him for past election interference and to deter him from a repeat offence. Before leaving office, Barack Obama directly confronted Moscow about the hacking in late 2016, and confiscated known Russian spy havens after the election as retribution.[30] Yet his successor is facilitating Russian hacking by taking such a soft line that he's practically inviting further foreign manipulation. Immediately after the election, Trump began looking for ways to lift longstanding sanctions on Russia, rewarding Putin for orchestrating an unprecedented cyberattack on Americans and the machinery of their elections.

Fortunately, public pressure from both State Department officials and a bipartisan effort in Congress prevented Trump from lifting sanctions as the full scope of the Trump-Russia collusion investigation began to come into view.[31] But that didn't stop Trump. He also considered returning the spy havens that Obama had confiscated—buildings that had been used to carry out Russian espionage on US soil.[32]

To be fair to the new president, he did sign a sanctions bill into law that further punished Russia. But Trump made clear that he was signing begrudgingly and that he opposed new sanctions. In fact, it is highly likely that Trump only green-lighted the measure to avoid the embarrassment of having his veto overridden by his own party in Congress. Worse still, Putin's retaliation for the new sanctions bill was to expel more than 700 diplomats working at the US Embassy in Moscow. For any normal president, this would have precipitated a savage response. In 1986, President Reagan retaliated in kind when the Soviet Union expelled US diplomats; in 2001, when the FBI caught a double agent who had allegedly been spying for Moscow, the George W. Bush administration expelled dozens of Russian diplomats and publicly slammed the Kremlin.[33] Trump instead chose to thank Putin—for saving the US government some money by expelling diplomats who had put their lives at risk in a difficult environment to serve America.

Nobody knows exactly why Trump refuses to criticize Vladimir Putin, a homicidal thug and a despot who kills journalists and murders dissidents. But regardless of his baffling reasons for acting as Putin's apologist-in-chief, the US president has been tested by a foreign adversary who has already shown his willingness to manipulate an American election, and he has failed that test. In 2018 and 2020, he will be tested again—unfortunately, the Russians have no real reason to fear the consequences of even more brazen efforts at election interference. Why would they, having only received a slap on the wrist in 2017? Like the child who faces no consequences for raiding the cookie jar, they will be back.

Finally, it's important to recognize that Russia's manipulations in 2016 were not even close to the nightmare scenario. The worst possible foreign meddling in November 2018 would be a full-on breach of voting machines and voting systems, wherein the foreign power deletes names from the voter roll on the eve of the election and then changes votes on election day. If that occurred, some people would cast their ballot for their preferred candidate only to have it invisibly switched within the voting machine itself. Those voters would never know their votes had been changed, and even once the tampering had been identified, very little could be done to verify the validity of each individual vote. The United States would face an unprecedented choice: hold another election, or accept a government formed of candidates who may only have won because the elections were stolen via hacking and espionage. Accepting such a government would take away a key foundation of our government's ability to work on behalf of the people: the perception of democratic legitimacy. Civil unrest would surely rise under this nightmare scenario, as the losing side of the election would openly question whether the winning side had actually won or had merely been installed by the Kremlin. It would accelerate toxic polarization and usher the American body politic into a far more destabilizing fragmentation. In Côte d'Ivoire, for example, a country I've worked in previously, the revelation that the winner of the 2000 presidential election had rigged the vote caused mass street protests, and the candidate who had lost (according to the official, rigged tally) was swept into power. Two years later, a civil war broke out. We cannot allow anything remotely close to this scenario in the United States.

If President Trump creates a permissive environment for foreign election hacking and simultaneously engages in mass voter suppression, Republicans could retain power illegitimately in 2018. If Trump maintains those tactics into 2020, he could win reelection even if he is overwhelmingly unpopular. And, even if Trump loses, he has already planted the seed of doubt in a quarter of Americans, who will presumably falsely believe that a Democratic victory in either election proves Trump right: that millions of noncitizens voted illegally. As with many of his most authoritarian tactics, Trump's attempts to affect the voting process could fail in his aims, yet still inflict immense damage on American democracy. After all, democracy relies not just on elections but on a shared perception across party lines that the voting was conducted freely and fairly, in accordance with longstanding democratic principles. Those principles are now under attack, and need protecting. The very nuts and bolts of American democracy are at stake.

6

DIVIDE AND RULE

Idi Amin was born in Koboko, an arid little Ugandan village less than a mile east of the border with the Democratic Republic of the Congo. His mother, a self-proclaimed sorceress, enrolled young Idi in a local school, but it didn't last. He dropped out by fourth grade. Instead, he received a practical education in the British colonial army. From his service, he soon boasted that he knew "more than doctors of philosophy because as a military man I know how to act."[1]

Amin's cocky self-assuredness grew as he rose through the ranks of the army. After Uganda gained independence in 1962, he continually received promotion after promotion. In 1970, President Milton Obote made him the commander of Uganda's armed forces. But, as Amin's ambitions clashed with Obote's leadership, a rift developed between the two former friends. Obote demoted Amin, as rumors spread that the president was also plotting to arrest him. Rather than allowing himself to be demoted, Amin went on the offensive. In January 1971, while Obote was abroad, soldiers loyal to Amin seized the main airport. Tanks rumbled through Uganda's capital, Kampala. Heavily armed soldiers surrounded Obote's residence, in case he tried to return clandestinely. The coup d'état succeeded; General Idi Amin became President Idi Amin.

As with any good narcissistic, power-hungry egomaniacal dictator, though, "President" simply wouldn't suffice as a title. Amin eventually came up with something grander and somewhat more eccentric: "His Excellency, President for Life, Field Marshal Al Hadji Doctor Idi Amin Dada, VC, DSO, MC, CBE, Lord of All the Beasts of the Earth and Fishes of the Sea, and Conqueror of the British Empire in Africa in General and Uganda in Particular."[2] The title reflected a megalomania that would lead to hundreds of thousands of deaths as Amin consolidated power.

But his ability to consolidate power was hampered by the shaky foundations that accompany a regime that came to power in a coup. After all, if Idi Amin could topple a government, couldn't someone else topple him? So, he started to destroy the army. His thugs crammed thirty-two army officers perceived as lingering Obote loyalists into a tiny cell at Makindye Prison in Kampala. Amin's soldiers lit a stick of dynamite, tossed it into the cell, and closed the door as the men were blown to pieces.[3] In his first year in power, Amin executed roughly two thirds of the Ugandan army—about 6,000 men in total.[4] He also established brutal security forces soon after his coup, to help him maintain control across his fiefdom. Several groups were tasked with rounding up and murdering perceived enemies. The Butcher of Uganda, as he soon became known, had a penchant for cruelty. He built a torture chamber in Mengo Palace, where his prisoners were placed on a platform above water with a strong electrical current running through it. They were given the choice of jumping into the water or dying at the hands of torturers. In the end, many didn't get to choose; countless victims died of asphyxiation instead, stacked like matches into a tiny concrete matchbox full of more despair than oxygen.[5]

As Amin's ruthlessness consolidated his grip on power, he faced a dawning realization: his enemies were growing by the day.

Unified, they could destroy him. Splintered, he would destroy them. So Amin followed a tried and tested playbook that dictators and despots throughout history have used to amass power and deflect blame: divide and rule. Mastered by the Romans, Caesar used the strategy to defeat the Gauls; Machiavelli preached it for princes. It became a foundational strategy for tyranny. Autocrats are rarely universally loved and are often universally loathed—or would be, if the population focused on their failures. But too often, despots cleverly deflect blame from their own governance failures, and project them onto another group: usually one that is deeply unpopular with the rest of the people. This is why scapegoats are a sweet nectar for budding despots.

Idi Amin desperately needed some convenient scapegoats. The Ugandan economy in 1972 was mired in poverty. In today's dollars, the average Ugandan subsisted on about $0.50 per day, and an annual income of $149.[6] At the time, a significant portion of Uganda's economic elite was of Asian origin, traders brought in during the British colonial period and their descendants. For Amin, they offered a ripe target: he could blame them for Uganda's economic woes while whipping up nationalist fervor. That strategic one-two punch would shield his regime from accusations of corruption and economic mismanagement. After all, if it was all the Asians' fault, it couldn't be Idi Amin's fault too.

In 1972, Amin ordered the expulsion of all Asians from Uganda. As a cynical political strategy, it was perfect. They looked different. They stood out. And he tapped into prevailing attitudes across the country. Many native-born Ugandans saw those of Asian background as thieves of Ugandan wealth. So Amin announced that they needed to go—a notion that came to him, he claimed, during a vivid dream. He accused Asian Ugandans of "sabotaging the economy" and "encouraging corruption"—two crimes of which he himself was certainly guilty.[7] Nonetheless, Uganda's Asian community was given a ninety-day grace period to leave the country. As Amin saw it, it was time to put Ugandans first: "We are determined to make the ordinary Ugandan master of his own destiny," he argued. "And above all to see that he enjoys the wealth of his country. Our deliberate policy is to transfer the economic control of Uganda into the hands of Ugandans, for the first time in our country's history."[8] Ethno-nationalist fervor soared. Xenophobia carried the day. Ugandans cheered as Asians fled. And, for a time, Idi Amin's rule had never been more popular. Scapegoating had worked.

Of course, the Ugandan economy quickly collapsed. Amin's purge led to international isolation and a complete loss of foreign investment. Again, Amin deflected, blaming those new economic woes on a British conspiracy against him. Ugandans, he claimed, were not the victim of his rule, but of migrants who took Uganda's jobs and wealth, aided by conspiratorial neocolonial enemies aiming to undermine Idi Amin from the shadows. The tried and true tactic of divide and rule diverted blame away from Amin's regime—but only for a time. In 1979, Ugandan exile groups united against Amin, overthrew him, and forced him into permanent exile. By that time, of course, he had held onto power for eight years—almost a decade's worth of damage to Ugandan society, politics and the economy.

Donald Trump is nothing like Idi Amin. But Amin's brutal, tyrannical rule was enabled by a tactic now co-opted—obviously to a far lesser extent—by the Trump presidency. On so many counts, Trump's first year in office has been an abject failure, brought about by bumbling incompetence and an inability to stay on message. But if there's one thing that's been astonishingly consistent—even systematic—throughout Trump's life, campaign, and presidency, it's his view of the world through the lens of his own whiteness. That lens has served him well politically, allowing him to tap into white cultural alienation in the face of a world—and an America—that is becoming more equal. Such alienation became a tinderbox underneath the presidency of America's first black president, Barack Obama; all Trump needed to do was light the match. The ensuing fires have acted as a smokescreen for Trump's failures in the eyes of his political base. Once again, scapegoating is working.

Donald Trump is a 71-year-old white man, born eight years before *Brown v. Board of Education* began to desegregate all American schools. He turned eighteen shortly after Martin Luther King Jr. gave his famous "I have a dream" speech in Washington. In other words, Trump is a product of a post-war age in which slavery had ended but African-Americans were officially and systematically placed below white Americans in the social hierarchy of the United States. This does not, of course, excuse racial resentment or stoking the fires of racial politics. Many Americans who grew up at the same time as Donald Trump have deliberately turned their back on an American past that turned its own back to minorities. Still, the tortured, decades-long evolution of Trump's views on American minorities foreshadowed his overt targeting of ethnic and religious minority groups during his presidency.

The first mention of Donald Trump in what he would later call the "failing *New York Times*" was in 1973, under the headline "Major Landlord Accused of Antiblack Bias in City." The article reported charges filed by the US Department of Justice over Trump's alleged "discrimination against blacks in apartment rentals." The government's filing documents outlined its case that Trump "refused to rent or negotiate rentals because of race and color."[9] Trump settled the case with the government but never officially admitted any wrongdoing. A decade and a half later, in 1989, Trump paid a reported $85,000 to take out a full-page ad in *The New York Times* calling for the "Central Park Five" to receive the death penalty.[10] The "Five" were young criminal defendants in a grisly rape and assault that had left a 28-year-old investment banker in a coma within New York's Central Park. The youngest defendant was fifteen when Trump called for him to be executed.

The case fit perfectly with America's history of presuming the guilt of non-white suspects accused of assaulting a white woman. The stories the boys told were so contradictory as to be nonsensical; nor did they match the evidence. They were interrogated while sleep-deprived and without attorneys present, and told that they could go home if they confessed. Under that pressure, several of the teenagers said that they had stabbed the victim—even though her corpse showed no stab wounds.[11] Any diligent prosecutor would have seen these as red flags. But it seemed that the more important color in this case was black. It is well known and well documented that assumptions tend to be made in such cases due to conscious or unconscious racial bias. In 2014, Trump defended his presumption of the Five's guilt by remarking that "these young men do not exactly have the pasts of angels"—in fact, none had any prior arrests, let alone convictions.[12]

It turned out that the "Central Park Five" were innocent. DNA evidence later exonerated all five of the defendants of any involvement in the crime, after they had unjustly spent between seven and thirteen years behind bars. To add to the certainty of this injustice, the real culprit confessed. Matias Reyes, a convicted rapist and murderer already serving a life sentence, admitted that he had acted alone in the gruesome assault. His DNA was a full match. And yet, despite a universal acknowledgement by law enforcement that the four African-Americans and one Hispanic member of the so-called "Central Park Five" had been wrongfully accused, convicted, and imprisoned, Trump continues to insist on their guilt. In October 2016, when asked about the case, Trump not only refused to apologize, but actually doubled down on his insistence that the five were guilty. It was a perfect moment of Trumpian delusion, ignoring clear and acknowledged evidence that he was wrong about a clear-cut racist miscarriage of justice.

Three years after Trump's ad calling for the Central Park Five to be executed, one of Trump's casinos had to pay a $200,000 fine because it had granted a request from a high-stakes gambler to only have white males deal his cards.[13] Disturbing statements and attitudes of this nature have continued into the new century. In 2005, Trump floated the idea of having his reality television show, *The Apprentice*, directly pit black against white, telling a radio audience that he was mulling "an idea that is fairly controversial—creating a team of successful African-Americans versus a team of successful whites."[14]

These incidents are far from an exhaustive list. Trump has repeatedly behaved in racist ways and made racist remarks throughout his decades in public life. But then, in 2011, something changed. Trump realized that race relations were a hugely consequential touchstone in American politics—particularly after three years of Barack Obama as America's first non-white president. He discovered birtherism.

It started with a phone call. In early 2011, Donald Trump got in touch with Joseph Farah, a well-known conspiracy theorist in right-wing online circles and the publisher of WorldNetDaily. com. Farah had a colorful history of producing completely fabricated fake news. His website published a bizarre and unhinged claim that Democrats had a secret plan to create concentration camps inside the United States;[15] Farah had also recently published a six-part series arguing that that soybeans caused homosexuality.[16] Then, he started claiming that Barack Obama had not been born in the United States.[17] After his previous scoops about the hidden secrets of soybeans, who wouldn't view him as a credible source? At least, Trump saw it that way. "What can we do to get to the bottom of this?" he asked. "What can we do to turn the tide?" A couple of weeks later, Trump started dragging the absurd, debunked, racist idea into the political mainstream, one interview at a time. On ABC's "The View," he planted suspicion: "Why doesn't he show his birth certificate?" On Fox News, he said he wanted to see Obama's birth certificate for himself. On NBC, Trump explained that "I'm starting to think that he was not born here."[18]

Barack Obama was born in Hawaii, as American as I am. But as Trump continued to promote the racist lie of birtherism, it seeped into the political mainstream. Largely due to Trump's constant interviews promoting the lie, a Gallup poll from that period found that only 38 per cent of Americans believed that President Obama was "definitely" born in the United States.[19] As a man who responds to attention more than anything, the response only pushed Trump to repeat his preposterous claims. He next reached out to Jerome Corsi, a conspiracy theorist who had previously claimed that September 11 was an inside job;[20] that Americans were being "enslaved" by scientific research showing that fossil fuels are a finite resource;[21] and, yes, that Barack Obama was not born in the United States.[22] Trump called up Corsi, and began repeatedly declaring that he had dispatched a team of researchers to Hawaii to get to the bottom of his totally bogus claim. "They cannot believe what they are finding," Trump boasted on ABC's "The View."[23] But it didn't end there. On 6 August 2012, Trump tweeted: "An 'extremely credible source' has called my office and told me that @BarackObama's birth certificate is a fraud."

It appears that Trump never actually dispatched anyone to Hawaii, that—shockingly—he lied about that too. Dr Alvin Onaka, the Hawaii state registrar at the time, told *The New York Times* through a spokeswoman that "he had no evidence or recollection of Mr. Trump or any of his representatives ever requesting the records from the Hawaii State Department of Health."[24]

All of this poisonous nonsense was bonkers. The worst part is that it worked. Before Trump dragged the birtherism conspiracy into the mainstream, Obama had already released his birth certificate. He later released the long-form certificate too. Clearly, none of this would have happened if Obama were white. Nevertheless, even in late 2016, an NBC News survey showed that only one in four Republicans agreed with the statement "Barack Obama was born in the United States." Nearly half disagreed, while about a third indicated they were unsure.[25] For people who wanted to see Barack Obama, the nation's first black president, as an illegitimate one, Trump sold them a racist lie that fit their narrative. This is how Donald Trump emerged as a pre-eminent force in the Republican Party.

Since then, Trump has found new targets to add to his laundry list of bigotry: Mexicans and Muslims. When he descended his escalator in Trump Tower to announce his candidacy for the Republican presidential nomination in June 2015, he signaled that his campaign would be predicated on nativism, xenophobia, and a crusade to protect white women from darker-skinned rapists (never mind that the world would soon hear Trump boasting about repeated sexual assault in his infamous *Access Hollywood* tape).[26] He also claimed that most undocumented Mexican migrants to the United States—more than 11 million people in all[27]—were violent criminals: "They're bringing drugs. They're bringing crime. They're rapists. And some, I assume, are good people."[28]

In December of that year, Trump shifted from race to religion. He called for a "total and complete shutdown of Muslims entering the United States until our country's representatives can figure out what the hell is going on."[29] In a country founded by pilgrims facing religious persecution, Trump was calling to ban people based on their faith. It was the most un-American statement made by any US presidential candidate in modern history. And still, his support among the largely white Republican base grew.

Three months later, David Duke, the former grandmaster of the Ku Klux Klan, endorsed Trump. Jake Tapper of CNN asked Trump whether he would disavow Duke and the KKK. Trump was evasive—so evasive that it's worth reproducing the full text here:

TAPPER: I want to ask you about the Anti-Defamation League, which this week called on you to publicly condemn unequivocally the racism of former KKK Grand Wizard David Duke, who recently said that voting against you at this point would be treason to your heritage. Will you unequivocally condemn David Duke and say that you don't want his vote or that of other white supremacists in this election?

TRUMP: Well, just so you understand, I don't know anything about David Duke, okay? I don't know anything about what you're even talking about with white supremacy or white supremacists. So I don't know. I mean, I don't know. Did he endorse me? Or what's going on? Because, you know, I know nothing about David Duke. I know nothing about white supremacists. So you're asking me a question that I'm supposed to be talking about people that I know nothing about.

TAPPER: I guess the question from the Anti-Defamation League is even if you don't know about their endorsement, there are these groups and individuals endorsing you. Would you just say unequivocally you condemn them and you don't want their support?

TRUMP: Well, I have to look at the group. I mean, I don't know what group you're talking about. You wouldn't want me to condemn a group that I know nothing about. I'd have to look. If you would send me a list of the groups, I will do research on them and certainly I would disavow if I thought there was something wrong. You may have groups in there that are totally fine—and it would be very unfair. So give me a list of the groups and I'll let you know.

TAPPER: Okay. I'm just talking about David Duke and the Ku Klux Klan here, but—

TRUMP: Honestly, I don't know David Duke. I don't believe I've ever met him. I'm pretty sure I didn't meet him. And I just don't know anything about him.[30]

Any normal person—and certainly any serious presidential candidate—knows that you should condemn and disavow support from the Ku Klux Klan and anyone who avows membership of it, whether or not you've heard of the specific Klansmen under discussion. (Trump, by the way, has in the past spoken publicly and repeatedly about David Duke, so it's impossible that he had no clue who he was).[31] But for the nativist wings of the Republican Party that still buy into white supremacist garbage, Trump's hesitation was enough for them; the support from those dark corners of American society continued to pour into his primary campaign. In fact, open white supremacists were positively jubilant at Trump's refusal to explicitly and immediately condemn David Duke. On the neo-Nazi online newsletter, *The Daily Stormer*, one blogger wrote that it was "the best political thing I have seen in my life." William Johnson, of the white nationalist American Freedom Party, said of the interview: "I couldn't have asked for a better approach."[32]

All of this was part of a "wink, wink" signaling system—known as dogwhistle tactics—that allowed Trump's statements to be understood as acceptance of bigoted movements and white nationalists, without him having to say anything along those lines. Not that he was afraid to—Trump re-tweeted bogus statistics that grossly exaggerated black crime. Twice, he re-tweeted a Twitter account called WhiteGenocideTM, which was full of anti-Semitic content and claims that minority groups were trying to purge America of its whiteness.[33] After the first re-tweet in January 2015, the reaction on *The Daily Stormer* was jubilant: "He willingly retweeted the name," they rejoiced in disbelief. "The name was chosen to raise awareness of our plight. He helped propagate it. We should be grateful."[34]

The hints of bigotry began being directly linked to Trump's primary campaign. At around the same time that Trump re-tweeted WhiteGenocideTM, a white supremacist political group called American National Super PAC started funding calls on Trump's behalf in Iowa. The calls told prospective Republican primary voters to support Trump in order to promote whiteness: "We need smart, well-educated white people who will assimilate to our culture. Vote Trump."[35] In early July 2016, as the Republican candidate, Trump tweeted an image of Hillary Clinton surrounded by piles of cash with a stylized six-pointed star that looked awfully similar to a Star of David. When it came to spreading bigoted tropes about unpopular minority groups, it seemed, Trump was an equal opportunist. Then, he hired Steve Bannon—a man who had boasted about his media empire (Breitbart) as "the platform of the alt-right" (a sanitized, euphemistic name to reflect white nationalists who want to be more acceptably portrayed in mainstream circles).[36] Suddenly, the fringe was alarmingly close to power. And then came 8 November 2016.

According to exit polling, Trump was doing far better than Clinton among white voters, particularly men. A popular narrative around this disparity quickly emerged: this was the forgotten working class in the Rust Belt, galvanized by Trump's promises on trade. Surely, there were some Trump voters who fit that mold—but most evidence doesn't reflect that optimistic thesis. Instead, there is a growing consensus among data analysts, political scientists, and pollsters that some of the strongest predictors of support for Trump tended to be not socioeconomic, but cultural and racial. The die-hard Trump voters in the Republican Party had a median household income of roughly $72,000—$15,000 above, not below, the median income in America.[37] But the mythology stuck. Trump was supposedly riding a wave of economic populism, fueled by destitute, out-of-work coal miners, never mind that this was statistically impossible, as there are more yoga instructors than coal miners in the United States these days.[38]

Pretty much every way you could slice the data, Trump won the white vote, across the economic scale. According to Edison Research, amongst white women, Trump beat Clinton by nine points. Amongst white men, he trounced her by a margin of 31 per cent.[39] Of course, the disparity between white votes for Democrats and for Republicans had already been growing before Trump. There are millions of white Trump voters who cast their ballots for various reasons unrelated to race or culture. But studies that control for other demographic factors tended to find racial resentment as one of the most powerful factors in predicting support for Trump's candidacy.[40] Saddling up with ethnic and religious scapegoating, he rode cultural alienation and racial resentment all the way to the White House.

Trump was not the first primary candidate to pander to the extreme of his party base when hoping to wrap up a party's nomination—that's not remotely abnormal. But Trump's first year in office has not been a pivot back toward the middle, as presidents usually ensure. Instead, it has been a full-on push to pander to that same base, including its culturally alienated white nationalist elements, who see themselves as the victims of a system slowly swinging toward a more equal nation.

Once in power, Trump cranked up the signaling aimed at reassuring white voters that he was a "law and order" president who would address minority crime. In early 2017, Trump's administration began publishing lists of crimes committed by immigrants.[41] Even though study after study shows that immigrants commit crimes at a lower rate than native-born Americans, Trump's administration singled them out,[42] using government resources to direct negative attitudes toward an already unpopular group—a common scapegoating tactic. Then, Trump's Department of Homeland Security opened a special hotline for people to call in and report "crimes committed by removable criminal aliens."[43] The hotline was quickly swamped by anti-Trump pranksters, posing as patriotic "victims" reporting thefts and abductions by literal criminal aliens, sometimes narrating entire plots of *X-Files* episodes to describe their supposed ordeals.[44] But this wasn't funny. It was hauntingly familiar to victims of past authoritarian government scapegoating.

Then, in late July 2017, Trump endorsed police brutality—which disproportionately affects minority communities. Speaking to law enforcement officers in Long Island, New York, Trump instructed them to be rough on suspects when taking them into custody. "And when you see these towns and when you see these thugs being thrown into the back of a paddy wagon—you just see them thrown in, rough—I said, 'Please don't be too nice.'" In case there was any doubt whether he was explicitly endorsing police violence, Trump added, "Like when you guys put somebody in the car and you're protecting their head, you know, the way you put their hand over? Like, don't hit their head and they've just killed somebody—don't hit their head. I said, 'You can take the hand away, okay?'" The police attending, to their shame, laughed and applauded.[45] But police chiefs across the country denounced Trump's incitement to police violence, which was counterproductive to repairing already (understandably) frayed relations between police and minority communities. In just one of many examples, two years before Trump's Long Island speech endorsing "thugs" being tossed into the "back of a paddy wagon" and treated "rough,"[46] African-American Freddie Gray had been handcuffed and tossed into the back of a police van in Baltimore and given "a rough ride." Officers didn't buckle him into the back of the van. According to prosecutors, they drove aggressively, speeding up, slowing down abruptly, making sharp turns aimed at tossing Gray around as much as possible. When they arrived at the station, Gray was dead.[47]

A fortnight after Trump's endorsement of police brutality, emboldened white neo-Nazis and Ku Klux Klansmen descended on Charlottesville, Virginia for one of the largest white supremacist marches in decades. The young men, who in the past may have been worried enough about appearances to cloak themselves in white hoods, marched openly through the town carrying torches and shouting "Blood and Soil!" and "Jews will not replace us!"

The following day, protests swelled as decent Americans marched to signal their disdain for such open bigotry and hatred. During the protests, a white supremacist drove his car through a crowd of such peaceful counter-protesters, killing 32-year-old Heather Heyer. It was a domestic terrorist attack, but not one that conformed to Trump's racially tinged definition of terrorism. Trump repudiated the violence on "many sides," drawing false moral equivalence as he equated neo-Nazis and Klansmen who had taken an innocent life with those who protested their hatred.[48] Trump even went so far as to say that there were "very fine people" in the rally, which had featured swastikas, Nazi flags, known Klansmen, and an array of anti-Semitic and other far-right chants.[49] The message was not lost on Trump's white supremacist supporters. *The Daily Stormer*'s reaction was euphoric: "No condemnation at all. When asked to condemn, [Trump] just walked out of the room. Really, really good. God bless him."[50] A few days after his complete moral failure in responding to Charlottesville, President Trump re-tweeted Jerry Travone, an anti-Semite who, four days earlier, had written on Twitter that "we have enough of these Jews where I live lol someone else take them."[51]

Trump's vague condemnation of Charlottesville, his false moral equivalence of "many sides" and "very fine people" fit the pattern of his earlier refusal to unequivocally condemn David Duke of the Ku Klux Klan. Ambiguous responses are common to politicians of all stripes, but not on Charlottesville. Furthermore, Trump is an unusual mainstream political figure in that he is never vague in any other statements. When he dislikes something and wants to condemn it, he doesn't mince his words. In his time on Twitter, he's called people "moron" 52 times; "dummy" 77 times; and "loser" a record 245 times. When Nordstrom pulled Ivanka Trump's products from their stores due to their dismal sales numbers, Trump lashed out at them directly, aggressively, and by name. But when white supremacists carrying Nazi flags marched through an American town and then murdered an innocent protester, he was as vague as when he refused to immediately disavow support from the Klan.

Thankfully, Trump then got his act together and belatedly criticized the white supremacists. They had "no honor," he said. They were "desperate" and "pathetic." They were "a total embarrassment." They were "weak and ineffective" and lived "at the bottom of the barrel." And finally, he returned to his favorite insult: they were "losers."

Actually, that's not true at all. These weren't insults that Trump hurled at neo-Nazis. They were his words for his 2015–16 Republican nomination rival Jeb Bush,[52] a respected former governor who ultimately dropped out of the race. If only we had a president who was as harsh on white supremacists as he is with luxury department stores and political rivals, then we'd be in better shape as a country. But we don't. Trump is Trump. He's not likely to change. And his inability to clearly and forcefully condemn white supremacy was yet another "dog whistle" to white nationalist groups, signaling that he is willing to tolerate the intolerable.

Whether by strategic logic or by bigotry, Donald Trump is systematically stoking religious and racial divides in the United States as he demonizes minority groups in the eyes of an intolerant segment of the white population. He has brought a hallmark of creeping authoritarianism into the United States: scapegoating. In Trump's portrayal, African-Americans tend to be inner city criminals. Mexicans illegally in the country are rapists; Muslims hate the United States. And white supremacist rallies are home to some "very fine people."

Racial tensions didn't arrive with Trump. Even after the Civil Rights Movement, American race relations have long been poor, with subtle bigotry lingering on in cultural attitudes and political decision-making. In early 2017, I drove the backroads through deep red territory—from rural Pennsylvania to West Virginia, Kentucky, and Indiana. I spoke to Trump voters in diners, cafes, gas stations, and at Bud's Gun Range in Lexington, Kentucky while trying my hand at shooting an AR-15 assault rifle. They all loved Trump.

Later that same evening, I struck up a conversation with an African-American couple at a bar down the road from the gun range. The wife had a high-flying job, made a generous living, and drove a flashy red sports car. She told me that she had finally taken to taping her most recent pay slip to the dashboard of the car because she had been stopped by the police on five separate occasions and asked, "How can you afford this car?" That never happens to white women—for the same reason that white presidents don't get asked to produce their long-form birth certificate by reality television personalities. Next to the pay slip on the dashboard, she had taped her driver's license, so she wouldn't have to reach for anything that an officer could mistake for a weapon if she were pulled over. She was taking this precaution just a few miles from a gun shop where I saw white people in the parking lot openly carrying guns without a second thought. "This stuff has been going on forever," she told me, "but since Trump won, people are a bit more open about it and I feel a bit more unwelcome."

Since that conversation, Trump has only escalated his decision to inflame racial divides. He has expanded his divide and rule tactics to include another tried and true strategy of despots: conflate criticism of government policies with a lack of patriotism. Mark Twain famously said that "patriotism is supporting your country all the time, and your government when it deserves it." Donald Trump agrees with that statement, or at least he did in 2014 when he tweeted it in implied reference to his disdain for Barack Obama's presidency. But now that it's him in the White House, Trump has flip-flopped. Rather than accepting dissent in pursuit of a more just government as a form of patriotism, Trump has started painting minority athletes who are protesting racial injustice as unpatriotic ingrates.

In late 2016, San Francisco 49ers Quarterback Colin Kaepernick began sitting during the singing of the national anthem at the start of football games. He did so in protest at police killings of black citizens. For some veterans, Kaepernick's protest was insulting. Nate Boyer, a former green beret who played in the National Football League in 2015, met with Kaepernick. The two men agreed on a productive solution: Kaepernick would kneel rather than sitting, just as soldiers kneel at the graves of fallen comrades to show their respect.[53]

Still, Kaepernick's kneeling protest cost him his job. NFL owners, including seven who had donated $1 million each to Trump's inauguration,[54] effectively blackballed him from playing in the league. Trump deliberately resurrected the issue at a September 2017 rally in Alabama, driving a racial wedge into the country to deflect from his pending legislative failures. In his remarks at the rally and on Twitter the same day, Trump called Kaepernick a "son of a bitch" and called on anyone who kneeled during the national anthem to be fired.[55] Aside from the authoritarian tinge of a president calling on private citizens in a football league to be fired for their political views, Trump used his attack on Kaepernick as a way to suggest that people who protest the government are actually protesting the country. In the days that followed, he tweeted about the NFL protests dozens of times.

By focusing public attention on the kneeling protests, Trump accomplished three common despots' goals in one fell swoop. First, he further divided the population over the issue, making it easier for people to turn on each other than to unify against him. Second, he conflated dissent with a lack of patriotism in the minds of his supporters—criticizing government failures was akin to disrespecting the flag, and by extension, the nation. Third, he distracted the public from his own failures, both short-term and ongoing. As he was tweeting about disrespecting America, there were Americans struggling to survive in Puerto Rico in the aftermath of Hurricane Maria. His administration has been criticized for its initially slow response—a response that might have been faster had Trump been focused on hurricane relief rather than quarterbacks. Moreover, as he pointed national anger at Kaepernick, Trump's proposed health care reform bill was collapsing in the US Senate. The NFL debate dominated headlines, even as one of Trump's major campaign promises fell apart.

Throughout his campaign and his presidency, Trump has weaponized racial divides, directing white populist anger toward minorities rather than toward a post-recession economy that has failed many Americans. He has brought racial resentment out into the open, trading hidden prejudice for overt bigotry in the political mainstream. In the process, Trump has capitalized on a tactic that many aspiring strongmen, like Idi Amin, have used in the past: deflecting blame onto an unpopular group (or, in academic speak, telling an "in group" that an "out group" is to blame for all of their woes).

This, of course, does not mean that comparisons with the world's worst tyrants are justified. But by driving a wedge through American society, buying him time with governance failures as he continues to lay his shortcomings at the feet of Mexicans, Muslims, and other minorities, Trump has borrowed a tactic battle-tested by warlords, despots, Machiavellian princes, and now the president of the United States. And maybe, just maybe, it will work—if we let it. But if Americans see beyond the race baiting and dog whistles, they can focus on real solutions to underlying drivers of economic victimhood, like inequality and automation.

The principle of democracy, to its core, is about equality and inclusion. Donald Trump's vote counts as much as that of a Muslim-American living in Michigan or a Latino voter in Arizona. But his attack on democracy through divide and rule tactics is not just about social and political exclusion of minorities, placing "real" Americans—white and Christian—above those who look different or worship a different God. It's also a cynical political tactic. When the Ugandan economy collapsed under Idi Amin despite the expulsion of the Asian population, he just had to find another scapegoat to blame. When Amin blamed the British for his troubles, he delivered a classically authoritarian double punch: blaming unpopular groups for his own failures while also using their unpopularity to justify a greater consolidation of power.

Trump has now created a dangerous and explosive authoritarian tinderbox, should something truly horrible happen during his time in office. He has divided the country, paving the way for him to rule with fewer checks. It's not a long leap to imagine Trump saying that he needs more authority to restore "law and order" in the event of a terror attack, or a particularly grisly violent crime by an illegal Latino immigrant. In that case, his scapegoating has not yet entered its most dangerous phase. Let's do more than hope that it never will; we should work to make sure that it can't. United, we must stand together, in defense of democracy.

7

FLOOD THE SWAMP

In the early 1970s, you couldn't find Gbadolité on a map. It was a sleepy little village in the Congo, a provincial backwater mired in poverty and devoid of development, whose people lived in mud-brick huts. Then, the most corrupt despot in African history arrived in his signature leopard-skin hat and transformed a destitute village in a destitute country into an obscenely opulent African Versailles, a monument built by Congolese dictator Mobutu Sese Seko—to himself.

Mobutu stole from his people on an epic scale, looting billions of dollars worth of his country's mineral wealth while his people struggled against starvation and disease. His conflicts of interest were endless, as he pillaged state-run enterprises for his own benefit and struck mineral deals that diverted profits directly into his own pocket. He changed the country's name to Zaire in 1971 and made it his personal fiefdom. There was no distinction between the interests of his country and his own personal financial interests; instead, he ruled for a constituency of one—himself.

Congolese children were malnourished; Mobutu built an enormous runway in the jungle so that Concorde jets could fly in from Paris to provide him with the freshest delicacies, baked the same day. Most Congolese would save scraps of goat meat for a special occasion; Mobutu served his guests eel and antelope, imported foie gras and freshly-caught salmon, all delivered to the world's elite on custom-built conveyer belts that would bring the food into the dining area from his overflowing kitchens. He sipped on Tattinger champagne and vintage *grand cru* wines from the 1920s, brought up from his cellar, which was widely considered to be one of the finest wine collections in the world.[1] Just miles outside his palace, Congolese workers toiled to buy basic necessities and had no running water. Mobutu decorated his palace with oil paintings and stained glass, surrounded by imported Italian marble, a pair of enormous swimming pools, and his extravagant bed, which mystified guests by rising up hydraulically through the floor of his gilded bedroom.

Mobutu's nauseating display of wealth in one of the poorest countries on Earth was made possible by his authoritarian kleptocracy, in which the line between political and economic power was erased. Businesses that had ties to Mobutu thrived as he doled out contracts and wealth on a whim, while businesses that crossed him collapsed. The elite economy was inseparable from his inner political circle, so that political power was economic power, and vice versa.

In such systems—from Mobutu's Zaire to Putin's Russia to Chavez's Venezuela—being politically connected is the only surefire way to become rich. Those who control the levers of the state dole out the fruits of the economy. And, while it is the case that political power confers economic benefits in Western democracies, there are ethical lines that cannot be crossed. The integrity of the democratic process relies on politicians following ethical norms—the soft guardrails of democratic conduct that, although not necessarily enacted into law, are enshrined in tradition and decency. If those ethical lines are blurred or crossed, the democratic link between the people and their political representatives is severed. After all, democratic accountability is predicated on the notion that politicians should act in the interests of the citizens they represent, rather than endlessly pursuing another zero on the end of their own bank balances. That is why politicians must avoid conflicts of interest that pit their own financial interest against the well-being of the people. When politicians face the choice between the two, almost all fail the test. Democratic ethical norms exist to pressure politicians to succumb to the better angels of their own fallible natures.

When it comes to basic democratic ethics, Donald Trump must have said, "You're fired" to his better angels long ago. Trump is not a full-blown kleptocrat by any means—but he is trampling on norms of American ethics, and likely getting richer as a direct result of his presidency. He pledged to "Drain the Swamp!" during the presidential campaign. Instead, he has flooded it to a level unseen in modern American history.

In the year since his election, Trump has blurred the line between his personal financial interests and the interest of the American republic. He has, in the process, created three major problems for American democracy. First, Trump's apparent profiting from the presidency is an inappropriate abuse of power that undermines democratic integrity. Second, as Trump tramples ethical norms, he is widening the scope of what is acceptable in American politics, paving the way for further abuses in other areas of government. Third, Trump's foreign business interests have created a dark web of entangling conflicts of interest that threaten to compromise both him and American security.

To understand the risks of violating ethics and conflict of interest guidelines, let's travel back in history to late 1939. In a few months' time, President Franklin Delano Roosevelt will be squaring off against his Republican challenger, Wendell Wilkie. Across the Atlantic, Hitler has begun annexing territory, assaulting neighbors, and threatening to expand his empire. Across the Pacific, Japan's emperor seems to be set on a collision course for war with the United States.

But let's imagine an alternative 1939. In this scenario, Wilkie accuses Roosevelt of having divided loyalties due to his company's secret business dealings in Japan and Germany. Roosevelt forcefully denies these allegations. "Japan and Germany have never tried to use leverage over me," FDR proclaims in one of his fireside chats. "I have nothing to do with Japan or Germany—no deals, no loans, no nothing." It's impossible to be sure, because Roosevelt declined to release his tax returns or allow any sort of independent audit of his financial entanglements or debts. Despite a few doubts among partisan rivals, the issue seems to dissipate as election day approaches. Voters reelect Roosevelt in November 1940 and Wilkie's accusations are, for a time, forgotten.

Then, in August 1941, just months before Japan launches a surprise attack on Pearl Harbor, intrepid investigative reporters discover that FDR had deceived the American people. In late 1939 and early 1940, while running for re-election, Roosevelt's business empire had been engaged in clandestine talks with aggressive autocratic governments in Berlin and Tokyo. He sought to build Roosevelt Tower Berlin and Roosevelt Tower Tokyo. Each project would have been a massive windfall for his personal wealth and Roosevelt was ready to cash in. The scandal tops headlines for a few days but then it is swept away by a massive natural disaster which makes everyone forget about FDR's prospective property development.

In this hypothetical scenario, Pearl Harbor doesn't get bombed. Japan has no need to attack Hawaii, because Roosevelt has quietly caved to Japanese demands. The United States doesn't enter World War II in the Atlantic theater. Roosevelt declines to stand up to Hitler or rescue Europe. Instead, Hitler and Hirohito use their financial leverage against Roosevelt and press him to make concessions behind the scenes. Roosevelt finally embraces the isolationist America First movement, publicly proclaiming that the United States cannot afford to be the world's policeman. But the real reason for his refusal to send American troops into battle is that Roosevelt knows how devastating such a conflict would be to his own wealth. Americans can't tell the difference. Who is to say why Roosevelt opposed engagement and embraced isolationism? It's impossible to know.

Without American involvement, Hitler achieves a favorable stalemate. Hirohito expands Japan's empire. When the war ends and FDR leaves office, he finally inks the deals that have been put on hold by the war. He attends the groundbreaking for Roosevelt Tower Berlin and Roosevelt Tower Tokyo, shortly before dying an incredibly rich man.

Of course, the scenario above is fiction. But how different is it from America's current predicament? The US president is already tangled in a perilous web of foreign financial conflicts. If Trump is not forced to divest from his business interests, we will be facing a question that we should never have to ask: were the president's foreign policy decisions—matters of war and peace—swayed by his desire to make more money for himself?

Sadly, we don't know the full extent of Trump's entanglements because Trump won't release his tax returns. Ever since Watergate, all presidential candidates have agreed to this, to show the American people that they are not compromised by foreign debts or beholden to any foreign interests that could influence their decision-making. In refusing, then, Trump is breaking with decades of precedent. He offers the flimsy explanation that he is being audited by the Internal Revenue Service.[2] But the IRS has repeatedly made clear that audits do not preclude public release of tax returns.[3] Trump's refusal also contradicts repeated previous pledges to let the public see his tax returns. In 2014, he declared "If I decide to run for office, I'll produce my tax returns, absolutely. And I would love to do that."[4] Democracy has a way of holding politicians accountable, but it only functions if politicians are forced to be transparent with their citizens. Without the tax returns, it's not possible for citizens to hold their billionaire president fully accountable—or even to know whether, or when, he is making US foreign policy with his wallet.

Some of Trump's conflicts are visible without needing a tax return. There were no Roosevelt Towers in Japan and Germany, but there are Trump Towers in multiple foreign locations. After being accused of having compromising business interests in Russia during the 2016 election, Trump said, not in a 1940s fireside chat but in a tweet, "Russia has never tried to use leverage over me. I have nothing to do with Russia—no deals, no loans, no nothing."[5] Trump denied several further times that he had any financial ties to Moscow—but, in late August 2017, it became clear that these repeated denials were just another lie. It turns out that, while Trump was a presidential candidate, he had sought a licensing deal for a major commercial venture: Trump Tower Moscow. Worse, Trump's business associate working on the deal was none other than Felix Sater.[6] Sater had been arrested in the early 1990s for stabbing a man with a broken cocktail glass during a bar fight and he has gone on to plead guilty to a variety of nefarious dealings related to the Russian mafia.[7] He's not exactly the whistle-clean business partner you'd want the president of the United States to associate with. But beyond Sater's dark past, we now know that Trump actively sought business dealings with Russia.

Those dealings would require a good relationship with Vladimir Putin, as he is widely known to interfere in business when political adversaries are involved.[8] At the same time that Sater was working on a Trump Tower Moscow deal, he was also seeking to get Putin "on board" to help Trump get elected. As discussed in Chapter 5, e-mails unearthed in August 2017 show that Sater believed the business deal with Moscow was critical to ensuring that the Kremlin would fully buy into the effort to get Trump elected. So is the American president being driven by financial, rather than national, interest when it comes to diplomacy toward Russia—America's chief foreign policy adversary on most issues? While the Trump Tower Moscow project was put on hold before Trump was elected, it is still an obvious benefit that the president could expect to gain if he stays on good terms with Putin. After leaving office, it is highly likely that Trump will seek to deepen further his business relationships in Russia. It's a clear ethical conflict. And yet, Trump gets away with it.

Of course, the prospective Trump Tower Moscow project is less compromising than the real brick-and-mortar Trump Towers dotted throughout the world—many of which stand in the capitals of countries run by despicable despots. A few months into his presidency, a transcript of a phone call between Trump and President Rodrigo Duterte of the Philippines was leaked to the press. During the call, Trump praised Duterte for the "unbelievable job" he was doing dealing with "the drug problem."[9] He was referring to an anti-drug initiative that is actually a state-sponsored murder campaign. Duterte's death squads kill people in cold blood in the streets. An estimated 7,000 have already been slaughtered. Most victims are poor. There is substantial evidence that the police often kill first, plant drugs on the victim second, and then falsely claim self-defense third.[10] Trump endorsed this barbarism on the phone call. Then, to make matters worse, he invited Duterte—a bloodthirsty despot who previously bragged about personally killing people by tossing them out of a helicopter—to the White House.[11] This is not usually an honor bestowed on those who, like Duterte, have publicly stated their aspiration to become the Hitler of their country.[12] So why roll out the red carpet for this monster?

There is plenty of evidence that Trump admires authoritarian strongmen. But here, the answer may be simpler. Trump Tower Manila is due to open in late 2017. Duterte's government can determine whether this happens as planned, or not. It could also revoke the project's licenses and turn it into a giant cash sinkhole, a real estate boondoggle that damages Trump's brand. Never subtle, Duterte appointed Trump's business partner as an official envoy to the US government. Jose Antonio broke ground toward Trump Tower Manila alongside Eric Trump and Donald Trump Jr. Now he is one of Duterte's representatives in Washington, working with the Trump sons on Trump Tower Manila while simultaneously working with their dad on US foreign policy toward the Philippines.[13] Then, of course, there are Ivanka Trump's business interests. She has product patents pending in the Philippines; if the patents are not approved, it could cost her a bundle.[14] Trump has plenty of personal reasons to cozy up to a murderous despot; the United States does not.

Trump's properties in Istanbul create another glaring conflict of interest in Turkey, a NATO ally that is rapidly transforming from a deeply flawed democracy into a dictatorship. Turkish President Recep Tayyip Erdogan has conducted months of authoritarian purges, jailing journalists and attacking dissidents.

In early 2017, when Erdogan held a rigged referendum that decimated the last remaining remnants of Turkish democracy, President Trump was the first to congratulate him. The referendum consolidated Erdogan's personal power, giving him broad authority to rule by decree and even greater control of the judiciary. It abolished Turkey's parliamentary system and the office of prime minster, eliminating key checks on the president.[15] In celebrating its fraudulent result, Trump both undercut the US State Department and ignored Western election monitors who documented that the vote was rigged. Why did he offer such inappropriate and immediate praise? Trump himself has hinted at the answer. When asked about his business interests in Turkey, he admitted that he had "a little conflict of interest."[16]

But there's nothing little about it. The Trump properties create ethical quagmires. What happens if Turkey continues to oppose US interests in the Middle East by attacking Kurdish fighters that the US seeks to empower in the fight against ISIS? Will Trump pursue America's interests, or his own? And what happens if Erdogan continues consolidating power and realizes his seeming ambition to be a dictator? Will Trump speak out for democracy, or will he remain silent so that his properties are not confiscated? The problem is, even if Trump does the right thing for the right reasons, we'll never know. There will always be that doubt, because there will always be the compromising—and not fully known—factor of his business interests potentially influencing his thinking. And that calls into question the integrity of all his foreign policy decision-making.

Trump's first foreign trip as president illustrated his compromised position. Since World War II, every US president has first traveled to a democratic ally—either Canada or a Western European nation—to reaffirm the durable alliances founded on shared democratic values. Trump abandoned that tradition. Trump's Air Force One first touched down outside the United States in Saudi Arabia, a longstanding US ally, but also a brutal monarchy that abuses human rights and rejects even the basic trappings of democracy. Dissidents in Saudi Arabia lose their heads for speaking their minds. American presidents have accepted the strategic value of an alliance with the Saudi kingdom, but they have also at least paid lip service to the human rights concerns and applied nominal pressure for democratic reforms. Trump abandoned wholesale even a pretense at such attempts to influence the Saudis, insisting that he was not there to "lecture" anyone.

So why the shift? Well, it could be that Trump has an ideological commitment to putting "America First," with hard-nosed international relations that reject values-based foreign policy. That's certainly possible. But it's also possible that Trump played nice with the butchers of Saudi Arabia because he is beholden to them for past favors they have done for him personally, and in hope of future favors too. In 2016, Trump registered eight companies in Saudi Arabia. Each of them seems to be linked to a development project in Jeddah, the second largest Saudi city.[17] But the government in Riyadh has even more leverage over Trump, because of his past. Specifically, Saudi Prince Alwaleed bin Talal Alsaud has bailed Trump out twice, including buying one of his glitzy yachts when the Trump-brand casinos in Atlantic City were going bust.[18] Even if Trump doesn't ink any new deals during his presidency (as he says he will not), praising the Saudis as president will indisputably pay off when Trump leaves the White House and cashes in on political goodwill. Conversely, if Trump actually did the right thing, his future business deals would be jeopardized. It was both noteworthy and puzzling that Trump's notorious travel ban for seven majority-Muslim countries excluded Saudi Arabia, the country that produced most of the September 11 terrorists. Was its omission from that list tied to Trump's business prospects? We may never know.

Past presidents have been guilty of colossal human rights failures too—from President Clinton's failure to intervene in Rwanda to President Obama's failure to cope with the tragedy of the Syrian civil war. But at least Americans never had to wonder whether Clinton failed to intervene in the Rwandan genocide because he was worried about Clinton Tower Kigali, or whether Obama failed to stand up to Assad in Syria because his daughter Malia had a clothing line pending in Damascus.

Moreover, we never know exactly where the next foreign policy crisis will arise. Already, the United Arab Emirates has joined Saudi Arabia in a major, unexpected diplomatic dispute with Qatar, and during his trip to Saudi Arabia Trump sided unequivocally against Qatar—even though Qatar hosts a major US military base that is critical to America's "War on Terror." Trump has properties in the UAE, but none in Qatar. His only business arrangement there was with Qatar Airways, which previously leased space in Trump Tower Manhattan, but pulled out of its lease before Trump took office.[19] Did the weighing up of Trump's property in Dubai, UAE versus a broken Qatar lease in New York affect American foreign policy? Again, we can never know for sure.

The prospective risks are just as harrowing as the conflicts of interest that have already emerged. If the US State Department wants to launch a fresh crackdown on international money laundering, will Trump Tower Baku cause Trump to go soft on Azerbaijan? This web of financial ties limits Trump's actions on the global stage; in short, his business holdings are both an ethical quagmire that undermines democratic accountability, and a national security risk.

Unfortunately, the problem doesn't end with Trump. It extends to his immediate family, many of whom he has put in his administration. Most notable, of course, is Jared Kushner, his billionaire son-in-law. The biggest albatross hanging over the Kushner family is 666 5th Avenue in New York City, a building that has them $1.2 billion in debt. The family has sought—and is still seeking—financing for the project from foreign entities including governments and funds based in Qatar, China, Israel, France, Saudi Arabia, and South Korea.[20] They haven't found anyone to bail them out—yet. But the requests for funds create a clear ethical conflict of interest. Will countries that invest in 666 5th Avenue be treated better in US foreign policy? Will those that refuse be punished? South Korea's sovereign wealth fund declined to invest in Kushner's building, and now Trump's administration is pressing to axe the US-South Korea trade deal.[21] Are the two decisions linked? It's impossible not to wonder if Trump would be more lenient with South Korea had they come to the rescue of his son-in-law.

Moreover, as part of the Russia investigation, Bob Mueller is looking into a previously undisclosed meeting between Kushner and Sergey Gorkov, the head of the Kremlin-controlled VEB bank. Was Kushner reaching out for Russian financing? As his father-in-law is fond of saying, "we'll see what happens." In the meantime, though, Trump and his entourage are a bunch of walking, talking conflicts of interest. American foreign policy can never be independent unless they divest their major assets—something President Trump has flatly refused to do, even while keeping his tax returns hidden. It's a major affront to a system of government that only functions properly with transparency.

But Trump isn't just flooding the swamp with conflicts of interest. He's also getting rich in the process.

Washington DC was no paragon of clean government before Donald Trump arrived in the White House. Lobbying has grown out of control. There are roughly 10,000 lobbyists in DC, about eighteen for every member of Congress. Worse, these lobbyists disproportionately represent well-heeled interests that can be out of step with the best interests of the average American. A recent study from Princeton University showcased that Congress usually ends up doing what lobbyists for the rich and powerful want, even if it conflicts with the preferences of the average voter. So, yes, Washington has long catered to the wealthy. But the current administration is the first time in modern history that the president of the United States has directly and blatantly used his power to enrich himself while in office.

Take Mar-a-Lago, Trump's lavish members-only golf club in Palm Beach, Florida. Shortly after winning the presidency, Trump recognized that the "Winter White House" would be more valuable since the president would frequent it. He doubled the joining fee from $100,000 to $200,000.[22] His other golf clubs create serious ethics issues too. According to impressive investigative journalism from *USA Today* that looked at golf handicap score websites to uncover pay-to-play political access, "at least 50 executives whose companies hold federal contracts and 21 lobbyists and trade group officials" were members at Trump golf clubs. Of those individuals identified in the *USA Today* report, more than two thirds played a round of golf at Trump's club on the same day as the president was visiting.[23] Maybe this is just a complete coincidence. It couldn't possibly have anything to do with the fact that they wanted a chance to mingle with—and influence—the most powerful figure in the country. This situation has no precedent in American history. As the report put it, for the first time ever, "wealthy people with interests before the government have a chance for close and confidential access to the president as a result of payments that enrich him personally." These figures include defense contractors, lobbyists for foreign governments, "and the leader of a pesticide trade group that sought successfully to persuade the Trump administration not to ban an insecticide [that] government scientists linked to health risks."[24]

We've been reduced to digging through golf handicap websites in order to identify who is getting access to the president, because he won't release official visitor logs for public review. President Obama published his, but Trump has ended that practice. He also refuses to release the logs for the private Trump golf clubs where he has spent roughly a quarter of his presidency so far.[25] The Trump administration is operating in the shadows, particularly when money is at stake.

Trump's flashy new Washington DC hotel, the Trump International Hotel, is housed in the historic Old Post Office building, owned by the US federal government. As a result, Trump is both the tenant and the landlord—his administration presides over decisions that directly affect a hotel he owns as a private citizen. Furthermore, other than the White House itself, the hotel is the only venue in DC that Trump frequents. As a result, it has become a hive of activity for those who wish to curry favor with the president. Before the 2016 election, the government of Kuwait had a longstanding reservation to celebrate its independence day at Washington's Four Seasons. Then, a few days after Trump's victory, it canceled its reservation, switching to— you guessed it—the Trump International.[26] Kuwait may have been the first, but it won't be the last.

The hotel isn't even subtle about the links. If you want to fork over $974 a night (plus taxes and fees, of course), you can have the privilege of staying in the "Ivanka Suite." The Ivanka Suite, named after the president's beloved daughter (who happens to have unfettered access to the Oval Office), is just five blocks from the White House, where Ivanka Trump acts as senior adviser to her dad. The other rooms don't come cheap either, often starting around $500 per night. No surprise, then, that it has turned a hefty profit. Financial disclosures show that the Trump Organization has pocketed roughly $20 million from the hotel since the spring of 2016—all while Trump was either the presumed Republican candidate or the elected president.[27] Those receipts are likely to rise over time as lobbyists and foreign governments alike splash the cash to buy access to or favor with Trump.

The Trump International in DC is far from an isolated example. The president stands to make about $14 million in the sale of a Brooklyn housing complex in a deal that must be approved by his own administration.[28] His golf clubs have advertised his possible presence as a selling point for Trump-branded weddings. And it's no coincidence that his financial disclosure filings show that his revenues have jumped most at properties that he frequently visits. Of course, with each visit, the Secret Service agents who protect him must often use government money to pay for Trump Organization items, from hotel rooms to golf carts. Every time the president goes on vacation, it's not just that American taxpayers foot the bill, as with any president—it's that the money goes directly into his pocket.

The fig leaf we are offered to cover these ethical conflicts is the *canard* that Trump's sons are running the business for him. But they themselves are not even attempting to maintain the illusion of a separation between themselves and their father. Instead, they routinely tweet out White House talking points. Worse, they are using his power to cash in on the political gravy train for themselves, too. In October 2017, Donald Trump Jr is slated to speak for thirty minutes at the University of North Texas for a fee of $100,000—the highest sum ever paid in that speaking series.[29] The organizer of the event was a prominent Republican donor who has been advising and lobbying President Trump on corporate tax cuts. The idea that Trump's sons are running his business empire at a proper distance from his political machinations is absurd. Even if someone else were managing a building he owned, he can't unlearn the fact that he has expansive real estate holdings. Without a full divestment, any decisions he makes related to tax policy or real estate will be obviously and unreasonably influenced by his own personal interest. His daughter, Ivanka, has also suggested that she and her husband have gone far enough in divesting by putting assets in a trust—but the trust is managed by direct family members. All of these are abhorrent conflicts of interest and a violation of the spirit of every ethical guideline out there. But it's not technically illegal, and Trump and his family are taking advantage of that unfortunate gray area.

The Trump administration has also fully embraced the revolving door of Washington lobbyists, redirecting the swamp directly into the White House. At the end of 2016, Michael Catanzaro was a high-flying lobbyist for the oil and gas industry, hoping to get the federal government to roll back environmental regulations that were costly for his clients.[30] By early 2017, he was in the White House, presiding over the rollback of those very regulations. Then there's Chad Wolf, who spent years working for a client to push the TSA, the airport screening agency, to adopt a new piece of technology for evaluating carry-on luggage. Now he's the TSA's chief of staff, evaluating the very piece of equipment that he was previously lobbying for.[31] Trump also appointed a lobbyist for the bottled water industry, who promptly announced that the National Park Service would reverse its ban on selling bottled water at its pristine parks.[32] These conflicts of interest were made possible by Trump, who quickly reversed President Obama's ban on lobbyists being hired by agencies that they had lobbied in the previous two years. The man who promised to "Drain the Swamp!" has opened the floodgates instead.

Trump granted more waivers for lobbyists joining his administration in his first four months in office than Obama did in eight years.[33] And, of course, Trump's pledge to "place a lifetime ban on White House officials lobbying on behalf of a foreign government" only lasted until his appointment of Michael Flynn as his national security adviser, the day of his inauguration. Flynn had previously been paid more than half a million dollars to lobby on behalf of Turkey as an "unregistered foreign agent."[34] Cabinet officials in the Trump administration have also treated the White House budget like a slush fund for their personal travel. Former Secretary of Health and Human Services Tom Price (now resigned) accrued more than $1 million of expenses to fly around on a series of private jets, even when a commercial ticket to the same destination would only have cost taxpayers a few hundred dollars.[35] Meanwhile, Secretary of the Treasury Steve Mnuchin is being investigated by his own department for requests to use a government jet for his honeymoon and for traveling to Kentucky on the taxpayer dime seemingly to get a better vantage point from which to view the August 2017 solar eclipse. Perhaps fittingly, the spot he picked was atop Fort Knox, where the US government stores its gold.[36]

Finally, there's the Hatch Act of 1939, which prohibits using official government power to promote some forms of political activity or economic benefits. President Trump's social media director was officially chastised by the Office of the Special Counsel after using his official Twitter account to call for a sitting

Congressman to be defeated in a primary,[37] while White House counselor Kellyanne Conway directly used her position to promote Ivanka Trump's product line. "Go buy Ivanka's stuff is what I would tell you," she said from the White House briefing room in February 2017, "I'm going to give a free commercial here: Go buy it today, everybody."[38] That's repulsive for anyone who believes in government ethics, of course, but now that violating ethical standards has become the new normal in Trump's America, it seems like a blip on the horizon.

After just the first few months of resisting this horror, continually pressing for greater disclosures, further divestments, and more transparency, Office of Government Ethics Director Walter Shaub finally decided that he had put up with enough. How can you work on government ethics in an administration that regularly shows disdain for them? He resigned during the summer of 2017, saying that his advice was being ignored.[39]

The swamp of lobbying and pay-to play access schemes that subvert the democratic process and push the government to deliver most for those who least need it is not of Donald Trump's creation. But throughout his presidential campaign, he bellowed that he would "Drain the Swamp!" Not only has he failed to do so, he's actually wallowed in the swamp. His supporters have been hoodwinked, deceived by a man who has disregarded ethical guidelines and bent every rule that cannot be legally broken. In the process, he's trampling on a core tenet of democracy: that public service should be dissociated from private interest. Kings may rule their kingdoms to get richer, and dictators may abuse their people for profit. But in democracies, nobody is supposed to get rich while in office.

Trump is not to blame for a system that allows him to get away with ethical violations, but he is exploiting the presidency in new and dangerous ways that undermine American democracy. The abuses documented here have happened in less than a year in power. More ethical violations will surely follow—especially if there is no real pushback resulting from past abuses. To shore up the integrity of our system of governance, we need to stop him, his family, and his cronies, by converting ethical gray areas into black and white ones where you go to jail if you cross the line.

In the meantime, Trump supporters who believed that their hero would ride into Washington and fix a broken system should be honest with themselves about what he has done. At the next campaign rally, those in red "Make America Great Again" hats should be chanting, "Flood the Swamp!" Because that is what President Trump has already done, and his cesspool is corrupting our democracy.

8

THE DEEP STATE

Few people have contemplated their own murder as openly as Benazir Bhutto of Pakistan. It ran in the family. Her father, Zulfikar, who had served as Pakistan's prime minister in the mid-1970s, was hanged in prison after being ousted by a military coup. Her youngest brother, Shahnawaz, was poisoned. Pakistani police shot her older brother, Murtaza, a little over a decade later under suspicious circumstances. Being a Bhutto in Pakistan seemed to bring a death sentence with sinister regularity. Benazir, the surviving daughter, went into exile twice to avoid a similar fate.

But in early 2007, she returned to Pakistan, hoping to reclaim power again as the country's first female head of state. She pledged to rein in the shadowy and powerful network of military and intelligence forces that had been the power behind elected officials in Pakistan for decades. This made her plenty of enemies who would have preferred her to return not as prime minister but in a casket. Keenly aware of threats on her life, she made repeated requests for additional security.[1] Instead, she got less. Police patrols outside her house were reduced. She asked for permits to allow her bodyguards to carry guns; they were denied. Equipment she was given to defend herself, like jamming devices that could disrupt remote-controlled bombing attacks, did not work. In late

October 2007, she wrote an e-mail to a trusted friend: "Nothing will, God willing happen ... I have been made to feel insecure by [the government's] minions."[2]

On the afternoon of 27 December 2007, Bhutto hopped into a custom-made bulletproof Toyota Land Cruiser. She had just finished addressing rapturous, adoring crowds in Rawalpindi, 12 miles southwest of Islamabad. The election loomed in just over a week, and spirits in her political camp were high. As her car began to leave, so many of her supporters swarmed the vehicle that the driver had to stop. Bhutto opened the sunroof of the bulletproof cruiser, emerged into the dimming light of the late afternoon, and waved to the cheering crowd, her white headscarf billowing in the breeze. Moments later, a young man approached the car, pulled out a weapon, and fired three shots in quick succession at Bhutto's head. She jolted, slumped forward, and then slunk down, dying, into the bulletproof car. A split second later, the same gunman or an accomplice detonated a suicide vest. The explosion rocked the square. Bhutto was pronounced dead soon afterwards.[3]

There is no consensus on who ordered the killing of Bhutto. The Pakistani military establishment and intelligence directorates, often referred to as Pakistan's Deep State, lay the blame on Islamist terrorists. But many of Bhutto's supporters remained unconvinced. For decades, the so-called Deep State had engineered assassination plots, coups, murders, and cover-ups.[4] As a result, it became impossible to take political leadership or spokespeople for political institutions at their word. If the military said Islamist militants killed Bhutto, then her supporters were prone to believe the opposite. A cloud of suspicion descended on Pakistan, and millions were left wondering whether the government had played a role in Bhutto's untimely death.

Such is the price of politicized institutions. In politics, when citizens believe that the military, or a government agency, or the courts are simply the tool of a specific partisan or "deep state" interest, trust dies. Without it, democracy is impossible. Donald Trump and his entourage are in the process of politicizing American democratic institutions, killing off trust in government as they paint government agencies, scientists, courts, and intelligence agencies as political opponents rather than as the collective bedrock of the US government. And the term they use to describe these institutions should be familiar to the people of Pakistan: the "Deep State." This concept, which originated in Turkey and has since spread to Pakistan and Egypt, refers to a sinister arm of the government that rules from the shadows. The interventions of the Deep State are always nefarious and often bloody: false flag operations; assassinations; purges; or bombings against civilians carefully orchestrated to seem the work of the political opposition.[5] This is a real "deep state." Such dark forces should seem completely alien to the functioning of American democracy within the United States.

Unless, that is, you listen to Donald Trump's administration and inner circle. Who is the American Deep State, you might ask? The answer is not to be found in shadowy assassinations or bombing plots as in Turkey or Pakistan. Instead, it seems, the insidious Washington puppet masters out to get Trump are hiding in plain sight, disguised as geeky legislative analysts who score the projected cost of proposed legislation. Yes, indeed, according to Trump and his political allies, these dastardly plots are hatched by the independent, nonpartisan Congressional Budget Office, which has been quietly plotting world domination one legislative markup at a time. The CBO wields not the gun of an assassin but the subtler, deadlier spreadsheet. Their latest false flag operation?

Assessing the cost and impact of the Trump-backed health care proposal that went down in legislative flames in the summer of 2017. Or so prominent Trump supporter Newt Gingrich would have you believe: "Here's the Congressional Budget Office as part of the deep state doing a hit job on the Senate Republicans," he claimed.[6] And of course, because this is the world of Trump, it wasn't just a deep state hit job. The White House also deemed the CBO to be "little more than fake news."[7] That designation meant that the CBO could be lumped in with all the other fake news outlets out there, referred to by Trump as the "enemy of the American people."

The Congressional Budget Office is neither deep state nor fake news. It is not the enemy of the American people. And if it were partisan (which it is not), it's hard to see how it would be biased against the Trump administration. Its leader, Keith Hall, is not just a Republican, but one who was headhunted for that job by Trump's then health and human services secretary, Tom Price.[8] Since 1974, Republicans and Democrats alike have relied on the Congressional Budget Office for independent, nonpartisan estimates of the effects at stake in legislative proposals. Their reports, which are saturated with well-researched statistics, cost curves, and confidence estimates, could put a well-caffeinated nerd to sleep in minutes. But they serve a crucial function in a democracy: they are the legislative scorekeepers that everyone can trust. That is, until Donald Trump came along. Now, Trump supporters view this longstanding, nonpartisan, Republican-led entity as a deep state tool for the Democrats to stick it to the president. At first glance, this makes no sense—unless you understand that undercutting the gravitas and authority of independent institutions is crucial to eroding democracy and amassing greater power.

All despots try to politicize institutions, depicting any that are independent and stand up to the "preferred" narrative as enemies of the people and stooges of political opponents. Trump may be completing this politicization more out of impulsive anger toward an unfavorable cost estimate than as part of an ideological authoritarian strategy, but the impact is the same. Talk about CBO estimates to Trump supporters and those who know what you're referring to will quickly dismiss it as the deep state, or, if you're lucky enough to find a full disciple, the deep state's fake news.

Within less than a year in office, Donald Trump has successfully dragged several core institutions of American democracy into the political fray. In the process, he has convinced millions of his supporters to distrust unbiased sources of information. If any part of the US government doesn't immediately bend to the will of the Trump administration, it is quickly labeled as a weapon wielded by the deep state. Or, in the case of Bob Mueller, the FBI special counsel in charge of the Russia investigation, as the tip of the "deep state spear" seeking to bring down President Trump—as Gingrich so colorfully put it.[9] Trump also re-tweeted a monologue by Sean Hannity of Fox News arguing that, in the context of the investigation, the "deep state" was "a clear and present danger to this country and to you."[10] It isn't just the Congressional Budget Office that has come under fire. It's also been NASA, the courts, intelligence agencies, science, and the military. The politicization of these institutions comes after decades of declining trust in government, which makes Trump's efforts all the more dangerous. On this score, the United States is nowhere near Pakistan, to be sure, but Trump is dragging America closer. And we've seen in the case of Trump's war on journalism what happens when civic trust breaks down: democracy dies a slow but certain death.

Here's a depressing thought experiment: list all the public institutions, government agencies and media outlets in American politics. Now, narrow it down to all those that you believe would be considered unbiased and objective by large majorities of both Democrats and Republicans. If anything is left on your list, it's longer than mine. In a May 2017 survey, just one in five Americans say Washington can be trusted to do the right thing "always" or "most of the time."[11] There is no single organization or institution that a majority of Americans trust "a great deal." It's gotten so bad that fewer people trust the government now than they did after the Watergate scandal.

Most Americans used to be able to trust the courts. Now, for the first time, they are looking to a president who not only criticizes and disagrees with court rulings as others have, but engages in personal attacks on individual judges, including on the basis of their skin color. Most Americans believed that NASA was above the political fray, that the agency that put a man on the moon would be driven by science rather than politics. In the Trump era, thanks to his comments and his appointments to such agencies, even science has been politicized. And, of course, Trump has openly attacked intelligence agencies while trying to bend them to his will, at the same time as injecting the White House with an unprecedented level of military counsel. In time, these decisions will lead to an erosion of trust in the few remaining bastions of across-the-aisle credibility in Washington.

Let's start with NASA. After winning the election but before taking office, a Trump adviser suggested that it was time to do away with what he called "politically correct environmental monitoring" at NASA—by which he meant climate change research.[12] This isn't particularly surprising given that Trump had repeatedly tweeted climate change denialisms such as "The concept of global warming was created by and for the Chinese in order to make U.S. manufacturing non-competitive." To bolster such claims, Trump offered such ironclad evidence as: "I'm in Los Angeles and it's freezing. Global warming is a total, and very expensive, hoax!"[13]

Trump is, of course, wrong. There is no scientific debate. Climate change is real, and even the tiny minority of climate change deniers tend to accept that the planet is warming but argue that it is not due to human activity (they are incorrect). But given Trump's withdrawal from the Paris climate accords and his history of absurd and incorrect statements on climate change, it's understandable that scientists worried their research would be suppressed—particularly after it had been branded as "politically correct environmental monitoring" by a senior Trump adviser. So, in early August 2017, a group of scientists leaked their latest climate change report to *The New York Times* before it could be buried by the Trump administration.[14] That's a truly shocking canary in the coal mine—when researchers from thirteen government agencies, including NASA feel the need to leak the latest findings of a clear scientific consensus for fear that their government would refuse to publish it.

Trump confirmed that their worries were justified a few weeks later when he announced his pick to head NASA. Typically, the NASA administrator is either a career member of NASA staff, or a scientist, an astronaut—anyone, really, who has deep and abiding expertise in the mission of the agency. President Obama's choice to head the agency was Major General Charles Bolden, an aviator and test pilot for the Marine corps who served as an astronaut for fourteen years.[15] He earned multiple science degrees before joining the Marines and was awarded ten honorary doctorates for his contributions to scientific research and space exploration. In short, he was precisely what NASA administrators are supposed to be. The same was true of George W. Bush's NASA appointees, including Mike Griffin, an aerospace engineer who had previously headed the Space Department at the Johns Hopkins University Applied Physics Laboratory. If you go through the history of NASA, it doesn't matter whether the president was a Republican or a Democrat, the administrator was someone who was highly qualified to pursue the mission free from political agendas or partisan ideology.

In September 2017, Trump announced that Representative Jim Bridenstine of Oklahoma would now head the world's most important space agency. Bridenstine's degree in business and psychology don't exactly reassure that he's prepared to lead NASA into the twenty-first century. He may once have directed an air and space museum in his native Oklahoma,[16] but that hardly prepares you to head NASA. He does have one credential unique to him as a NASA administrator, though: he has been a climate change denier. "Global temperatures stopped rising 10 years ago," Bridenstine said in a 2013 speech on floor of the House of Representatives. "Global temperature changes, when they exist, correlate with sun output and ocean cycles."[17] Actual scientists tend to point out that this claim is, of course, wrong. With Bridenstine's appointment, NASA has become yet another partisan pawn in Trump's game. Democrats and Republicans alike have been outspoken in opposition to this politicization of NASA, most notably with Republican Senator Marco Rubio of Florida condemning the appointment by saying it is "important" that NASA "remain free of politics and partisanship."[18]

Unlike the until-now pure NASA, the Environmental Protection Agency has long been politicized in previous administrations. But Trump's systematic approach to that process—to the detriment of objective scientific research—is new. Scott Pruitt, the Trump-appointed head of the EPA, has denied that there is any link between CO_2 and climate changes, a view that is repudiated by 99 per cent of climate scientists. (Many of the 1 per cent who disagree have been employed by polluters to produce rival studies aiming to muddy the waters of an otherwise crystal clear scientific consensus.)[19] Since Pruitt's appointment in February 2017, one outspoken climate scientist within the EPA has been involuntarily reassigned to another job—as an accountant.[20] There has been a systematic effort to prop up industry voices while drowning out scientific ones.[21] Of course, this amounts to a damaging attack on core institutions of democratic government, because environmental protection agencies are supposed to provide unbiased scientific assessments of risk before political decisions are made on how to mitigate them. In Trump's EPA, the risks are being whitewashed and buried. But it's not just science that is under attack as institutions become politicized.

The courts are a cornerstone of democratic government. They provide the foundational pillar of rule of law, which separates arbitrary authoritarianism from the democratic legal framework essential to government of the people, by the people, and for the people. Trump, however, has crossed an important line in the separation of powers between the judiciary and the executive by overtly attacking not just the courts generally but also judges individually.

In June 2016, Trump was facing a plethora of lawsuits alleging that he had committed fraud in setting up Trump University. The allegations included reports from former Trump University staff that they were pressured to make high-cost sales pitches to prospective "students" based on misleading claims about who would be teaching them. Many students were led to believe that Trump himself would be actively involved, only to realize that their instructors teaching them about real estate investment often had never conducted any real estate transactions themselves.[22] Trump eventually settled the fraud suit after his election, by paying $25 million.[23]

The judge assigned to the case was Judge Gonzalo Curiel, who was born in Indiana, the son of Mexican immigrants who came to the United States shortly after World War II. Curiel's father worked in an Indiana steel mill and became a naturalized American citizen.[24] Judge Curiel himself was therefore neither Mexican nor an immigrant; he was an American-born son of Indiana. Still, before the suit was settled, Trump saw fit to attack Curiel because of his Mexican heritage, claiming that he would be biased against the then presidential candidate. Trump called on Judge Curiel to recuse, simply because his parents had been born in the country that Trump had been demonizing during the campaign. "I've been treated very unfairly by this judge," Trump argued. "Now, this judge is of Mexican heritage, I'm building a wall." Trump continued: "He's a member of a society where—you know—very pro-Mexico and that's fine, it's all fine, but I think—I think—he should recuse himself."[25] As Republican Speaker of the House Paul Ryan put it at the time: "Claiming a person can't do their job because of their race is sort of like the textbook definition of a racist comment."[26] Still, candidate Trump's poison had been injected into the well, encouraging the public to believe that the courts and their representatives are not independent arbiters of law, but biased by their own race and therefore untrustworthy.

But it gets worse. As president, Trump has depicted the courts system—the bedrock of American rule of law—as a deep state ploy to derail his agenda. Trump has also tried to politicize the courts by suggesting that, in their quest to uphold the American constitution, they will have blood on their hands for any future terrorist acts. When courts ruled that Trump's travel ban targeting seven

Muslim-majority nations was unconstitutional in early 2017, Trump tweeted that the "courts are political!" Candidate Trump had called for "a complete and total shutdown" of Muslims entering the United States in December 2015,[27] but when a judge ruled against Trump's order, Trump tweeted: "Just cannot believe a judge would put our country in such peril. If something happens, blame him and court system. People pouring in! Bad." This tweet itself was a lie. Nobody was pouring into the United States, and the vetting procedures that had always been in place were still in place. But Trump nonetheless made a statement inviting Americans to blame any future terror attacks or violence from foreign nationals on courts who were simply doing their job: interpreting whether or not an executive order was constitutional.

As Trump ratcheted up popular anger at the proper functioning of American courts, his White House doused the flames with a healthy amount of gasoline by issuing a statement that suggested judges now had blood on their hands for upholding the Constitution: "This San Francisco judge's erroneous ruling is a gift to the criminal gang and cartel element in our country, empowering the worst kind of human trafficking and sex trafficking, and putting thousands of innocent lives at risk."[28] There was, of course, no evidence to support that statement. Further, Trump tweeted that "because the ban was lifted by a judge, many very bad and dangerous people may be pouring into our country." Again, no evidence was offered to support this claim, and in the last twenty years no Americans have been killed in a terrorist attack by nationals originating from any of the countries subject to Trump's travel ban.[29]

But Trump's vociferous and visceral criticism, not only of the courts system but also of specific judges, provided plenty of fuel for Trump surrogates to fan the flames and suggest that the judiciary was also part of a "deep state" plot against Trump. Sean Hannity of Fox News, a close confidant of the president who sometimes dines at the White House, shrouded the normal functioning of the judicial system under a cloud of sinister suspicion. "All of this is happening because of the deep state," he claimed. "It's now the deep state gone rogue. The deep state against the American people. The deep state against the outcome of an election—a free and fair election in this country. And the deep state that is now actively seeking to take out your president."[30] Alex Jones of *InfoWars*, a notorious cesspool of bogus conspiracy theories, took it further, claiming that the rulings were part of a plot to assassinate the president.[31]

Of course, crackpots like Jones say crazy things all the time. NASA was even forced to respond to an allegation made on his radio show in the summer of 2017 that the agency was running a secret slave colony on Mars.[32] But Trump appeared on *InfoWars* during the campaign and has repeatedly praised Jones for his "amazing reputation."[33] Through his actions and his words, Trump has been breathing fresh life—and now presidential legitimacy—into those who seek to further politicize the judiciary, supposedly an extension of the clandestine plot to undermine Trump's agenda. The courts are just doing their job. They are part of the American system of democratic checks and balances. But now, millions of people who accept the "truth" of Trump's pronouncements falsely believe that judges with Mexican heritage, or judges who believe in the authority of the American constitution in a democratic framework, are part of some deep state conspiracy. Rebuilding trust will be both difficult and time-consuming.

Then, we have the intelligence agencies and the military. Democracies accept that intelligence agencies must operate in the shadows, a rare dose of acceptable opaqueness in an otherwise transparent system. But that consensus is derived from necessity and is predicated on the shared belief that intelligence agencies work with the best available information to provide informed risk estimates to politicians who must then make decisions. That consensus—and the authority and independence of intelligence agencies—is threatened when politicians attempt to attack intelligence agencies for coming to conclusions at odds with their own political ideology; or to prod the agencies into producing politically motivated findings rather than dispassionate, objective ones.

Ironically, Trump's favorite argument to discredit intelligence agencies comes from a previous attempt to politicize them: "I remember when I was sitting back listening about Iraq, weapons of mass destruction. How everybody was 100% sure that Iraq had weapons of mass destruction. Guess what? That led to one big mess."[34] It is true that in 2002 and 2003, policymakers in George W. Bush's administration tried to use their political leverage to sway intelligence assessments toward their preferred narrative. There was precedent for this, too: in one case documented by Richard K. Betts in his study *Enemies of Intelligence: Knowledge and Power in American National Security*, an intelligence officer was reassigned because his views were not what the administration wanted to hear when it came to discussing the risk of weapons programs in Cuba and Syria.[35] In the run-up to the war in Iraq, senior Bush administration officials publicized intelligence findings without contextualizing the uncertainty surrounding them. They refused to publish dissenting views. And they put an effective gag order on any of those who held dissenting views from voicing them publicly. In other words, America went to war for a decade on the basis of politicized intelligence assessments.[36] The danger is real.

Yet, if Trump truly believes that Iraq was a blight on the intelligence community's record, then his response should be to seek to keep politics out of its assessments. Instead, during the year since his election, Trump has demonstrated the opposite aim: to attack intelligence agencies when he doesn't like what they say, and to pressure them to say more of what he does like to hear.

Nine days before taking office, Trump compared American intelligence agencies to those operating in Nazi Germany.[37] He has referred dismissively to their clear consensus that the Russian government interfered in the 2016 election as "fake news," a "witch hunt," and "a Democrat EXCUSE for losing the election" (as we've seen, this latter deflection makes no sense, because the FBI investigation began several months before the election took place).[38] These attacks seem absurd to many Americans, but they are persuading millions. In a June 2017 NBC/*Wall Street Journal* poll, only 53 per cent of Americans said they believed that Russia had interfered in the 2016 election—despite the unanimous conclusion of the intelligence community. For self-identified Republicans, 65 per cent said they did not believe that the Russian government had interfered, while 78 per cent of self-identified Democrats believed (correctly) that it had.[39] This partisan split is a disaster for the role of intelligence agencies within a democracy. Just as democracy cannot function properly if only one party believes the media, so too will democracy wither if the government's intelligence assessments are believed by one party and openly dismissed by the other.

Furthermore, there is burgeoning evidence that Trump is seeking to draw the intelligence community directly into the partisan fray. As former Deputy CIA Director David Cohen has argued in *The Washington Post*, Trump has been demanding "intelligence to support his policy preference to withdraw from the Iran nuclear deal."[40] At first, the intelligence community provided an objective assessment that Trump didn't like—that, whether or not you like the nuclear deal struck between President Obama and Iran, the Iranians do appear to be holding up their end of the bargain. With that analysis in hand, Trump grudgingly re-certified that Iran was doing its part in the nuclear deal. But, shortly thereafter, he commissioned a working group within the White House and, according to *Foreign Policy*, told them "that he wants to be in a place to decertify 90 days from now and it's their job to put him there."

In other words, Trump is asking for intelligence estimates that affirm his pre-ordained preference. He's aiming to base foreign policy decisions not on objective assessments but on pre-determined political ideas. As Cohen aptly argues, billions have been invested "in the aftermath of the episode regarding weapons of mass destruction in Iraq—to ensure that finished intelligence is objective, properly qualified, based on all available sources and free of political considerations. When the president demands intelligence to fit his political desires, this investment is squandered and our national security endangered."[41]

Nobody knows how this will all play out with the Iran deal specifically—even if Trump re-certifies the deal on 15 October, it is up for continual review; he will likely be looking for further excuses to de-certify on each occasion. More importantly, Trump's willingness to attack intelligence agencies openly when they say inconvenient things is dangerous—especially given his seeming penchant for pressuring them to produce intelligence he likes. As with the Congressional Budget Office, citizens in democracies cannot make informed decisions if the realm of partisan battles expands to include independent assessments made by objective government agencies. Unfortunately, as the polling is showing, Trump's politicization campaign is working.

Finally, the next area to watch will be the military. In public opinion surveys from Pew Research, the military and the police are the only state institutions that command "quite a lot of confidence" from a majority of Americans.[42] That, in and of itself, is unhealthy for a civilian-led democracy. But Americans now feel they must trust seasoned generals to manage an often-unhinged president. The secretary of defense, General James Mattis, was only appointed after a waiver was granted allowing him to serve in civilian office sooner than would normally be allowed after exiting the military.[43] The scandal-plagued General Michael Flynn was dismissed as Trump's national security adviser in February 2017 and replaced by another general, H.R. McMaster.[44] Finally, Trump named General John Kelly as his chief of staff after dismissing Reince Priebus in the summer of 2017. These military men in key civilian posts join the Joint Chiefs of Staff—six generals and an admiral—who also advise Trump on military and foreign policy matters.

Therefore, if you add in Senior Advisor to the President Jared Kushner and Advisor to the President Ivanka Trump, a significant proportion of those advising the president of the United States are either members of his family or generals. This is unfathomable in other functioning democracies. It's hard to imagine German Chancellor Angela Merkel or British Prime Minister Theresa May surrounded by a cadre of men in uniform, jockeying for influence against a daughter and son-in-law. This is banana republic stuff. If this staffing pattern existed in some other country, with generals being hailed as saviors rescuing the people from the civilian leader, alarm bells would be going off for every pro-democracy monitoring group in the world.

The alarm bells have been muted, however, because the generals seem to be the steadying hand that keeps Trump from his darkest and most destructive impulses. For most Americans, the necessity of finding seasoned professionals who can stop Trump from his craziest tweets or his most impulsive behavior eclipses any considerations about the dominance of civilian rule in the democratic system.[45]

But an important line has not just been crossed but also blurred. As with many features of Trumpian behavior, the modern American precedent lies with President Richard Nixon, who made General Alexander Haig his chief of staff while his presidency spiraled into scandal.[46] Even so, Trump's warrior advisers represent an unparalleled influence of military figures in a civilian administration. Perhaps, in the Trump era, these steadying hands are a justifiable violation of that sharp line between civilian and military rule. But we do need to be vigilant and ensure that this does not become the new normal in American politics. If it does, this one last bastion of widespread, bipartisan trust—in the military—may also be sacrificed. If that happens, and the military becomes perceived as an extension of a specific political party or politician, then American democracy will truly be poisoned beyond repair.

Certainly, partisan debates are essential to democracy. They allow citizens to consider options before making key choices. But government institutions—courts, scientific advisers, the Congressional Budget Office, intelligence agencies, and the military—should be shielded from the insidious influence of partisan polarization. Americans may not agree on tax policy, health care, or foreign policy, but they must agree that judges, intelligence analysts, or budget forecasters are not part of a shadowy deep state plot to subvert Donald Trump. That belief is as absurd as it is toxic for democracy.

Unfortunately, it is now also widespread. As with so many of Trump's attacks on democracy, he doesn't need to be an effective president to spread this false perception—he simply needs to repeat these baseless attacks over, and over, and over. Eventually, they stick in the minds of millions of his supporters. As their thoughts are poisoned against the core institutions at the heart of democratic governance, democracy itself gets a little poisoned too. In such an environment, creeping authoritarianism can grow like a weed, feeding off mistrust and conspiracy theories. In that sense, Trump's toxic rhetoric is fertilizing the weeds. And it's going to take years, perhaps decades, to restore healthy democratic soil once Trump leaves office.

9

TAKE YOUR KIDS TO WORK DAY

From 1989 until his death in 2016, Islam Karimov ruled the Central Asian nation of Uzbekistan as a ruthless dictator. To improve his public relations with the international community, Karimov sought to soften his image. Instead of being seen as a bloodthirsty autocrat (which he most certainly was), why not try to make people see him as a doting father instead? Karimov began to project his eldest daughter Gulnara as an extension of his personalist regime. She was just seventeen when her father ascended to power.

Gulnara stood by her father's side as he turned the newly independent Uzbekistan into a totalitarian state, a terrifying autocracy where dissent ensured either a death sentence by torture or a one-way ticket to a barbaric jail cell. Karimov's regime engaged in forced child labor, in some years systematically pushing children into backbreaking work picking cotton.[1] In 2003, an inquest initiated by Western governments found evidence that two dissidents had been tortured and then boiled alive.[2] Karimov had the "compassion" to return the disfigured, boiled corpses to their families, a gesture that was somewhat undercut by the fact that family members could plainly see that the fingernails of their loved ones were missing—haunting clues of unspeakable torture.[3]

Gulnara Karimova was supposed to be the regime's velvet glove. She was Ivy League-educated, a comfortable fixture amongst the American cultural and economic elite. Back in Uzbekistan, she sought to promote various causes. She organized a marathon for charity. She was a patron of the arts. She launched a new micro-credit project for rural women in farming. To outsiders, she was the heart that her father sorely lacked. And everyone seemed to hope that she could restrain her father's most brutal and misguided impulses.

But while Gulnara was promoting the image of a socially conscious philanthropist filled with compassion, she also took advantage of her position as a despot's daughter. She gallivanted with pop stars and celebrities. She organized a concert for Sting in Uzbekistan. Karimova even became an Uzbek pop star herself, cashing in on her powerful connections to create slick music videos and forge a carefully crafted glamorous cult of personality. She used the stage name GooGoosha, her father's pet name for his favorite daughter. The music video of her first hit, *Unutma Meni* ("Don't Forget Me") takes place in a surrealist dreamscape as a baby blue sports car floats toward a golden city in the clouds. The imagery clearly resonated with her family's rise over the oppressed people, completely divorced from the daily realities of hardship created by her father's authoritarian kleptocracy.

In the process, the dictator's daughter became fabulously rich. According to documents published by the Organized Crime and Corruption Reporting Project, Karimova amassed an estimated $1 billion from telecoms and other businesses in exchange for political influence with her father.[4] With all that wealth secured, she also moved into the world of fashion and jewelry. In March 2009, the dictator's daughter rolled out a new jewelry line called GULI, which she then turned into a broader brand selling clothes and interior design items. In 2011, she set off for New York, accompanied by American pop star JoJo, to promote a new fashion line drawing on traditional Uzbek dress. "We've been showing in Milan and we had a lot of interest in Europe," she boasted to reporters fawning over her lines.[5] But when she tried to return with new styles for the catwalk a year later, Karimova was banned, after Human Rights Watch raised concerns about her father's regime and its systematic record of torture and abuse.[6]

Like many despots, President Karimov elevated his family not just to wealth but to power. It wasn't enough to make Gulnara absurdly rich. Uzbekistan's despot also wanted his daughter to be seen as an extension of his own presidency on the global stage. She became a senior figure at the Uzbek delegation to the United Nations in New York starting in 1998. She represented her country at the Uzbek embassy in Moscow from 2003 to 2005. In 2008, she was made Permanent Representative of Uzbekistan to the United Nations. And in January 2010, she was named as the Uzbek ambassador to Spain. Through all these posts, she was her father's apologist to the world's leaders, playing up her role as a "modern woman," distant from the medieval aspects of the regime.[7]

Gulnara was everything her doting father hoped for—offering a princess-like, glamorous image of the Uzbek regime, outwardly charitable and well-spoken, the soft edge to his harder brutality. In the public eye, she was a jewelry designer turned diplomat, a pop star turned political titan. In the shadows, though, she was cashing in on her father's power. And, crucially, she provided political cover for her father's regime on the national and international stage.

Sound vaguely familiar?

Despots run their countries like a family business. Nepotism is a hallmark of authoritarian societies, but an improper stain on democratic ones. Donald Trump has now blurred that line. Of course, Trump's administration is nowhere near the abomination of Karimov's regime. However, there are striking parallels between Gulnara Karimova and Ivanka Trump, the US president's eldest and favorite daughter. Trump sees Ivanka as part of his presidency, a "secret weapon" to be deployed to charm world leaders and highlight the glamor of his administration's "brand." Like Gulnara, Ivanka is Ivy League-educated, a cosmopolitan social butterfly, an occasional model, and the owner of her own jewelry line and a business empire aimed at women. Ivanka mirrors Gulnara in cultivating a charitable persona. And both daughters have perpetually breathed life into the myth that they can soften their father, swaying each president to become more socially progressive.

At the G-20 summit in Hamburg during the summer of 2017, Trump took a page straight out of Islam Karimov's playbook by using Ivanka as a sort of stand-in senior diplomat, allowing her to take his place among the world's most powerful leaders.[8] There was Chancellor Merkel of Germany, President Xi of China, and then First Daughter Ivanka Trump of the United States. Add those parallels to the comically expansive senior role that Trump has given to Ivanka's husband, Jared Kushner, and you've got a full-blown case of nepotism that is usually only seen in the world's palaces. If pressed, nobody in the Republican Party would seriously argue that either Kushner or Ivanka Trump would be genuine contenders for advisory roles in any other administration; they are solely employed in this White House because they are related to Donald Trump. This is nepotism personified. And it's dangerous for democracy.

Of course, Donald Trump is not the first American president to engage in nepotism. John Adams made his son an emissary to Prussia in 1797.[9] After the Civil War, Ulysses S. Grant appointed his cousin as the chief American diplomat in Guatemala. In total, Grant ended up appointing nearly forty family members, from customs officers to White House ushers.[10] Dwight Eisenhower gave his son an assistant staff secretary post.[11] And, perhaps most famously, John F. Kennedy made his brother, Robert, the US attorney general. Since then, however, several anti-nepotism laws have been passed to restrict the practice. It's true that even after this legislation Bill Clinton did appoint his wife, Hillary, to head a task force on health care reform in the 1990s. The effort flopped, and Clinton took considerable political heat for the appointment. It was clearly a mistake.

Donald Trump's nepotism is far more dangerous. Rather than rewarding family members with exotic but unimportant posts (like Grant) or as part of a liaison team with Congress (like Clinton), Trump is using unqualified family members as his main advisers. Every major decision President Trump has made in almost a year in office has been influenced by two relatives with no government experience, no understanding of policy nuance, and no real expertise. This would be understandable if Trump were being advised on jewelry design, how to run a fashion business, or New York real estate development. But he's not. He's being advised on counterterrorism, trade deals, and how to cope with the threat of a nuclear North Korea—by people who don't have a clue about any of those issues. Moreover, Trump has placed a dizzying array of important tasks on his son-in-law's plate. Kushner is working on them without proper oversight, giving him wide latitude to make vital government policy without accountability. There is no other way to put it: Donald Trump's daughter and her husband are two of the most powerful people on Earth, and they have that power exclusively because they are related to Donald Trump.

Trump's relationship with his daughter—politically and personally—is not normal. Ivanka Trump is the daughter of Donald Trump's first wife (Czech supermodel Ivana Trump), whom he divorced after cheating on her with Marla Maples—who then went on to become Trump's second wife.[12] What's even more confusing than this complex family tree is Trump's perpetual sexualization of his daughter. This began, disturbingly enough, when Ivanka was still a teenager.

While watching Ivanka host the Miss Teen USA pageant in 1997, he reportedly turned to the reigning Miss Universe, and quipped: "Don't you think my daughter's hot? She's hot, right?"[13] Ivanka was sixteen years old. Since then, he has endorsed describing Ivanka as "a piece of ass"[14] and called her "very voluptuous" himself.[15] In 2003, on the raunchy *Howard Stern Show*, Trump boasted, "My daughter, Ivanka. She's 6 feet tall, she's got the best body."[16] A year later, he told *New York* magazine, "Let me tell you one thing: Ivanka is a great, great beauty. Every guy in the country wants to go out with my daughter. But she's got a boyfriend."[17] And perhaps the grossest moment of all occurred with Ivanka right by his side. Trump smiled mischievously at his eldest daughter on the set of the morning show *The View* in 2006 as he told the world that Ivanka "does have a very nice figure. I've said if she wasn't my daughter, perhaps I'd be dating her."[18] Presumably, every viewer's skin crawled at the mental image of 60-year-old Donald Trump dating his 24-year-old daughter, but these revealing moments matter. Aside from their generally troubling insights into one of the most important father/daughter relationships in the world, they also expose another violation of democratic norms: even if they weren't family, in a healthy, functioning democracy the president shouldn't be hiring anybody to whom he clearly and publicly relates in such a personal—and sexualized—way.

Whatever the precise nature of his feelings, Trump is close to his daughter, and she looks up to him. Since graduating from the Wharton Business School at the University of Pennsylvania (impressively, it must be noted, with *summa cum laude* honors), Ivanka decided to try to follow in her father's footsteps. She started working on real estate deals. She formed her own company, selling designer jewelry and fashion items. She modeled on the side. Over time, her business flourished—growing the wealth that she had acquired from birth. That wealth expanded even further in 2009, when she married young real estate and media baron Jared Kushner.

By 2015, the New York power couple had emerged as "the" powerful couple in Trump's surging presidential campaign. With a skeletal staff and Trump's instincts as the main driver of campaign strategy, close confidants started to run the show. Kushner and Ivanka Trump were increasingly calling the shots, alongside Trump's other politically active children, Donald Jr and Eric. At one point, Kushner's role was so large that *The New York Times* referred to him as the "de facto campaign manager."[19] Kushner spoke with former Secretary of State Henry Kissinger, Speaker of the House Paul Ryan, and media mogul Rupert Murdoch.[20] In short, behind the scenes, Trump's family members served as the real power brokers for the early stages of an upstart campaign that shocked the world.

There was also an obvious tension between Jared and Ivanka's social circle and the campaign they were powering. The New York social elite with which the power couple rubbed elbows tended to be far more socially progressive than Donald Trump's campaign. As Trump called Mexicans rapists and led chants of "Build the Wall!" at campaign rallies, Ivanka and Jared found themselves increasingly under fire as the enablers and apologists. Indeed, at two critical points in the campaign, they enabled and apologized in ways that would prove crucial to Trump's political survival.

In early July 2016, right before the Republican National Convention at which Trump would accept the Republican nomination, a member of the candidate's staff tweeted the image showing a Star of David and stacks of money alongside the accusation that Hillary Clinton was the "Most Corrupt Candidate Ever!"[21] As we've seen in Chapter 7, this was just one, profoundly anti-Semitic example of the Trump campaign's persistent tribalization of American society. The tweet prompted outrage from Jewish Americans, who objected to the fact that a man seeking to become president of the United States had shared an image that seemingly originated from a white supremacist website targeting Jews. Nonetheless, Trump did not publicly apologize for the post.

Enter the secret weapon: Jared and Ivanka. The couple are Jewish (Jared from birth; Ivanka converted before she married Jared). Kushner therefore had real standing to speak out in favor of his father-in-law, to defend the indefensible. He published a letter called "The Donald Trump I Know," in which he argued that Trump's team had just made a careless mistake.[22] This implausible letter provided Trump crucial political cover at a vulnerable moment. Journalists moved on.

Ivanka has served the same function when it comes to scrutiny of Donald Trump's views on gender. Trump has been consistent in his awful comments about women. In 1992, he told *New York* magazine that, when it comes to women, "you have to treat 'em like shit."[23] It doesn't get much clearer than that. And in the early stages of the primary campaign, he responded to presidential hopeful Carly Fiorina by saying, "Look at that face. Would anyone vote for that? Can you imagine that, the face of our next president? I mean, she's a woman, and I'm not supposed to say bad things, but really, folks, come on. Are we serious?"[24]

For decades, then, Donald Trump has been a misogynist who is open about his misogyny. But when allegations surfaced during the campaign, Ivanka stepped in to limit the fallout from her father's alleged sexual misdeeds. When he was publicly accused of groping a woman, Ivanka went on CBS *This Morning* in March 2016 and said, "He's not a groper. It's not who he is ... he has total respect for women."[25] Her unequivocal defense of her father helped to stop the political bleeding; by the day after this interview, most of the media's Trump stories were centered on his willingness to hold talks with Kim Jong-un of North Korea. Seven months later, the *Access Hollywood* tape emerged in which Trump boasted about serial sexual assault: "When you're a star, they let you do it. You can do anything. Grab 'em by the pussy. You can do anything."[26] Ivanka pushed her father successfully for a public apology, but Trump went immediately back to dismissing his comments as "locker room banter";[27] his daughter went straight back to promoting his campaign while claiming to be a champion for women's equality.

When Trump won the election, there was rampant speculation about whether the relatives who had served as key campaign confidants would soon become staff members with top security clearances. At first, the president-elect denied on Twitter that they would,[28] and was backed by his transition team, who told *The New York Times* that Trump would not be seeking security clearances for his children.[29] Despite that claim, Ivanka was behaving very much like a senior adviser to her father. She participated alongside her husband in meetings with Prime Minister Shinzo Abe of Japan and would later dine with Chinese President Xi Jinping. These honors are typically reserved for secretaries of state or vice presidents who have decades of direct experience in diplomacy or international affairs, not someone whose professional experience primarily revolved around building a fashion business—or purchasing New York apartment units.

Nonetheless, by the time President-Elect Trump became President Trump on 20 January 2017, he had already appointed Jared Kushner as a senior adviser to his White House.[30] It raised red flags with ethics experts and anti-nepotism advocates, but the appointment stuck. Kushner formally became one of the most powerful men in the world by his personal proximity to the president of the United States. He didn't just have the president's ear, but also the familial bond and the official title to match. Then, Trump put him in charge of just about everything. Mockingly referred to as the Secretary of Everything, Kushner was tasked with: bringing peace to the Middle East, criminal justice reform, serving as a liaison to Mexico, acting as a point person for China, solving the massive opioid crisis decimating rural America, and reforming the entire federal government.[31] The extreme breadth of Kushner's tasks prompted the satirical publication *The Onion* to run the headline: "Jared Kushner Quietly Transfers 'Solve Middle East Crisis' to Next Week's To-Do List."[32] Even the most seasoned political operator would have found the scope of his portfolio impossible to manage. For a young political novice whose experience in government wouldn't stack up favorably against that of a junior postman, the entire thing was laughable—or it would have been if the stakes weren't so high.

The White House announced on 20 March 2017 that Ivanka would be given a security clearance and a West Wing office, but would not be an official member of the administration;[33] a week later, she announced that she would, in fact, have a formal (unpaid) title[34]—all of which the Trump transition team had insisted would not happen. Nonetheless, Ivanka now had an office next door to Deputy National Security Adviser Dina Powell—

who had previously served as a senior diplomat at the top levels of the State Department under George W. Bush. To those working in the White House who had devoted their lives to decades of public service, the appointment of Ivanka, the glamor princess of Trump Tower, had to be a striking insult. After all, Ivanka was so inexperienced in politics that she hadn't even voted for her father in the New York primaries. She and her brother Eric had forgotten to register before the deadline.[35] And yet, the businesswoman with no government experience who hadn't even registered to vote is now one of the most powerful women on the planet, advising her father on decisions that have life-changing consequences for billions of people.

But, as Gulnara Karimova of Uzbekistan has shown us, nepotism isn't just about becoming politically powerful. It's also about becoming richer in the process. When Ivanka introduced her father at the 2016 Republican National Convention, she wore one of her own fashion items: a blush "Studded Sheath Dress" that retails for about $140. Not to miss an opportunity to use the Trump political platform to make money, her official personal account tweeted out "Shop Ivanka's look from her #RNC speech" with a link to the dress for sale on Macy's.[36] On 15 November, just a week after her dad had been elected as the next president, she was interviewed on the CBS program *60 Minutes*. Shortly after the interview aired, Ivanka Trump's brand circulated a "style alert" along with an image of Ivanka wearing "her favorite bangle" during the interview. Of course, there was a prominent link to purchase it for the lowly price of $10,800.[37] It was a direct attempt to profit from the political power bestowed on her father. In December, she tried to auction off a charity coffee date for the bargain price of $67,888.[38] Perhaps she was just absurdly naïve and oblivious, but the coffee date auction was rightly viewed as a direct attempt to sell access to the president-elect's daughter in a way that is simply unacceptable in democracies governed by ethics guidelines. Under intense but completely justified criticism, Ivanka canceled the event.[39]

For a person as rich as Ivanka, however, the real way to translate political power into wealth isn't one bangle or blush dress at a time. That's amateur hour compared to using political influence as a way to get favorable treatment in new and highly lucrative markets. On 6 April 2017, Ivanka Trump and Jared Kushner joined President Trump at his exclusive Mar-a-Lago club with President Xi of China. As they dined and ate "beautiful chocolate cake," Trump informed his Chinese counterpart that he had just ordered an attack on Syria. That same evening, China also approved new trademarks so that Ivanka could sell "handbags, jewelry, and spa services" in China.[40] Peter Riebling, a trademark lawyer in Washington DC, told National Public Radio that the approval of these trademarks was highly unusual in how quickly they were processed: "What's interesting about these applications is they sailed through incredibly quickly compared to what is normal in China, under normal trademark practice."[41] In other words, for a businesswoman who didn't share a last name with the US president, the same trademark would likely have been languishing for many more months, or even years.

China also has serious leverage over Ivanka, meaning that they have serious leverage over the Trump administration. If you buy a pair of Ivanka Trump shoes, odds are that they were made in a factory in China. (Her business has come under scrutiny for the labor practices at some of these factories, many of which have involved documented physical abuse and 12- to 14-hour work days.)[42] Just as the Trump entourage's business ties to Russia have been flagged as problematic (see Chapter 5), the direct link between Ivanka's personal wealth and her business operations in China makes her vulnerable to foreign influence. If the Trump administration helps China, she might profit more. If the Trump administration angers China, it could dent her personal bank account.

A few weeks after Ivanka and Jared met with President Xi at Mar-a-Lago, Jared Kushner's relatives were in China. The Kushner family business was touting the EB-5 immigrant investor visa program.[43] The family stood to profit from the EB-5 scheme, as it could lead to lucrative investments in Kushner properties. Any such sales pitch was improper, however, given the family's ability to influence the parameters of the visa program. By August 2017, the Kushner family was reportedly under investigation for that effort.[44]

Since her father took office, Ivanka Trump has made at least $12.6 million, according to financial disclosures filed over the summer of 2017.[45] Jared Kushner failed to disclose more than seventy assets on financial disclosure forms, and did not disclose roughly $1 billion in debts.[46] He has amended his financial disclosure form at least thirty-nine times so far.[47] The couple have taken minimal steps to separate themselves from their business empires and the conflicts of interest that accompany them. Ivanka has objected to that accurate characterization in interviews, arguing that she put assets in a trust—not a blind one, as is typical with presidential divestment, but one run by her in-laws.[48] As ever in Trump world, it all somehow stays in the family.

Nepotism is a serious threat to the integrity of democracy. Obviously, the most basic problem is one of fairness and merit. Better qualified public servants deserve to be in the roles inhabited by Jared and Ivanka. But that's hardly the most damaging aspect of Trump's nepotism. Far more worrying is that his reliance on them in the White House pushes his administration toward what political scientists refer to as "sultanism." In those regimes, what matters is not expertise, official roles, or bureaucratic procedure; instead, what matters is your relationship to the president. On this count, Trump is a paragon of the regime type. As Anne Applebaum of *The Washington Post* argues, "One of the things that distinguishes rule-of-law democracies from personalized dictatorships is their reliance on procedures, not individual whims, and on officials—experienced people, subject to public scrutiny and ethics laws—not the unsackable relatives of the leader. That distinction is now fading."[49]

Applebaum's "unsackable" line is crucial. Imagine a situation in which National Security Adviser H.R. McMaster holds a certain view on a particular strategic threat from a foreign power. In this hypothetical, McMaster is aware that Jared and Ivanka hold the opposite view—perhaps because they have business interests at stake, hold personal biases, or are simply uninformed. McMaster will need to pick his battles in those situations, choosing when to cross Jared and Ivanka and when to keep his powder dry. This dilemma would never arise in a normal administration, because national security advisers would never need to worry about alienating family members of the president when giving candid and well-informed advice. But the Trump White House is certainly not normal. Ivanka Trump and Jared Kushner have developed a real power center inside the most powerful building on Earth.

Worse, Ivanka believes (probably accurately) that in the White House hierarchy, she is on par with the chief of staff. When General John Kelly was appointed in late July 2017, Ivanka tweeted that she was looking forward to working "alongside" him.[50] Coming from any other White House adviser, that tweet would rightly be seen as insubordination toward a superior. For Ivanka, this is just the way she has always been with her father—

exceptional. And, unfortunately, Trump probably does listen to her more than to his other advisers.

Neither a businesswoman nor her real estate developer husband are qualified to be the top advisers to the president of the United States. Neither of them has ever worked in government. Neither has studied policy issues in any depth. Jared and Ivanka don't have a clue what they're doing compared with any previous White House advisers. Given President Trump's own lack of government experience and poor grasp of policy problems—worse than any other president in modern history—they are like the blind leading the blind. In this White House, relying on the advice of unqualified relatives is even more dangerous than normal.

During the Civil War, Abraham Lincoln managed to steer the country through its gravest existential threat because he relied on a "Team of Rivals" approach. He picked the best and brightest minds, including some of his former political adversaries, to advise him. Lincoln asked them to debate their points of view, aiming to sway his opinion with the strength of their arguments, their expertise, their wisdom from decades of public service.[51] Donald Trump has a Team of Relatives instead. It's a threat to the rules-based, expertise-driven functioning of modern American democracy, which eschews personalist power centers and asks people to serve their country, not their father or father-in-law.

In Uzbekistan, the dictator eventually turned on his daughter. In 2015, Gulnara Karimova vanished. In 2017, the BBC reported that she was thought to have been under house arrest, and the Uzbek Prosecutor-General's Office asked the Russian authorities to freeze Russian real estate in her name.[52] She has disappeared from public view. Ivanka, on the other hand, is still one of the most prominent faces of her father's administration.

10

THE DESPOT'S CHEERLEADER

Donald Trump probably doesn't have a set of pom-poms, but he should buy some for all the cheerleading he has already done for global strongmen. He admires brutal dictators; praises monsters who abuse human rights; and endorses the tactics of cruel tyrants. He's not content just to attack American democracy at home, but is undermining it abroad too. Champagne corks have been flying around the world's palaces since 20 January 2017—or they should be. Thanks to Trump, now is one of the best times to be a dictator or despot since the end of the Cold War. He has transformed US foreign policy significantly in his first year in office—for the worse. Under his leadership, America's place in the world is in disarray, because the face of the nation seemingly has no moral compass or principles.

On 16 March 1988, 11-year-old Kamaran Haider was playing in his family's garden in the Iraqi Kurdish town of Halabja. Kamaran looked up into the sky and saw specks in the distance, flying fast toward him. His father quickly shouted for him to take cover in the makeshift shelter he had dug for the family in their little plot of arid land. The Haider family crammed together underground as the first wave of Iraqi jets screamed overhead. An instant later, napalm exploded on the town. Wave after wave of jets followed, blanketing the town with bombs and smoke. In the next attack, the white smoke was replaced by a yellow haze, and the family began smelling a faint whiff of what seemed to be apples or garlic.

Kamaran's mother realized immediately that they were being exposed to chemical gas. She quickly tried to cover her family's mouths and noses with wet towels or papers, whatever she could find in a rushed scramble to protect them. But curiosity got the best of Kamaran's older brother, 14-year-old Rewar, who impulsively rushed out of the shelter to investigate what was happening. His mother tried to stop him, then followed him out into the smoky fog, calling for him to come back to the shelter. Moments later, she found her son, dead in the street. "Rewar is dead!" she shrieked, stumbling back into the shelter. As she entered, she stumbled, collapsed, and dropped dead herself. Kamaran watched her die at his feet and then passed out, drifting in and out of consciousness for days.

When Kamaran came to, he stumbled out into a ghost town, strewn with corpses. His mother and brother were dead; that much he already knew. But he soon discovered the body of his sister, clutching her lifeless brother. "I could see my father dead in front of the bathroom, far from the shelter," he later recalled. That was one of the last sights he saw. Soon, his eyesight failed. Blinded, he could still feel blistering burns across his skin. But despite his injuries, Kamaran was one of the rare few in Halabja— he survived.[1]

An estimated 5,000 others had not been so lucky.[2] Some died gruesome, slow deaths as their bodies were chemically corroded by a vast cloud of gas that could seep under door frames and into lungs. Others died instantly. A BBC reporter who arrived soon after the attack reported seeing one corpse, frozen in the midst of biting a piece of bread.[3] Another was smiling, as if in the middle of laughing. How these people had died depended on how directly they had been hit with the gas and what kind they had inhaled.

The Iraqi air force, at the orders of its brutal tyrant, Saddam Hussein, had dropped a deadly cocktail of chemical agents on thousands of Kurdish civilians: VX nerve gas that shuts down the body's nervous system until breathing stops and the victim asphyxiates; sarin, which causes incredibly painful violent convulsions and frothing at the mouth, torturing men, women, children, and babies until they succumb to a colorless cloud that is twenty-six times deadlier than cyanide;[4] and the lethal World War I-era agent that Kamaran and his family might have smelled, mustard gas—which can kill slowly, blistering the skin with massive burns.

Those who survived the initial gas attack faced an enormous risk of dying from future complications related to the chemical exposure. Kamaran still suffers from short-term memory loss, a cruel irony that leaves him with a vivid recollection of watching his mother die in front of him but an inability to recall recent events. In addition to the 5,000 who died outright, an estimated 7,000 to 10,000 others were severely injured.[5] Most were civilians.

Donald Trump has spoken about the barbaric Halabja attack. But he remembers the worst chemical attack in modern history as a moment when the international community's outrage was overblown. It was a moment, to Trump's mind, that showed we shouldn't have worried too much about Saddam Hussein—if this "overblown" tragedy was the worst he could do. Trump mocked the international condemnations that followed the Halabja attack before an adoring crowd of his supporters. "Saddam Hussein throws a little gas, everyone goes crazy! 'Oh, he's using gas!'" Trump went on to praise how Saddam used such attacks to maintain stability at the time. "They go back, forth, it's the same. And they were stabilized."[6] For a man who shocks us so much that we have grown somewhat numb to it, this callousness still makes one shudder: the candidate who went on to become the president of the United States minimized the importance or seriousness of a genocidal chemical attack that killed thousands of civilians, including countless young children.

Then, to clarify his admiration for some other aspects of Hussein's ruthless despotism, Trump praised his handling of terrorism in Iraq—which involved arbitrary arrests, extrajudicial killings, and grisly torture. "But you know what?" Trump said at a rally. "He did well? He killed terrorists. He did that so good. They didn't read them the rights. They didn't talk. They were terrorists. Over. Today, Iraq is Harvard for terrorism."[7]

Of course, Trump didn't just want to praise Saddam Hussein's brutality and torture for the sake of it, but as an example. He publicly argued in favor of the United States government using torture—a crime under both international and American law. During the campaign, he expressed his belief that "torture works,"[8] despite just about every military official in the United States disagreeing, saying that it's most likely to produce flimsy information you want to hear rather than valuable or even accurate intelligence.[9] Then, Trump took it one step further. Rather than limiting his endorsement of torture to previously used tactics, like waterboarding, he said he would bring in "waterboarding and a hell of a lot worse."[10] Let that sink in for a moment: the current American president, the so-called "leader of the free world," has openly endorsed the usage of extreme methods of torture, even though he knows it would be indisputably illegal. For the time being, his advisers have reined him in—there is no evidence that the United States has permitted or ordered torture during Trump's time in office. His open praise of the practice is nonetheless a troubling wake-up call.

Trump's disdain for human rights and his endorsement of brutal atrocities did not end when he became president. Instead, he has used the pulpit of the most powerful office in the world openly to praise state-sponsored murder campaigns, while pledging to stop "lecturing" nations on the atrocities that they conduct within their own borders.[11]

Just before President Trump was elected, mass atrocities were well underway in the Philippines. One evening in early October 2016, Benjamin Visda was having a quiet evening eating cake and celebrating at a family birthday party.[12] The unemployed father of two had succumbed to a drug addiction, but he had worked hard to quit and was finally clean. However, his name was still on a Filipino government "wanted" list of known drug users—a group subjected to large-scale extrajudicial killings since President Rodrigo Duterte had taken power earlier that year. Around 11pm, a woman approached Visda and asked him to get her some "shabu," the local word for methamphetamine. Visda refused; he had worked hard to get clean, he explained. After the encounter, Visda ventured off to a nearby shop to buy some food.

Security cameras in the area captured what happened next. Men in masks can be seen grabbing Visda, yanking him toward and forcefully putting him on the back of a motorcycle. The headlamps of several other motorcycles fill the screen with light as they too surround him. He is sandwiched between two masked men. They quickly speed away. Visda's family hears the commotion outside their home and rushes out. They chase after the motorcycles, but to no avail.

Twenty minutes later, Visda's lifeless body was dumped outside a police station. The police claim it was a buy-bust operation and that Visda had tried to buy "shabu." In their official version of events, he tried to reach for an officer's gun while handcuffed, so they shot him. But that's not what the footage shows. He is handcuffed, and forcefully tossed onto the back of a motorcycle by masked men who speed away. In the video, he is alive and does not struggle.[13]

Thousands of state-sponsored police executions in the Philippines follow the same pattern. Police claim that they shot or stabbed a victim in a shootout, or for resisting arrest. But the bodies almost never show signs of any of that. Instead, they have usually been executed at close range, or tortured for hours, or stabbed dozens of times and left to die. Usually, the corpses' heads are wrapped in packing tape—the telltale sign that they have been killed in this so-called drug war. Often, they have signs taped to them, as warnings that anyone selling or even just taking drugs—or anyone affiliated with those who do—may end up facing the same fate. In a single night in August 2017, police in the Philippines killed thirty-two people. According to Amnesty International, at least 7,000 people—many of them low-level addicts—have been killed, roughly half of them directly by police (there are credible reports from human rights groups that police have also paid vigilantes to do their dirty work for them).[14]

This isn't a total shock to people who have followed the rise of President Rodrigo Duterte, culminating in his election in 2016. Duterte is a monster. During his presidential campaign, he said that if he were elected, he would kill up to 100,000 criminals in his first six months in office.[15] He warned that he would treat journalists as "legitimate targets of assassination."[16] He also reminisced about the grisly gang-rape and murder of an Australian missionary who was killed while he was mayor of Davao. "When the bodies were brought out, they were wrapped," he recalled during a rally. "I looked at her face, son of a bitch, she looks like a beautiful American actress. Son of a bitch, what a waste. What came to my mind was, they raped her, they lined up. Was I angry because she was raped? Yes, that's one thing. But she was so beautiful, I think the mayor should have been first. What a waste."[17]

On 27 April 2016, less than a month before his election, Duterte pledged that his presidency would be a "bloody" one.[18] Then, he made clear that he would absolve any officers who committed atrocities on his orders. "I will issue 1,000 pardons a day," he vowed. And then, he joked about how he would use his pardon powers to insulate himself from mass murder charges. "Pardon given to Rodrigo Duterte for the crime of multiple murder, signed Rodrigo Duterte," he said with a smile. The crowd laughed.[19]

Becoming president didn't seem to restrain Duterte from continuing such outbursts. Six months into the job, he boasted about having personally murdered three people as mayor. "I killed about three of them ... I don't know how many bullets from my gun went inside their bodies. It happened and I cannot lie about it."[20] He bragged about how he used to ride around on a motorcycle, looking for trouble, searching for people to kill. And, with a sick amount of swagger, he also laughed while recounting how he had previously taken a Chinese suspect up in a helicopter and tossed him out of the door to plummet to his death.[21] To top it all off, Duterte said he hoped he could stack up favorably with Hitler in history. "Hitler massacred 3 million Jews. Now, there is 3 million drug addicts. I'd be happy to slaughter them." Of course, Hitler massacred 6 million Jews, but the comparison stood.[22] Here was a man, aspiring to become president of a major American ally, boasting about personally killing people, vowing to kill a hundred thousand more, and aspiring to be the Hitler of the Philippines. At another campaign rally, he put it plainly: "If I make it to the presidential palace, I will do just what I did as mayor. All of you who are into drugs, you sons of bitches, I will really kill you. I have no patience, I have no middle ground, either you kill me or I will kill you idiots."[23] As Benjamin Visda's family knows, Duterte kept his word.

The West has been unequivocal in its opinion of Duterte. The European Parliament issued a statement in March 2017 condemning his extrajudicial killings,[24] and he has been harshly criticized by human rights groups and governments across the developed world. In response to Duterte's remarks during his 2016 campaign, President Obama sharply criticized him. The US State Department put pressure on him to scale back his extrajudicial killings and respect the rule of law.[25] In response, Duterte called President Obama a "son of a whore." Obama canceled any future meetings with Duterte.[26] He never invited him to the White House, refusing to imbue Duterte's brutal state-sponsored murder campaign with any sort of legitimacy or diplomatic acceptance.

His successor in the Oval Office has had the opposite reaction. A month after the EU resolution condemning Duterte, President Trump praised him in a phone call and endorsed his death squads. According to a leaked transcript of the conversation, Trump told Duterte, "I just wanted to congratulate you because I am hearing of the unbelievable job on the drug problem ... what a great job you are doing and I just wanted to call and tell you that." He explicitly praised Duterte's state-sponsored murder campaign of extrajudicial killings and torture. Then, Trump put the icing on the cake: "You are a good man ... if you want to come to the Oval Office, I will love to have you in [the] Oval Office. Anytime you want to come ... Keep up the good work, you are doing an amazing job."[27] This clearly wasn't just a tepid or even a strained acceptance of a necessary strategic relationship. It was a diplomatic bear hug. If you were Rodrigo Duterte and the US said those things to you, would you be more or less likely to continue committing mass atrocities? Take a wild guess.

In less than a year, President Trump has already shifted American foreign policy to be increasingly amoral—unconcerned with dictators or mass atrocities. Sure, even before Trump, the record of the United States on this front has been checkered. As I wrote in my previous book, *The Despot's Accomplice: How the West is Aiding and Abetting the Decline of Democracy*,[28] the United States has long been two-faced when it comes to promoting democracy around the world. In the Cold War, the United States helped actively topple democratically elected governments in places as diverse as Chile (Salvador Allende), the Congo (Patrice Lumumba), and Iran (Mohammed Mossadegh). After the Cold War ended, the United States made substantial contributions to genuine democracy promotion in regions across the world, from sub-Saharan Africa to Southeast Asia. But still, far too often, perceived geostrategic interest trumped democratic principles as the American foreign policy machine cozied up to brutal despots from Saudi Arabia to Uganda. While US presidents from Reagan and Clinton to Bush and Obama spoke of freedom and democracy, they also doled out billions of dollars of weaponry to places like Riyadh, helping a tyrannical monarchy oppress its people.

However, most countries, from Cambodia to Malawi, are not central to America's geostrategic ambitions. In these, the United States has tried to push for democracy. Leaders who blatantly rigged elections, jailed journalists or abused human rights would face the very real specter of international isolation, sanctions, or reduced foreign aid packages. These threatened punishments were a real and crucial deterrent; they stopped would-be despots from committing their worst cruelties. And, with the Soviet Union gone as a counterweight to American power, democracy spread rapidly. The number of democracies in the world roughly doubled from 1989 to 2006.[29] Experts were so optimistic that it became commonplace to believe that the world was on an inevitable and unstoppable march toward liberal democracy, taking root everywhere. It would be, as Francis Fukuyama famously wrote, "the end of history."[30] But, almost two decades into the twenty-first century, history has come roaring back in an ugly way, bringing with it power-hungry despots, dictators, and counterfeit democrats—those wolf leaders in sheep's clothing who claim to be committed to democracy but instead chip away at it while amassing more power.

For the last decade, democracy has been in decline. Autocrats are ascendant. Every year since 2006 has become more authoritarian globally than the year that preceded it. 2016 was yet another notch in this dismal streak: according to Freedom House, a think tank that monitors the state of democracy across the globe, sixty-seven countries drifted closer to authoritarianism in 2016, while only thirty-six made reforms bringing them closer to consolidated democracy.[31] Authoritarian populists are rising. From Hungary and Turkey to Rwanda, Venezuela, and the Philippines, such leaders have shored up their power in countries that once looked like promising outposts for democracy. In several liberal democracies beyond the United States, like Poland, core democratic freedoms are under threat. And most of those democratic declines took place before Donald Trump became president.

There are a whole host of reasons for this democratic decay (see *The Despot's Accomplice*). Western economies have seen wages stagnate while inequality has soared. The financial crisis was an earthquake for politics in the developed world, and we are still feeling the populist aftershocks. Finally, Western foreign policy has done a poor job at prioritizing long-term investments in democracy over cozy short-term relationships with despots and dictators. However, Donald Trump's presidency is consolidating those swirling anti-democratic winds into a perfect storm. He is the final major gust in the sails of authoritarianism's advance. After all, the past decade of democratic declines has taken place in an environment wherein there was at least some credible and serious pressure for genuine democracy in at least some places, coming from the White House. Now, we instead have a president who is openly disdainful of due process and journalists, while simultaneously embracing torture and endorsing mass state-led atrocities. Generally, however, Trump seems to have a limited interest in global affairs. This has allowed China, for instance, to take a central role in shaping international accords, past and future. At the 2017 Davos forum, President Xi, positioning himself as a leading champion of free trade and the fight against climate change, emerged as the pre-eminent defender of the system that the United States had built—and that Trump was trying to tear down.[32] These developments on the American side, combined with an insular turn in Europe as the EU grapples with Brexit, will inevitably lead to a world that is shaped to a greater extent by illiberal forces—particularly those in Beijing and Moscow.

Unfortunately, Donald Trump is empowering those illiberal forces by breaking with a longstanding American bipartisan consensus, and praising authoritarian rulers in both China and Russia. In fact, if you put all the names of the planet's worst despots into a hat and picked one out, odds are pretty good that Trump will not only have failed to condemn them, but will actually have offered explicit praise for them despite their ruthlessness. It is a stunning reversal of decades of foreign policy, shattered in less than a year of the Trump administration. As well as Duterte and Saddam Hussein, he has also praised Recep Tayyip Erdogan in Turkey, Vladimir Putin in Russia, Xi Jinpeng in China, and even Kim Jong-un of North Korea.

Throughout the campaign, Trump attacked China (better know as "Gi-na!" at his political rallies). But his criticisms were always rooted in trade policy, never China's internal governance or its authoritarian rule over more than a billion people. After Trump and Xi bonded at Trump's private Mar-a-Lago club in Florida, Trump has mostly stuck to kind words for the world's most influential authoritarian leader. In July 2017, hours after prominent human rights activist and Nobel Peace laureate Liu Xiaobao died in China while in state detention for his outspoken pro-democracy, pro-human rights views, Trump had nothing but ebullient praise for President Xi: "I think he's a very good man. He loves China, I can tell you. He loves China. He wants to do what's right for China."[33]

In contrast, Angela Merkel criticized Beijing and praised not Xi but the recently deceased Liu as a "courageous fighter for civil rights and freedom of expression."[34] Republican Senator John McCain, who has often filled the role of the Republican conscience on human rights, freedom, and democracy in the Trump era, said what the president should have: "Unfortunately, and as Dr Liu would have wanted everyone to remember today, this is only the latest example of Communist China's assault on human rights, democracy, and freedom."[35] He called the detention and death "barbaric" and slammed China for its "egregious" violation of basic democratic freedoms and individual rights. Secretary of State Rex Tillerson, to his mild credit, also released a statement, but stopped short of criticizing Beijing.[36] The White House's statement on Liu's death, via then Press Secretary Sean Spicer, also failed to condemn China's treatment of the activist.[37]

THE DESPOT'S CHEERLEADER

When it comes to Russia, the tolerance is even worse. The bizarre and dangerous Trump–Putin bromance began in June 2013, when Trump tweeted: "Do you think Putin will be going to The Miss Universe Pageant in November in Moscow—if so, will he become my new best friend?" Since that time, Trump has largely been providing the Kremlin with political cover within the American political mainstream. In a December 2015 Republican primary debate, when asked about Russian aggression, candidate Trump pivoted away from the question, in a classic moment of Soviet-style whataboutism (see Chapter 2). "Well, first of all, it's not only Russia," Trump answered. "We have problems with North Korea where they actually have nuclear weapons. You know, nobody talks about it, we talk about Iran, and that's one of the worst deals ever made. ... So, we have more than just Russia."[38] This was just a little over a year after the United States and its allies had imposed sanctions on Moscow over its invasion of Ukraine and annexation of Crimea.

During his primary campaign, while Trump was pursuing a business deal to build Trump Tower Moscow (see Chapter 5), Joe Scarborough on MSNBC's *Morning Joe* pressed him on the subject of the Russian president. Putin "kills journalists that don't agree with him," Scarborough rightly pointed out. In response, Trump scoffed. "He's running his country and at least he's a leader, unlike what we have in this country ... I think our country does plenty of killing also."[39] Trump had favorably compared Vladimir Putin to Barack Obama in a despicable statement of cowardly false moral equivalence, while secretly working on a deal with Putin to make some extra money for the Trump empire. Two days later, on 20 December 2015, Trump continued carrying political water for Putin, on ABC's *This Week*. When pressed over Putin's murders of journalists, which are well documented,[40] Trump couldn't have done a more magnificent job at defending Putin if he were the man's press attaché: "But, in all fairness to Putin, you're saying he killed people. I haven't seen that. I don't know that he has. Have you been able to prove that? Do you know the names of the reporters that he's killed? Because I've been—you know, you've been hearing this, but I haven't seen the name. Now, I think it would be despicable if that took place, but I haven't seen any evidence that he killed anybody in terms of reporters."[41]

Trump performed the same maneuver in January 2017 when asked about the death of Alexander Litvinenko, a Russian intelligence officer who defected to Britain before being poisoned in London. The British government had just published its findings, which clearly pointed to state-sponsored assassination by Andrei Lugovoi and Dmitry Kovtun, at the direct orders of Putin's security directorate, the FSB.[42] The evidence was overwhelming. Litvinenko was poisoned by the highly toxic, highly radioactive polonium-210, hardly a substance that you can buy at the local pharmacy. On primetime television, Trump argued, "If he did it, fine. But I don't know that he did it. You know, people are saying they think it was him, it might have been him, it could have been him. But Maria, in all fairness to Putin—I don't know. You know, and I'm not saying this because he says, 'Trump is brilliant and leading everybody'—the fact is that, you know, he hasn't been convicted of anything."[43] True, the Russian president hadn't been convicted of anything. But perhaps that had something to do with his status as an authoritarian despot who regularly makes a mockery of rule of law and cannot be extradited to face real justice in another criminal prosecution system. After all, if Trump's moral benchmark for autocrats abroad is tied to their criminal convictions, perhaps he's also unwilling to make any negative judgments on Fidel Castro, Chairman Mao, or Stalin. They "haven't been convicted of anything" either.

In subsequent interviews, Trump called Putin "a genius" and "a strong leader."[44] When asked about Putin and Ukraine, Trump vowed not to let Russia invade: "He's not going into Ukraine, OK, just so you understand. He's not going to go into Ukraine, all right? You can mark it down. You can put it down. You can take it anywhere you want."[45] Unfortunately for Trump, and for Ukrainians, Putin was already there, and had annexed Crimea—part of Ukraine.

Moreover, Trump has actually parroted Putin's exact words against Hillary Clinton, a patriotic American who had lost a hard-fought election and received more votes than he had. Trump tweeted, "Vladimir Putin said today about Hillary and Dems: 'In my opinion, it is humiliating. One must be able to lose with dignity.' So true!" Trump amplified Putin's voice, even though the Russian president had done more to undermine democracy than just about anyone on the planet. Putin has been America's main foreign adversary in achieving foreign policy goals for several decades. And here was the president-elect gleefully attacking a former secretary of state (who, in that role, had fought for US interests toe-to-toe with Putin), with Putin's own words. If any other Democrat or Republican had done the same thing, there would have been bipartisan outrage. But for Trump, it was just another crazy tweet, another numbing outburst that would quickly be replaced by the next insanity. After all, it also felt nothing more than a little blip when Trump called Kim Jong-un "a smart cookie."[46] This was the same brutal dictator who was threatening the United States with a nuclear strike. Trump said it would be an "honor" to meet him.[47] The president should be "honored" to meet a democratic ally. He should be "horrified" by one of the world's worst tyrants.

But Trump doesn't just praise awful autocrats. Even within the West, Trump is doing his best to boost illiberal forces that threaten to undermine genuine democracies. In his first major trip to Europe, Trump visited Poland and put its ruling party on a pedestal. Unfortunately, the Law and Justice Party has been systematically eroding Polish democracy since it took power in 2015. There have been authoritarian attempts to politicize the judiciary, giving politicians the ability to control Poland's courts. The European Union has harshly criticized Poland's attempts to undermine rule of law and violate democratic principles.[48] But its pressure was swiftly undercut as the Trump administration announced the president's intention to endorse Poland as a model for the West, in exchange for Law and Justice's promise of what Trump wants most: good optics with rapturous crowds chanting, "Trump! Trump! Trump!"[49] He knew that he couldn't get that in London or Paris or Berlin, where he is loathed by the public,[50] so he sold out democracy in a friendlier major European nation, in exchange for a good photo opportunity.

Trump's statements and actions are enormously consequential. The president's words matter. His behavior matters. What Trump says or does provides a signal to despots, dictators, and aspiring autocrats everywhere. The signal so far has been clear: your leash just got a lot longer. In the past, backlash from Washington may have deterred leaders from indulging their worst authoritarian fantasies. But now, there's a new sheriff in town and his golden badge says TRUMP. If you abuse your people, roll back democracy, or consolidate power, America won't have much to say about it. Rest assured, despots globally have received the message. Over time, Trump's amoral foreign policy, putting autocrats on a bizarre pedestal of admirable strongmen, will make the world a significantly darker and more authoritarian place. Democracy will almost certainly continue to fade, likely faster than before.

THE DESPOT'S CHEERLEADER

I have traveled extensively across the world, including living in eleven different countries long enough to have a gym membership there. I've met with despots, their advisers, and their adversaries in sub-Saharan Africa, Southeast Asia and the Middle East, and behind the former Iron Curtain. I've interviewed hundreds of people living under authoritarian regimes or counterfeit democracies, including many who have risked their lives fighting to create a genuine democracy. The striking thing in each country, from Togo to Madagascar or Belarus to Thailand, is that what goes on in Washington makes headlines everywhere. The world pays attention to the words and actions of the president of the United States. They are right to—it is the most consequential and powerful office in the world. But this also means that when Trump endorses torture, minimizes the importance of chemical gas attacks, or praises dictators rather than criticizing them, it leaves a lasting and influential impression.

Under Trump, does Prime Minister Orban in Hungary really have to worry about backlash from the Oval Office if he jails a few reporters, so long as he makes clear that they were the FAKE NEWS ones? If Putin decides to murder another opposition leader with a bit of polonium, whether in Moscow or in Milan, will Trump again provide cover for him and cast doubt on the allegations? If Duterte decides to toss someone else out of a helicopter, would Trump jeopardize Trump Tower Manila to criticize the government of the Philippines? If China continues its crackdown on pro-democracy youth movements or ramps up its censorship of the Internet, will Trump say anything or just keep insisting that Xi is "a very good man"? And if an authoritarian populist rises to power somewhere unexpected, will Trump chastise them for rolling back democracy? Don't hold your breath. Under Trump, it's open season on democracy. The president cares far more about whether leaders are nice to him or make him look good to the American electorate than he does about dictatorship or democratic decline. After all, he's been far harsher in speaking about Angela Merkel, the leader of a longstanding liberal democratic ally of the US, than about Vladimir Putin, a murderous despot. The signal that such a juxtaposition sends to America's democratic friends and dictatorial foes alike is pretty unmistakable.

There's also more than rhetoric going on here. Trump is trying to enshrine his amoral, pro-despot foreign policy into changed policy priorities and slashed budgets. The United States already punches below its weight, in proportional terms, on foreign aid. On average, the twenty-nine top donor nations in the OECD devote about 32 cents of every $100 in their economies to international development aid. For the United States, the figure is about 18 cents. Trump has proposed slashing that already disproportionately low budget by a further $9 billion per year. If his proposal were enacted, the US would fall further behind comparable governments, leading Americans to spend about 13 cents of every $100 in the economy on foreign aid.[51] This is not just an abstraction or a budget line to the hundreds of millions of people around the world in receipt of this aid every year, in the form of support for hospitals, combating malnutrition, or, yes, promoting democratic reforms.

The United States government is also considering deleting democracy from its diplomatic priority list altogether. In internal discussions within the State Department in August 2017, Trump's administration proposed ending any reference to democracy in its mission statement.[52] This would be a stark reversal from its longstanding commitment: "The Department's mission is to shape and sustain a peaceful, prosperous, just, and democratic world and foster conditions for stability and progress for the benefit of the

American people and people everywhere."[53] The new proposed mission statement is only about advancing safety and prosperity—nothing about justice or democracy. Of course, with Trump at the helm, this should come as no surprise. That does not make it any less shocking or horrifying for career diplomats and foreign service officers, many of whom have devoted careers to advancing human rights, democracy, and justice.

President Ronald Reagan used to invoke the image of America as a shining "City upon a Hill," a beacon to the oppressed peoples of the world. In his farewell address, Reagan put it like this: "After 200 years, two centuries, she still stands strong and true on the granite ridge, and her glow has held steady no matter what storm. And she's still a beacon, still a magnet for all who must have freedom, for all the Pilgrims from all the lost places who are hurtling through the darkness, toward home."[54]

Of course, Reagan's administration promoted democracy in some places while getting in bed with terrible tyrants elsewhere. We must not whitewash that dark Cold War history. But his imagery was still apt. The United States, more than any other major global power in human history, has devoted considerable power, force, and money toward making the world more democratic. In many cases, it has succeeded—just ask South Korea, Japan, or Germany. And for much of the world, Washington has been a beacon of hope and freedom while billions of innocent victims lived in a dark corner of the world, under the shadowy rule of oppression and tyranny. The Washington blueprint for how to structure a democratic society had serious credibility from Sierra Leone to Slovakia and from Bolivia to Bangladesh. It was often put on a pedestal as an example of a powerful, functional democratic state worthy of admiration and emulation.

For billions worldwide, that is no longer true. The election of Donald Trump—the disarray, the chaos, the incompetence, and his complete lack of moral leadership—have damaged perceptions of America abroad. A June 2017 Pew Research survey showed that, between Barack Obama and Donald Trump, confidence in America's president to do the "right thing" in global affairs fell 75% in Germany; 71% in South Korea; 70% in France; 61% in Canada; 57% in the United Kingdom; and 54% in Japan. Unsurprisingly, confidence in America's president has risen by 42% in Russia since Trump took office.[55] Even more stark is how America is now viewed as favorably as China. In a similar Pew survey, 49% of respondents in thirty-eight different countries reported a positive view of the United States; that figure was 47% for China, a statistical tie. It's a marked shift. The same survey three years earlier had given America a fourteen-point lead over China in global views, but that lead has collapsed with the rise of Trump to just two points.[56] It's a catastrophe for American soft power, the ability of Washington to inspire action abroad without having to use hard power—military force. More and more countries now aspire to build their own version of China, instead of their own replica of America.

The fading sheen of the United States under Trump is a terribly sad and destructive change. For decades, the West has stood for a powerful idea: that people everywhere should rule themselves. Everyone should have a meaningful say in decisions that affect their lives. Since the end of the Cold War, Washington has had a deeply flawed foreign policy, but has nonetheless helped to double the number of democracies across the globe. That's an important triumph, and Trump is putting it at risk.

There is a simple truth in geopolitics: the world is shaped primarily by those that are powerful enough to do so. That pits the United States and Europe against Russia and China. The former are liberal democracies; the latter are illiberal authoritarian regimes. Europe is already sharply divided, partly by the EU's inability to articulate a common foreign policy from its splintered membership; partly from ongoing financial crises; and partly from the ongoing saga of Brexit. The European Union is therefore unwilling or unable to serve as a white knight that can ride in and help support democracy around the world. That puts even more pressure on the United States. Unfortunately, with Trump's America First rhetoric—bashing NATO while praising Putin and endorsing torture—it's not even a fair fight any more. As Trump drags the United States away from its longstanding stated commitment to supporting democracy beyond its borders, the world will be shaped more and more by an increasingly aggressive Russia and a rising China. That's great news for dictators, and terrible news for the pro-democracy forces fighting them.

It's also terrible news for the United States itself. The greatest foreign policy investment that the United States ever made was the Marshall Plan, which rebuilt Europe after World War II. Americans shipped huge sums of their hard-earned dollars across an ocean. What did they get in return? Their future allies. Their most reliable trading partners. And, yes, peace and democratic prosperity in the region of the world that had twice erupted into world war. The payoff was huge, but it took long-term vision and a serious investment.

What would Donald Trump say about the Marshall Plan today? In his transactional worldview, it would be a colossal waste of money. It would be a "stupid deal" made by "morons," who are "laughing at us." And that's where Donald Trump gets America and its place in the world completely wrong. As a businessman, he concluded a series of short-term deals that allowed him to make a quick buck and then get out. As president, his approach is broadly similar. It will likely be catastrophic, as the blinders of short-term transactional diplomacy lead, inevitably, to long-term disasters. But beyond that, America is a country that stands for—or stood for—a powerful set of values. Donald Trump is turning his back on them. As he does, yet another casualty of his presidency will be the vitality of democracy around the world—withering as the White House looks on, Trump clutching his proverbial pom-poms and leading cheers from the global sidelines in Washington.

11

THE GHOST OF DESPOTISM YET TO COME

A WARNING IN FOUR ACTS

"I am in the presence of the Ghost of Christmas Yet To Come?" said Scrooge.

The Spirit answered not, but pointed downward with its hand.

"You are about to show me shadows of the things that have not happened, but will happen in the time before us," Scrooge pursued. "Is that so, Spirit?"

The upper portion of the garment was contracted for an instant in its folds, as if the Spirit had inclined its head. That was the only answer he received...

"Are these the shadows of the things that will be, or are they shadows of things that may be, only?

...Assure me that I yet may change these shadows you have shown me, by an altered life!"

Charles Dickens, *A Christmas Carol*

In his timeless Christmas classic, Charles Dickens uses three spirits to show Ebenezer Scrooge the errors of his penny-pinching ways. The most powerful of the three omniscient ghosts in shifting Scrooge's behavior was the Ghost of Christmas Yet to Come, a spirit who floats the miserly Scrooge into the not-too-distant future to make clear what will happen if he continues drifting through life as a heartless cheapskate. Horrified by the vision, Scrooge implores the spirit: "Are these the shadows of the things that will be, or are they the shadows of things that may be, only?" Happily, it turned out to be the latter, and Scrooge had enough time to repair the damage—before it was too late.

The same is true for Americans. There is enough time to mitigate the worst damage from Trump's ongoing attack on American democracy. We can save it. But we need to recognize what we're facing first. None of the scenarios that follow will be the full picture of reality, but it is likely that each of the four visions presents part of America's future. We get to decide what to do with these warnings. The survival of American democracy depends on citizens rejecting apathetic indifference and embracing constructive action. The chapter unfolds as a warning in four acts. Act I: Democratic Decay; Act II: the Forerunner; Act III: American Authoritarianism; and, ending on a high note, Act IV: The Trump Vaccine. Like Scrooge, we can see these warnings and either simply let such harrowing possibilities come to pass, or ensure that they do not. The choice is ours.

Act I: Democratic Decay

It's early 2020, and President Trump is up for reelection. The distant memory of his improbable upstart victory over Hillary Clinton has faded from public consciousness. The constant uproar over Trump has long since died down. After all, how long can one stay outraged? It's tiring. It's old news now, and life must go on. Plus, many Americans are starting to wonder: maybe he's not so bad? After all, most of them still have the same job. Most still have the same daily routine. And most are paying lower taxes today than they did in 2016. Of course, the Fake News pessimists who can't handle Trump's winning streak keep saying that corporations and the wealthy pocketed the bulk of the tax cut, but who wants to worry about that when you could buy a new car on credit borrowed against your recent tax rebate?

And why not try out a new car when so many crumbling roads and bridges have been rebuilt? That's thanks to Trump's trillion-dollar infrastructure plan, with a few million dollars thrown in to ensure that the roadside is dotted with pictures of our smiling president flashing the thumbs up every few miles to happy drivers. Of course, the Deep State so-called "Congressional Budget Office" estimate suggested that hundreds of billions of dollars from the infrastructure spending went directly to corporate profits, mainly to those who donated to Trump's re-election war chest. But who can trust those Obama-era holdovers anyway? It's hard to believe them when you can see with your own eyes a few new roads glistening with fresh black tar during your morning commute. At least we know that our eyes don't have a hidden agenda—more than you can say for the Deep State that's lodged in the DC swamp.

Some people who used their tax rebates to make major purchases on credit—like a new car—worry that it's unsustainable. But who can lecture us for taking on new credit card debt in the wake of working class people getting a modest tax cut? Surely not the US government. Between the infrastructure spending, the ramp-up of military spending, and a deep tax cut, they're in no place to lecture. Debt has soared, nearly matching what George W. Bush and Barack Obama added during the financial crisis (though the economy is now humming from their deficit spending), but many Americans feel that debt is a problem for the next generation to worry about. All of the new roads and new jobs and tax breaks have made millions of Americans worry less about other things that Trump has done in the past. Who really cares about all those negative stories these days? Americans tried for a year or so, but then it just became too much.

As the deluge of news beats people into a state of resigned apathy, Twitter has seen its traffic fall. CNN, MSNBC and even Fox News have seen viewership decline too. New forms of fun media were there to pick up the slack. They don't wallow in boring political stories. They are Snapchat, Instagram, and a new Apple social media app with a "news-free" option for those Americans who just can't handle the constant barrage of update after update on the latest alleged scandal. If Paris Hilton and Beyoncé are on Instagram and Snapchat, why bother with Twitter anymore? It's overwhelmed by trolls and bots anyway. And only truly old-fashioned people still read a newspaper these days.

In response to the loss of viewers, readers and users, some of the mainstream outlets seem to have softened somewhat on Trump. Maybe it's because he earned it? It's hard to tell why that subtle shift occurred. CNN's parent company, Time Warner, did finally receive approval from the White House for its merger with AT&T after months of inexplicable delays. For a while, it seemed that perhaps the merger would be rejected. But after Kellyanne Conway started appearing as a part-time paid contributor to the channel, the merger suddenly sailed through. The First Amendment still stands strong. Everyone is free to say what they wish. So why complain?

For many Americans, however, it has just become so hard to know who or what to trust. There have been so many fake stories pushed on social media and spread by bots on Twitter that it's hard to figure out what is real and what is not. Worse, with new artificial intelligence and machine learning software, there's a deluge of fake videos out there too. Did Obama really say that Trump "wasn't so bad" in a secret, leaked recording? Or did some group in Macedonia or Russia just splice it together to make it sound like that? It's hard to say. Who can be certain whether those documents about Trump's supposedly shady dealings in Azerbaijan are authentic? There are a lot of people out there who might want to make something like that up, so maybe it's better just to tune out all of it.

Pundits have grown tired of criticizing Trump, too. There were, of course, the early adopters of a more optimistic narrative—those who said that Trump became presidential when he spoke like a normal politician before Congress, or when he bombed a Syrian runway that one time, or when he visited hurricane victims. That all seems like a distant dream now given the never-ending news cycle. But even many of the longstanding holdouts have since softened. It's hard to go on day after day, pointing out the abnormalities, the crazy stuff, the allegations, the scandals. People who sound like broken records attacking President Trump don't make good television. After a time, they start to seem like zealots—even as they scream into the wind that they haven't changed their position, we've just changed what is politically acceptable. Nobody is listening anymore. Thankfully, those that are stuck on sour grapes about Trump can be replaced by someone who shows greater willingness to write a more compelling storyline. Nobody wants to hear that their democracy is withering on the vine—everyone wants a dose of hope, a new twist in this exhilarating and historical Trumpian saga, signaling that perhaps he has finally, mercifully changed.

Now, there *was* a fair amount of critical coverage around the release of Bob Mueller's federal Russia investigation report, which determined that it was "certain" that elements of Trump's campaign sought to collude and "highly likely" that they knowingly colluded with Russian assets at various point in an attempt to win the election. But the FBI seems to be doing a lot of investigating of Trump these days, so maybe the Trump base is right that the

FBI is infiltrated by a bunch of anti-Trump, pro-Obama Comey loyalists? And so what if law enforcement and intelligence agencies are right about what happened with Russia? Is collusion with a foreign adversary really a crime? We don't know for sure, because Trump issued several key pardons "to heal the nation and move on." At least that's what he said in the tweet.

Still, it did seem to ruffle an awful lot of feathers at the time—even in the Republican ranks, and beyond the usual suspects like Lindsey Graham and John McCain. But that all eventually died down too, especially after national security issues began to eclipse a scandal that really seemed like old news. Plus, when Trump ended the sanctions on Russia and simultaneously released a substantial amount of oil from the US strategic oil reserve, gas prices fell right in time for Labor Day road trips, and that was nice. Maybe Trump was right and it was more important to be friends with Russia? None of it really changed daily life in small-town rural America, after all. Maybe the Trump campaign's alleged collusion just helped us get to the point where we could focus on the real enemy: terrorists. That's also presumably why Trump didn't speak out when Russia formally annexed Belarus—or, as Putin put it, "reunited old friends." Who cares, anyway? Nobody in Belarus seems to be protesting. Russia is killing terrorists. Why make a fuss?

That's what the generals say, anyway. They've taken on quite a prominent role in the administration. A few of the Fake News outlets like *The Amazon Washington Post* and *The Failing New York Times* even reported that Trump had delegated all airstrikes and counterterrorism decisions to the military chain of command. There's not much civilian oversight, but pundits agree that the generals are "the adults in the room," so it makes sense to let them make more and more decisions. According to one article,

Trump used to ask for updates on the airstrikes every week, but he's changed that to every month. "It's always the same thing when they do these briefings," Trump has reportedly told his aides. "Just get on with killing terrorists and let me focus on the big picture." Some have said that the civilian death toll from airstrikes in places like Yemen and Libya, pockets of Syria and Iraq and even the Philippines has risen to its highest levels in US history. At least that's what was reported, but most Americans distrust the media—and the government—more than ever. When the White House is asked about it, they go back to a line that Trump used throughout his 2016 campaign: it won't answer those questions, because that would just give our enemies an advantage in understanding what we were up to.

The Democrats used to criticize the increasing military influence in government, but they stopped speaking out so much after losing the 2018 midterms. It was a strange election. Many states adopted the recommendations of Kris Kobach's "election integrity" commission, which made it harder for certain people to vote. Minority turnout fell considerably wherever those "reforms" were put in place. And then, it was an odd coincidence, but an array of Democratic House candidates in swing districts seemed to get hacked over the span of about two weeks before the election. A lot of their personal communications were posted online. There wasn't much polling so it was hard to see what the impact was on those races, but most of them lost. Several outspoken "Never Trump" political analysts were hacked too, laying bare their personal lives for everyone to consume at will online. Many of those pundits slunk away from public view. Everyone realized that publicly bashing the president made you a featured target for hacking and eventual publication by WikiLeaks. Many started to wonder if it was worth it. Turnout fell to record low levels again—around where it was in 2014, roughly 37 per cent of the eligible population.[1] That seemed low to a lot of activists because there were huge marches and demonstrations beforehand. There were also some reports of voters who had properly registered being turned away at the polls because their names no longer appeared in electronic databases. It was probably just an outlier, though. And the crackpot so-called "data scientists" who claimed to have found evidence that some voting machines had been tampered with? Some Americans believe that stuff, but most people think it sounds a bit too far-fetched. We've all had enough of so-called "experts" anyway.

Ivanka Trump has become the de facto secretary of state. For months before Rex Tillerson resigned, she began taking on more of a role as an "informal diplomatic envoy." This followed after she started holding high-profile meetings during the United Nations General Assembly first converging in New York in 2017. The backlash against that was limited, lasting less than a full news cycle, so Trump decided to ramp up her involvement. Of course, it was unavoidable that she sometimes met with people who could make decisions affecting her business interests.

There are still some killjoys who continue to bang on about Trump getting richer from being president. But who hasn't? Sure, previous presidents didn't use their position to enrich themselves while in office, but they still seem pretty rich to most Americans. Anyway, it's harder for Democrats to criticize Trump for blurring business interests with politics given that two names often discussed for the upcoming 2020 election, Mark Zuckerberg and Oprah Winfrey, have done precisely that. They haven't released their tax returns either, so why should Trump? Plus, an increasing number of the president's defenders openly wonder: is it a crime to profit from the presidency? Don't we value success and hard work in America? We should celebrate the Trump brand because it's now America's brand, they say. Polls have Trump narrowly leading a splintered field with plenty of independent challengers—but only time will tell if he'll be reelected.

Some of this will likely come to pass, some of it will not. It's hard to say for sure. But there's no doubt that democracy is slowly declining before our eyes. In some form, democratic decay will become our new normal. Even if we act forcefully and rapidly now, American democracy will have been fundamentally transformed by Trump's time in office. It is now a question of how much damage, rather than whether there will be any. But each of the harrowing prospects above is certainly plausible as a logical extension of several more years with Trump in the White House. Imagine if a book written in 2013 had predicted that the host of *The Celebrity Apprentice*, Donald Trump, would soon become president. People would have laughed. "Impossible!" they would have said. Yet, it happened. Are any of the specters outlined above truly more impossible to imagine?

Like the mythical parable that a frog will allow itself to be boiled alive so long as the water temperature increases slowly, American democracy is gradually melting away. The prospect of democratic decay is simultaneously the most likely and, in some ways, the most insidious. Of all the specters of the future, this is the hardest one to pinpoint. Does democracy die if people no longer trust the Congressional Budget Office? Surely not. But the violation of democratic norms, day after day after day, adds up. If we're not careful, democracy could fade in front of our eyes, until one day, we realize it's gone. But perhaps that's not quite how it will go...

Act II: The Forerunner

So far, the chief saving grace of American democracy has been Donald Trump's incompetence. He is a master of self-sabotage. When he builds up momentum from a genuine political win, he shreds it with an unhinged tweet or gaffe. Often, the greatest force undermining Donald Trump's presidency is Donald Trump.

But what if someone else came along to pick up the reins—someone who didn't routinely tweet absurd venom? What if that person could unequivocally condemn Klansmen and could make a coherent speech without a series of meandering lies? What if Trump's offensive statements and blunders were replaced by a polished political operator? What if a rising star in the Republican Party, who we'll call "Trump 2.0," had the policy substance and authoritarian impulses of Trump, but the style, persona, and charm of Obama or Reagan? In this scenario, Donald Trump could act simply as a forerunner. His impulsive, ego-driven attacks on American democracy could be built on by a strategic, policy-driven assault on it by a successor. We have no idea who Trump 2.0 might be. But let's imagine it, because it's a very real possibility for America's future.

It's 2021 and Trump 2.0 has just been elected president of the United States. In 2020, the Republican Party resurrected itself from the disarray of the 2018 midterms, when a combination of Trump's historic unpopularity and the still swirling questions about Mueller's Russia investigation culminated in the Democrats narrowly re-taking the House of Representatives. The Democrats started holding hearing after hearing, publishing Trump's tax returns and subpoenaing trucks full of documents. The Trump agenda was blocked, stuck in the mud of Trump's seemingly endless scandals. There was no major infrastructure bill, no meaningful tax reform, no full immigration overhaul. As a result, many Republicans began to turn on Trump more openly. They sensed, probably correctly, that he didn't stand much of a chance to be re-elected. A political civil war broke out within the ranks of the Republican Party. Of course, Trump's base remained solid, as 25 to 35 per cent of the American population stood by the president through thick and thin. That is, until a viable alternative arrived.

When Trump 2.0 emerged as a challenger to President Trump, most people scoffed at them. A member of the House of Representatives challenging the president from his own party? Surely the upstart candidacy would fizzle in a matter of weeks. But as soon as Trump 2.0 started making stump speeches, it became clear that this was someone to be reckoned with. They had the silver tongue of Obama when he wanted to make lofty speeches to a packed arena. But it was also clear that they had the personal warmth of Reagan. They could relate to coal miners in West Virginia and suburban soccer moms in Minnesota. Trump 2.0 wrapped up the Republican nomination.

In policy terms, they picked up where Trump left off. At their campaign launch, they announced that their campaign would revolve around three key issues: immigration, an economy that works for American families, and national security. That focus made sense. Immigrants are genuinely unpopular in the United States; they make a scapegoat almost as good as the media. The home of the brave is now home to millions who live in fear of terrorism. Tapping into that fear is politically expedient. And inequality got even worse under the Trump years, so there are a lot of downtrodden people out there looking for a helping hand.

In style, though, Trump 2.0 offers a sharp contrast. Where Trump said, "I alone can fix it," his successor delivered an uplifting message that "together, we can fix it." Whereas Trump's speeches were laced with dark imagery, an America under siege from crime and immigration, Trump 2.0 channels hope and optimism. Like Reagan's famous 1984 "Morning in America" television ad, this new Republican upstart highlights what is great about America and shows how much further it can improve. Immigrants are still scapegoated, but the new president assures everyone that families won't ever be broken up. It's Trumpism with compassion, something that independent voters can rally behind. Of course, Trump 2.0 does use some coded racial language like "our Southern heritage," but is always careful to explicitly condemn neo-Nazi groups, realizing that it's far more powerful for the authoritarian agenda to win over the center than the rabid right. Plus, after the vitriol and venom of the Trump era, Trump 2.0 has correctly figured out that Americans are yearning for a return to decency and civility in politics. Their youthful charm doesn't hurt either, as a contrast to the brooding 75-year-old Trump.

Every word out of Trump 2.0's mouth seems to be custom-made for the American middle class, but his/her policy ideas cater to wealthy establishment types that are funding the over-flowing campaign war chest. The Twitter feed is charming, witty and polished, but also funny. It never features an outrageous meme, never a spelling mistake, never a factual error. The speeches frequently mislead, but never involve outright false-hoods. The press openly muses about how difficult Trump 2.0 is to pin down, never speaking in specifics and rarely granting high-stakes one-on-one interviews. The voters don't care. Just as Obama focused on "hope and change" and "yes we can," Trump 2.0 has an instinct for uplifting catch phrases. They have an instinct for uplifting storytelling, building a narrative around their candidacy that makes average people feel like they're important characters in America's ongoing saga.

Trump 2.0 isn't afraid to borrow Trump's knack for belittling nicknames that cut to the core of an opponent's weakness—but always does it with a smile and a wink, to let voters know that he/ she isn't angry and that it's all in good fun. Just like Trump, his/ her rallies are high energy, but far more focused. Trump 2.0 is masterful at bringing the audience along for an emotional roller coaster ride, with carefully scripted villains to loathe and carefully scripted heroes to love. The players are the same as those singled out by Trump, but Trump 2.0 knows how to play with voters' heartstrings too, telling deeply emotional stories of hardworking single mothers in rural Kentucky or out-of-work steel workers clambering over impossible barriers that the Washington establishment had placed between them and their dreams. The rallies feel uplifting, heartwarming even, but they leave people with a sense of purpose as to who is the enemy.

Below the surface, some people believe that Trump 2.0 is a masterfully authoritarian figure. Trump paved the way for it, as people simply grew used to democratic norms being routinely violated. Moreover, as echoes of authoritarian populism entered the American political mainstream, the Democrats shifted their tactics to mimic it too. "Why bother with political norms if the Republicans won't?" they figured. As an unintended consequence, Democrats gave political cover to Trump's tactics. As soon as both sides started dismantling the political conventions that protect American democracy as we know it, the window of possible political actions opened much wider. Trump 2.0 is clearly capitalizing on an environment that is more permissive to authoritarianism than any other in modern American history.

Trump 2.0 mimics Trump's attacks on the press, but is more adept at it. Working with major Republican donors, they have set up a state media channel that broadcasts round-the-clock. It started off less partisan, but has been drifting closer and closer to providing exclusively positive coverage for the president. The administration used the victory of a major infrastructure spending bill to provide political cover for a systematic attack on transparency in government. Press briefings are now only held every two weeks and presidential news conferences every two months, subject to cancelation. The president no longer releases his/her daily schedule. They blunt criticism by regularly stating that they are more than happy to provide written answers to questions from the press—the president will pick five per week to answer. At first, people were outraged, but then, it just became the new normal—an experience that became familiar during Trump's four years in office.

Ethics guidelines have been relaxed considerably, and the Office of Government Ethics has been abolished. This was done over the 4 July weekend, when few were paying attention to politics and those outside the *New York Times* and *Wall Street Journal* readership wouldn't really care. It was a blip and then forgotten. Trump 2.0 also convinced Congress to change the appointment structure for the chairman of the Federal Reserve, allowing that position to be appointed along with the election of a new president, "in the interest of the engine of the American economy working together and not against each other," as Trump 2.0 said at one rally. The banks were skeptical but didn't really push back too much; after all, the new president assured all his/her donors that he/she would ensure the new chair delivered all of their economic priorities. The new president has also scrapped the traditional way of assessing the cost and effect of proposed legislation. Rather than using the Congressional Budget Office (which is now closed), Trump 2.0 has allowed political parties to establish their own analyst teams to provide public estimates of a given piece of legislation. The estimates are often widely divergent, so nobody really trusts any of them—providing much more latitude to lawmakers to claim what they think a given bill will actually accomplish.

The new FBI director is a close friend and longtime political ally of the president. So is the deputy director and several other appointed officials within the law enforcement and intelligence community. They are all loyal lieutenants to the president, but are extremely careful to steer clear of any impropriety. They always stay on the right side of the law, but nudge the needle in the president's favor on any matters involving him/her, little by little. Under new leadership, the federal law enforcement community is currently working on a bill with Congress that would create special protest zones in each city—for the safety of protesters, of course. After tragic deaths in places like Charlottesville, it only makes sense for people to exercise their democratic rights—in a space that law enforcement can easily defend. Most of the protest zones are far from the hustle and bustle of urban downtown areas, tucked away in safer, emptier spaces.

These changes did elicit some public backlash. Academics and pundits alike railed against the administration for days on end. But the sky didn't fall in. For most Americans, life carries on, the same as it did before. Plus, President Trump 2.0 is overwhelmingly popular, with approval ratings in the high 50s and low 60s. They deliver on their promises. Major public works programs are humming along, producing jobs from Alaska to Florida. The middle-class tax cut is well on its way to fruition. And the new Federal Reserve chairman is heating up the economy even more by setting interest rates as low as possible to prime the economic pump. So nobody listens to the pessimists who worry that a few government agencies have been shut down.

This vision of Trump 2.0 is not far-fetched. Donald Trump has already shown us the weaknesses built into our democracy. At its foundation, American government is predicated just as much on political norms as on law. If those norms become disposable, so does democracy. That's already dangerous under President Trump. But it could be far more dangerous with a President Trump 2.0, a man or woman who retains Trump's authoritarian impulses but is younger, more politically savvy, charismatic, eloquent, and strategically thoughtful. Let's hope that person never arrives—but plan on the assumption that they will.

Act III: American Authoritarianism

Donald Trump's damage to American democracy has been limited by the prosperity he inherited. When he took office, the economy was nearly at full employment. Wars in Afghanistan and Iraq had been relegated to low-level conflicts. No mass casualty terrorist attacks had taken place on American soil for a long while. In short, Trump inherited two impediments to building authoritarian power: a strong economy and a reasonably safe security environment. But there's no reason to believe that those two characteristics will be present throughout his time in office. If they are not, the risk to American democracy will magnify considerably. A national security threat or severe economic disaster is the only plausible avenue to genuine American authoritarianism—a scenario wherein democracy does not wither, but is uprooted completely. This is certainly contingent on a terrible disaster, so we must hope beyond hope that it does not arrive. But what might it look like if it does?

The 2019 terror attack was the worst in nearly two decades. Radical Islamist terrorists somehow slipped through the security net and detonated a dirty bomb—loaded with unrefined nuclear material—in the midst of the 4 July fireworks display on the Mall in Washington DC. There had been warning signs, of course; in 2016, police in the former Soviet Republic of Georgia—not for the first time—intercepted an attempt to purchase radioactive materials that could be used in the production of a dirty bomb.[2] Even so, one cell succeeded. The initial blast killed about a hundred people, but invisible radioactive particles began to settle all around the blast site. Thousands died from radiation poisoning in the subsequent days. Anywhere within a 2-mile radius of the blast—an enormous area—instantly became an uninhabitable radioactive wasteland. Experts quickly estimated the fallout from the blast, and predicted that tens of thousands more would develop cancer directly from the blast. Several hundred thousand on top of that also faced a heightened risk of cancer later in life. The particles, we have been told, will remain dangerous for two centuries, until hundreds of millions of dollars are poured into clean-up efforts. Decontamination will take years, but during that time, central Washington DC is effectively a no-go zone. The economic impact of the attack has been devastating.

Thankfully, President Trump was away from the blast site at his golf club in Bedminster, New Jersey and was safely evacuated to Camp David—the acting White House in the aftermath of the crisis. From the wooded outpost that in normal times primarily serves as a presidential getaway, President Trump declared a national State of Emergency. In a televised address, Trump invoked precedent from Abraham Lincoln during the Civil War and the *Korematsu* Japanese internment Supreme Court decision during World War II.[3] He announced that he would be suspending habeas corpus, allowing the US federal government the power to detain suspects indefinitely without trial. Then, he announced that he would be creating forced registrations of all Muslim-

Americans; that all mosques would be allocated a full-time government liaison; and that some would be shut down. Each Muslim-American or Muslim holders of green cards would be required to check in with an assigned law enforcement officer once per week, and would not be allowed to travel outside their state of residence. In cases where law enforcement couldn't handle the new mandated workload, National Guard members would fill in and do the monitoring for them. All Muslim-Americans are now also required to provide their social media passwords to the authorities. If they change them without notifying the authorities, they are arrested.

These measures don't come as a total surprise to those who remember Trump's 2015–16 statements suggesting that his administration would create a database of Muslims in the United States. In a November 2015 interview, for instance, Trump said, "There should be a lot of systems, beyond databases, we should have a lot of systems, and today you can do it." The reporter pressed him: "But for Muslims specifically, how do you actually get them registered in a database?" Trump responded: "It would be just good management. What you have to do is good management procedures and we can do that."[4]

Now, a "Good Neighbors" initiative, which encourages those who don't currently have job—including young people, the elderly, and the unemployed—to serve as volunteer surveillance deputies, has also been launched, advocated if not championed by those close to the president. It's an unofficial scheme, but its partisans regularly travel around the country reminding citizens that neighbors should watch each other because a good neighbor has nothing to hide. Unfortunately, in spite of the large increase in local surveillance, the initiative has failed to deter a spike of Muslims being lynched. "You can't cook an omelet without breaking a few eggs!" Trump tweeted, shortly after sending his thoughts and prayers to the families of the victims. Shortly after the attack, he signed the PATRIOT Act 2020, which drastically increased surveillance powers for the government without any warrants being required. Within hours of this becoming law, thousands of career intelligence staff resigned in protest, but their agencies continued without them. "GOODBYE DEEP STATE TRAITORS!!!" Trump tweeted.

Today, as the 2020 election approaches, Trump's administration is hinting at the possibility that the elections will need to be postponed. While it has stopped holding press briefings or press conferences under the State of Emergency, the White House did issue a vague press release about unspecified security threats that intelligence sources suggest may be further attacks aimed at disrupting the election. Given the catastrophe of the previous attack, they have suggested that it may be a national security imperative to delay the election by at least six months.

Normally, such an extreme move would generate protests, but those have been temporarily banned because of worries that another dirty bomb could target large groups of people conglomerating in a major urban center. The protest ban has pushed dissent online, where digital rallies are being held in support of Muslim-Americans and to press the Trump administration to hold the elections as scheduled, rather than giving into fear. But with an online platform, it is extremely easy for the Trump White House to see precisely who is speaking out most vocally against the government. Some of those critics have found themselves indicted before secret grand juries. Leaks from the cases suggested that they were held in secret for national security reasons, but the cases always seem to eventually fizzle. Still, in the process, the outspoken defendants amass enormous legal fees. Dissent in this new America is expensive.

Citizens see National Guard soldiers patrolling the streets daily, but it's not clear how many have been deployed, because reporting those numbers could jeopardize national security. Legal challenges to the presidential orders have been mounting, but Trump has vowed to ignore any Supreme Court order that he feels will not keep Americans safe: "Now is not the time for judges to worry about parchment!" he tweeted in a particularly memorable outburst from Camp David. "Now is the time to Make America Great by ensuring it Survives!" His approval ratings are at an all-time high, as a rally-around-the-flag mentality has gripped America. It's time to put politics aside. We are all on the same team now.

This scenario is unlikely. But Americans are underestimating how dangerous it is for a man with authoritarian instincts to be in power if and when a national security catastrophe strikes. Large-scale national security threats create seismic shifts in politics immediately. George W. Bush famously said during the 2000 presidential campaign that he didn't believe in "nation building." His views changed radically after September 11.

Trump has already suggested registering Muslims in a database. In August 2017, he tweeted that "Radical Islamic Terrorism must be stopped by whatever means necessary! The courts must give us back our protective rights. Have to be tough!"[5] It is hardly a leap of the imagination to believe that a mass casualty terror attack would magnify such impulses into something truly dangerous, not just for international security but also for American democracy.

I'm sure Trump is aware that President George W. Bush's approval rating was 51 per cent on 10 September 2001 and spiked to 90 per cent by 21 September in the aftermath of the attacks.[6] With Trump spending much of his time in office with an approval rating below 40 per cent, there is also the risk of the president leading the country to a national security crisis in an effort to capitalize on national unity. The American people's impulse to rally and support the commander-in-chief during times of crisis is a wonderful testament to its unity. But it's also a key vulnerability for our democracy if a demagogue is in office. We may face the threat of American authoritarianism sooner than we think if, God forbid, a mass casualty attack occurs on Trump's watch.

Act IV: The Trump Vaccine

A vaccine is a weakened form of a virus that is injected into the body to allow the immune system to recognize its own vulnerabilities and patch them up before the more virulent and dangerous strain invades. In the same way, there is the possibility that President Trump will act like a vaccine for American democracy. He is a weakened strain of demagoguery, a man who is more impulsive than ideologue, more simpleton than scheming strategist. There is no question that he is exposing the vulnerabilities of American democracy. The question, of course, is whether our democratic immune system is up to the challenge of generating the antibodies needed to repel the attack before it's too late. We, the electorate, are that immune system. Let's imagine this hopeful world, one in which American democracy doesn't just survive, but comes back stronger as a result of citizen backlash against the abuses of Donald Trump.

After Trump's first year in office, Americans realized something significant: the Founding Fathers had set up a pretty good system. It anticipated a demagogue becoming president. It anticipated a Congress corrupted by that figure. It just didn't anticipate both scenarios occurring in tandem and trampling basic political norms in the process. However, the Founding Fathers did give citizens the tools to fight back if American democracy was under threat. As a result, as we approach the 2020 elections, Americans can be proud of themselves. They have organized, agitated, and spoken out. Now, a raft of political norms is enshrined in law. They are no longer niceties that should be followed; they are legal requirements that must be followed.

Some of these new laws were passed the old fashioned way: through Congress. For example, in 2016 cabinet members were legally prohibited from promoting their own business interests while in office, but the president was not. That has changed, forcing President Trump to fully divest for the remainder of his term. Former heads of the Office of Government Ethics lobbied Congress to pass a more stringent nepotism law, barring direct family relatives from serving in a presidential administration in any official capacity. Any presidential relatives who hope to work in other branches of government must now have full qualifications and be subject to an independent hiring panel that blindly reviews their files against those of comparable applicants.

The Grassley-Feinstein FBI Act of 2018 explicitly prohibited the president from firing a director of the FBI while the Department of Justice is in the midst of an active investigation involving the president, his family members, or any of his close associates. Furthermore, it requires that firing an FBI director at any other point must be with cause, similar to the rules that govern dismissal of special prosecutors. President Trump, of course, vetoed the bill, but grassroots organizing paid off and the veto was overridden by bipartisan groups in both the House and the Senate.

John McCain decided to make his legacy one that would contribute to the reestablishment of American moral authority in the post-Trump era. He authored a proposed constitutional amendment that would explicitly prohibit the United States or any of its agents from knowingly engaging in or being complicit with the use of torture on suspects foreign or domestic. The amendment is still working its way through the process, but most analysts have suggested it will easily pass—ensuring that Trump's fantasies about bringing back "waterboarding and a hell of a lot worse" will remain just that. Meanwhile, the "Lock Her Up" Act of 2019 recently passed the House and is awaiting approval in the Senate. If signed into law, it would make it a federal crime for a presidential candidate to publicly call for their opponent to be jailed, or worse. Most people expect Trump to veto it, but this too may be overridden by Congress.

There was also a congressional push to force candidates to publicly release their tax returns in order to be eligible for the presidency. Unfortunately, Trump lobbied his allies in Congress aggressively, and the effort fizzled. But American citizens in the Trump era have proven resilient. Not to be deterred, they took the fight to the state level and began lobbying state legislatures to ensure that ballot access was tied to releasing tax returns. California was the first to pass that legislation, ensuring that Trump would certainly lose the popular vote in 2020 if he didn't make the disclosure. But the big victories were in Pennsylvania, Ohio, Florida, Michigan, and Wisconsin. Now that the bill has passed those swing states—which Trump won in 2016—it's clear that he will need to release his full tax returns or be guaranteed a defeat at the ballot box.

At the state level, activists and organizers have also successfully pushed to adopt automatic voter registration. This has been implemented in dozens of states now, ensuring that Trump's efforts to suppress votes under the Kobach Commission will be dead on arrival. The initiatives do not require people to vote, but citizens are automatically placed on the electoral roll in case they should choose to exercise their democratic right. Disenfranchisement will never completely disappear, but this effort has at least put voter suppression into its death throes.

Of course, there's no way to write a law that prohibits every possible destructive behavior that a future Trump could adopt. And there are some things that can't be legislated; it's difficult, for example, to imagine a law against presidential tweeting, or the criminalization of misleading or false statements from the White House podium. This means that legislation is not a panacea that will miraculously repair all the damage done to American democracy in the Trump era. Instead, the system itself needs to be reformed, and our political culture needs a serious overhaul. It will require an enormous amount of public mobilization. It will require a new ethos of citizen engagement. But it is possible. Then, and only then, will Trump act like a vaccine, showcasing democratic weaknesses, but giving us time to repair them so that American democracy stands stronger than ever.

As with Scrooge in *A Christmas Carol*, these four scenarios are things that *may* be, not things that *will* be. Most of the visions will not come to pass, but their haunting image should alarm us into action. There is still hope to ensure that the darkest scenarios do not become our future and that the rosiest ones do. There is still time. It's up to all Americans, and all who believe in American democracy. It's not too late to save it.

CONCLUSION

HOW TO SAVE DEMOCRACY

"There is nothing more arduous than the apprenticeship of liberty. It is not so with despotism: despotism often promises to make amends for a thousand previous ills ... The nation is lulled by the temporary prosperity that it produces, until it is roused to a sense of its misery. Liberty, on the contrary, is generally established with difficulty in the midst of storms."

Alexis de Tocqueville, *Democracy in America*

The future of American democracy seems bleak. Three more years of Trump could wreak havoc on the democratic system. Endless waves of anti-democratic rhetoric and behavior from a demagogue will erode even robust institutions. Trump is not a Democrat vs. Republican problem—he is an American problem.

Demagogues are nothing new. We have lessons from history that can teach us how to defend democracy. In ancient Athens, for example, there was no shortage of demagogues. They were populists, usually rich but not born from nobility, of a sort of *nouveau riche* class. They thrived on division and anger. Enter Cleon in the 420s BCE, a crude but charismatic demagogue.[1] Cleon talked tough, offered simplistic solutions, fabricated claims about his political enemies, and used litigation to attack his rivals. Cleon had few principles, but he had an instinct for brutality. And he took every opportunity to belittle his opponents.

Aristophanes, a contemporary Athenian playwright, decided to take on Cleon in a satirical drama called *The Knights*. In the play, Aristophanes personifies Athenians who flocked to Cleon as a gullible man named Demos (Greek for "the people," from which the word democracy arose). During the play, two slaves discuss the threat of demagogues and one astutely points out: "A demagogue must be neither an educated nor an honest man. He has to be an ignoramus and a rogue."[2]

Huey Long was the closest thing to a demagogue we've had in America. He rose in the 1930s, when the future of democracy also looked bleak. Across Europe, elected leaders were destroying fledgling democracies and replaced them with fascism. Communism took root to the east; tyranny ruled everywhere else. Meanwhile, in the United States, Long rocketed into political prominence by being divisive. He frightened people while simultaneously dazzling them with his clownishness. He became governor of Louisiana and then a US senator. He tried to hold both jobs at once, and even mobilized the Louisiana National Guard to help him retain this double role (he gave up eventually). Long set up a plainclothes police service that answered only to him; he controlled Louisiana politics, even when he was in Washington; he rewarded political allies and punished political enemies through a patronage system.[3] And his authoritarian impulses sometimes emerged from his thin skin: after founding Louisiana State University, he inserted a clause in its statutes such that the student newspaper was prohibited from criticizing him.[4] As Michael Kazin later wrote in *The Washington Post*, "Huey Long was the most entertaining tyrant in American history."[5]

Long broke political norms with glee, reveling in the press coverage that his outrageous conduct or comments generated. He craved the spotlight, and he knew how to place himself in it. In one particularly memorable encounter, Long met a German naval commander during an official state visit wearing only silk green pajamas and a bathrobe.[6] The elite was outraged; the masses loved it. "The lesson he [Long] learned from the incident was less the importance of diplomatic niceties than the value of buffoonery in winning national publicity," one scholar wrote of the occasion.[7] After a while, the spotlight simply followed Huey Long; he no longer had to chase it.

Long was planning to run for president as an independent in the 1936 election against Franklin Delano Roosevelt. He got worryingly close to the White House. Then, on 10 September 1935, Dr Carl Weiss assassinated Long, stopping his ambitions short. Long's demagoguery never made it to the Oval Office.

Violence is not the answer to demagoguery. We have a system in place to defeat would-be despots. That's because the Founding Fathers feared but anticipated the rise of despots and demagogues. They had a better answer: civic education and civic engagement. As Thomas Jefferson explained, those two forces were antidotes to toxic demagogues who played on passions rather than reason. And Horace Mann, the founder of public schooling in the United States, argued: "A republican form of government, without intelligence in the people, must be, on a vast scale, what a mad-house, without superintendent or keepers, would be on a small one."[8] In other words, without civic education and civic engagement, it would only be a matter of time before an opportunistic showman arrived on the political stage and dazzled his way to despotism.

Civic engagement in the United States has fallen over the last several decades. Polarization is at historic highs. The system itself is broken. Or, put more succinctly, a lot of people don't care about politics; those that do can't seem to find any common ground with "the other side"; and a distorted system fails everyone. Donald Trump is capitalizing on all three weaknesses of American democracy.

He has blurred the line between fact and fiction, using lies as a tool to create a cult of personality and convince his supporters that he can do no wrong. He has attacked the press, echoing Mao's and Stalin's rhetoric in calling free independent journalists the "enemy of the people." He called for his political opponent to be "locked up," but pardoned a political ally who ignored court rulings and abused state power for racist ends. Trump has politicized the rule of law, mimicking despots who seek to impede investigations threatening their political survival. He has ramped up efforts to suppress votes, turning to the wizard of voter suppression himself, Kris Kobach of Kansas, to spearhead the Orwellian "election integrity commission." He has followed in the footsteps of countless autocrats by stoking racial animosity to divide and rule. He has not "drained the swamp" of corruption, but flooded it with egregious ethics violations. He has politicized core institutions of government, ranging from scientific research and NASA to the courts and even the Congressional Budget Office. Trump has hired his family members and cronies for positions that they are unqualified to occupy. And he has exported his attack on democracy globally, by acting as a cheerleader for despots abroad.

Since Trump emerged as the Republican frontrunner in late 2015, I haven't been able to get the warning from Mikalai Statkevich, the Belarusian presidential candidate, out of my head: "You don't know how lucky you are. Never take your democracy for granted. You won't realize what it's worth until it's too late."

It has stuck with me because I've met countless people, such as Mikalai Stakevich in Belarus or Pravit Rojanaphruk in Thailand, who have risked their lives to fight for democracy. In my research,

CONCLUSION

I've grown used to a familiar pause in conversation, as a torture victim tries to find the right words to explain suffering that simply cannot be put into words, carried out by a cruel despot. How do you muster the means to describe having your fingernails pulled off one by one?

Despots don't just destroy the lives of dissidents or opposition leaders. They leave their countries in ruin. I've seen heartbreaking scenes of little kids scrounging for food in landfills. I've met dozens of activists who have been beaten for protesting. And I've talked to family members of dissidents who didn't survive such savagery. These are the horrors of kleptocratic autocracy. In sub-Saharan Africa, the Middle East, Southeast Asia, and parts of post-Soviet Europe, many have told me that they envied me—because I had won the lottery of birth and ended up as a citizen in a rich democracy. I have always tried to explain that the US is still deeply flawed, that it faces enormous challenges. "Yes," they would say, "but at least you have the power we all dream of: the power to change it."

Yet only 36 per cent of American adults voted in the 2014 Congressional elections,[9] and just one in four Americans can name the three branches of the United States government.[10] Instead of exercising our power to change and improve, we have let it wither on the vine. Even in the most recent election—one of the most consequential ballots in American history—only 61.4% of adult citizens voted.[11] That meant that less than 30% of American adults voted for Donald Trump to become president, while nearly 40% of American adults didn't vote at all.[12] Apathy beat Trump by 10 points, but he's in the Oval Office nonetheless.

Citizen apathy allows politicians to subvert democracy. Donald Trump is the leading culprit, but if Americans allow democracy to fade, we only have ourselves to blame. A common complaint that I've heard across the United States is that people didn't like the candidates in 2016. Fair enough. But we often get the candidates we deserve. In the 2016 presidential primaries—the process of selecting candidates to represent each party—7% of American adults voted for Hillary Clinton. Only 6% voted for Donald Trump. Nearly 75% of American citizens did not vote in the primary process at all.[13] Most let others choose for them who would be on the ballot, and then complained about it when they didn't like who won. Democracy is withering from our collective indifference.

Some say that they didn't vote because it doesn't make any difference. They're wrong. On the gubernatorial campaign that I co-managed in Minnesota, one of the key issues dividing the candidates was whether that state should accept funding from the US government to provide health care coverage to 220,000 more low-income and disabled people.[14] If we won, they'd get it. If we lost, they wouldn't. We won by a few thousand votes, out of more than 2 million ballots, and 220,300 more people received medical insurance. Every vote counts.

Some say they didn't vote in 2016 because the system is broken. Wages have stagnated; inequality has soared; most Americans feel powerless. Many of those justifiable complaints are manifestations of structural problems with democracy in the United States—too much money in politics; an unfair electoral system; the disproportionate influence of lobbyists; and politicians who are out for themselves rather than out for us. But we've allowed that situation to develop. It didn't happen overnight. It couldn't have happened at all, if citizens had fought the corrosion of American democracy tooth and nail—but we didn't. That's the bad news.

The good news is that we can build a better democracy. People abroad who live under true despots are powerless to change the system; they are the pawns of tyrants. Americans are not. In the United States, we must imagine a world in which democracy lives up to its promise; where collaboration, consensus, and compromise prevail over vitriol and Internet trolls; where people get a fair shake so long as they work hard and follow the rules; where justice is within reach; where our elected officials are qualified, skilled, and dedicated representatives; where liberty and justice for all is a reality, not an aspirational catch phrase. All are still possible.

Civic engagement is the key to unlocking a better future. But first, we must protect democracy from political order reverting to its natural state: tyranny. For most of human history, tyrants have dominated. Democracy is ancient, but it doesn't arise or thrive naturally or survive effortlessly. As Mark Twain put it, "I am a democrat only on principle, not by instinct—nobody is that. Doubtless some people say they are, but this world is grievously given to lying."[15] It's far easier and far more common for a ruthless strongman to take charge of subjects than it is for citizens to band together in pursuit of a better world. Collaborative democracy sometimes requires us to battle our basest passions. Ronald Reagan was right that we don't automatically pass democracy to future generations in our bloodstream. If we take it for granted rather than rallying to defend it, one day "we will," in the words of Reagan, "spend our sunset years telling our children and our children's children what it was once like in the United States where men were free."[16]

Democracy is worth saving. Right now, in the United States, it needs to be saved—before it's too late. It's far more difficult to resurrect democracy after it dies than it is to heal it when it's sick. Donald Trump is a symptom of chronic illness in our political system; he could not have won an election in a healthy, fully functioning democratic system. But now that he's in the

White House, his authoritarian impulses are weakening an already sick patient.

To defend democracy against Trump, we must return to those three harsh realities of American politics: too many people don't care about politics; too many who do care hate the "other side"; and the broken democratic system is failing everyone.

To cure what ails us—to face these problems and fix them—we need a new code of civic engagement that encourages far more citizen involvement. The aim of that engagement in the short term must be to elect more principled Democrats and principled Republicans—who will stand up to Trump's authoritarian instincts, at least on procedural grounds if not on policy—in the 2018 Congressional midterm elections. We must only elect those who will protect democracy rather than protecting their job or their party. We will have to work for long-term structural reforms that heal American democracy—fair redistricting without gerrymandering; reducing the role of money in politics; imposing stricter ethics; curbing the influence of lobbyists; introducing automatic voter registration that gives everyone the opportunity to vote; making election day a public holiday so that work duties never get in the way of civic duties; and investing more in civic education.

For now, though, let's start with building a new civic code. Current levels of citizen engagement aren't enough. Voting is good, but democracy requires more than just voting. Politicians are our employees, and we need to monitor their work—not just re-hire or fire them every couple of years. There are already encouraging signs that some aspects of civic activism are starting to bounce back. But, up until now, being an informed voter was the same thing as being a good citizen. Today, in an era of new threats, that's no longer good enough. We don't have to risk our lives for democracy like the Statkeviches and Rojanaphruks of this world, but we do have to make democracy more central to our lifestyles. Democracy is a daily duty.

There are small steps that we can all take to improve the health of American democracy and shore it up for future generations. First, vote—even in primaries and local elections. The candidates who win a primary or local election today can become the candidates we elect at the national level tomorrow. Barack Obama, for example, won just over 16,000 total votes in his first election victory, and a decade later he entered the White House with 69 million votes.[17]

Second, we can make our political engagement social. We mistakenly see citizenship as a private matter, one in which we don't want to step on anyone's toes by encouraging them to get involved. But the world that we will inhabit is shaped not just by our own choices, but also by those of people all around us. If we stay silent, and don't encourage others to speak out, then the voices of extremists are all we hear; if we all speak up, extremists get drowned out.

Third, we can all try to find common ground about democratic principles. Americans must transcend partisan squabbles to protect democracy. We can disagree without being disagreeable about particular policies, then close ranks around bedrock principles. Americans will get nowhere screaming into the wind if our words are only carried back to our own partisan "side." Polarization is a gift to would-be despots. Those who have successfully defeated despots or stood up to demagogues across the globe have learned this crucial lesson. In Tunisia, for example, I've witnessed heroic and inspiring efforts to find common ground—even between torture victims and those who were involved in their torture. They bridged those divides to build a better democracy, even winning a Nobel peace prize for their impressive resolve.

I first met Said Ferjani in Tunis in 2013, two years after the Arab Spring had uprooted a despot and planted the seeds of democracy. Ferjani had only recently returned to Tunisia from a long exile in the UK. In the late 1980s, Ferjani had plotted an ill-advised coup d'état against Tunisia's despot, Habib Bourguiba. But Ferjani's plot was beaten to the punch by Zine el-Abidine Ben Ali, who launched his own coup, which succeeded. Ben Ali became Tunisia's new dictator. Ferjani and his collaborators were arrested. Ferjani was tortured and beaten so badly that he slipped into a coma. He awoke nearly a week later with terrible injuries, including a broken back and spinal damage that still causes him wincing pain.[18]

Once Ferjani got out of the torture chambers and the prison, he was still trapped in Tunisia. The regime had barred him from leaving the country. Refusing to give up, Ferjani forced himself to rise from his wheelchair so he could practice walking far enough to get through airport security without raising the suspicions of the border police. After gritting his teeth and getting used to the pain, Ferjani was ready. He borrowed a passport from a friend and slipped through security onto the plane. He spent the next twenty-two years in exile in London. When the Arab Spring toppled Ben Ali's regime, Ferjani came home to Tunisia. Rather than seeking vengeance, though, he looked to build consensus on one overarching principle: that democracy must become a shared Tunisian value.

Ferjani and his political rivals could not be more different. He is a devout Muslim; they are secular. Ferjani was a torture victim; many of the older members of the rival political party were members or supporters of the regime that tortured him. Nonetheless, Ferjani has not just been willing to tolerate the "other side." He has developed friendships across Tunisia's political divide. How, I asked him, was it possible for him to have the personal courage to shake hands with people who had helped break his back? "We are conscious of the fact that any mistakes now could make democracy reversible," he answered.[19] It was as simple as that. Ferjani saw his role as larger than his own personal suffering. It has worked, as Tunisians face severe challenges but never lose sight of the democratic goal. They have put deep, fundamental, and even horrifying personal divides aside—to save democracy.

Thankfully, Americans don't need such courage. But if Said Ferjani can find common ground with his torturers, surely Democrats and Republicans can work together to protect democracy. If Mikalai Statkevich is willing to be beaten, abducted, and imprisoned for years in order to fight for democracy in Belarus, we should at least be willing to vote every few years or volunteer every few weeks to save ours. And if Tunisia can throw off the shackles of an entrenched dictator, then surely we can protect American democracy from a bumbling demagogue.

In the mid-1950s, another American politician with authoritarian impulses took center stage: Senator Joe McCarthy. McCarthyism, as it came to be known, fed on targeting perceived enemies of the United States. It painted critics of the government as traitors, and thrived on fear and division. McCarthy himself aimed much of his fire at the press: "The heads of every one of our intelligence agencies say that, except for communist utilization of the so-called respectable newspapers and radio stations, they could destroy the entire [communist] movement."[20] And when reporters had the gall to criticize McCarthy, he would question their patriotism, saying: "When you write stuff like that, you're helping the communists."[21]

On 9 March 1954, television broadcaster Edward R. Murrow helped bring McCarthyism down with one of his many principled monologues. "This is no time," Murrow argued, "for men who oppose Senator McCarthy's methods to keep silent." McCarthy's rise, he continued, had "caused alarm and dismay amongst our allies abroad and given considerable comfort to our enemies. And whose fault is that? Not really his. He didn't create this situation of fear, he merely exploited it—and rather successfully. Cassius was right. The fault, dear Brutus, is not in our stars, but in ourselves." With these words, Murrow underscored a crucial and powerful point: "We must not confuse dissent with disloyalty."[22]

Trump, like demagogues and despots throughout history, has tried to wrap himself in the American flag. He conflates critics with traitors; labels dedicated patriots as deep state infiltrators; and paints those who seek to improve the government as enemies who hate America. The American flag stands for precisely the opposite spirit to that of Trump's vicious attacks. It stands for the most powerful idea of all: the freedom of a citizen to protest a man like Trump, to speak out, and to work to build a better democracy without being ostracized, beaten or tortured.

Loyalty to America does not mean loyalty to Trump. He is acting like a despot's apprentice, borrowing tactics from authoritarian leaders I've seen elsewhere. It could happen here. Trump has put our democracy at risk, and in this moment of democracy in peril, he reminds us that we must sometimes fulfill the most important and, often, the most difficult duties of true patriots: to dissent and oppose.

ACKNOWLEDGEMENTS

I, too, am an apprentice—to better people.

My parents, Paul and Barbara, taught me most of what I know. They are saints. My mom sparked my interest in politics when I was seven years old. She ran for the local school board—and crushed her opponent with the clever slogan of "Vote Straight A's—for Barbara Klaas." My dad taught me never to be satisfied with "good enough." When I was a kid, I'd bring home a test. "98 out of 100," I'd say, beaming. "What happened to the other two?" he'd ask. They taught me that life is about relationships with people you care about, experiences you enjoy, and making the world better than you found it. They are and always have been there for me. They also saved me from committing social suicide when, at the age of ten, I asked them if I could become an American Civil War reenactor and they said no. I owe them everything.

My great friends, Marcel and David, taught me that life is too important to take yourself too seriously. From dog sledding in the Arctic Circle to shooting guns in Kentucky—while discussing politics all along the way—life is always better when you're around. If there's ever a contest for "best German" or "best Canadian," rest assured that you have each earned my vote.

Hundreds of brave people in Madagascar, Zambia, Thailand, Tunisia, Belarus, and Côte d'Ivoire spoke to me, often at great

ACKNOWLEDGEMENTS

personal risk. They taught me how lucky I am to have been born in a rich democracy—and how important it is to preserve and protect it.

A special thanks to the team at Hurst & Co, especially Michael, Lara, Jon, and Alison. Michael asked me to write this book. It would not exist without him. I am deeply indebted to him for his guidance, support, and friendship. Lara is to great editors what the Loch Ness Monster is to Scotland: many people claim such a thing exists, but you wouldn't really believe it unless you see it with your own eyes. She was endlessly patient and scarily efficient. On the western side of the Atlantic, a special thanks to Tony and Michael at Skyhorse, who believed in this project and invested in me.

Finally, Ellie, who is somehow still blind to the fact that she's out of my league, taught me that a long, stressful day can be wiped away by an instant together. I'm very lucky to have found you.

NOTES

INTRODUCTION: AMERICAN AUTHORITARIANISM?

1. Statkevich, Mikalai (2015). Former Belarusian presidential candidate. Personal interview, 17 December 2015, Minsk, Belarus.
2. Bernstein, Adam (2006). 'Alberto Stroessner; Paraguayan Dictator', *The Washington Post*, 17 August 2006, http://www.washingtonpost.com/wp-dyn/content/article/2006/08/16/AR2006081601729.html, last accessed 3 October 2017.
3. Risen, James and Sheri Fink (2017). 'Trump Said "Torture Works." An Echo Is Feared Worldwide.', *The New York Times*, 5 January 2017, https://www.nytimes.com/2017/01/05/us/politics/trump-torture-guantanamo.html?_r=0, last accessed 4 October 2017.
4. Vavreck, Lynn (2017). 'A Measure of Identity: Are You Wedded to Your Party?', *The New York Times*, 31 January 2017, https://www.nytimes.com/2017/01/31/upshot/are-you-married-to-your-party.html?mcubz=1&_r=0, last accessed 3 October 2017.
5. Klaas, Brian (2017). 'Gerrymandering is the biggest obstacle to genuine democracy in the United States. So why is no one protesting?', *The Washington Post*, 10 February 2017, https://www.washingtonpost.com/news/democracy-post/wp/2017/02/10/gerrymandering-is-the-biggest-obstacle-to-genuine-democracy-in-the-united-states-so-why-is-no-one-protesting/?utm_term=.ec611b4c5331, last accessed 3 October 2017.
6. Peckham, Matt (2013). 'Congress Now Less Popular than Head Lice, Cockroaches and the Donald', *TIME*, 8 January 2013, http://newsfeed.time.com/2013/01/08/congress-now-less-popular-than-head-lice-cock-roaches-and-the-donald/, last accessed 3 October 2017.
7. Badinelli, Andrew and Annie Goldsmith (2016). 'The Rise of Trump:

Harvard Professors Weigh In', *The Crimson*, 3 November 2016, http://www.thecrimson.com/article/2016/11/3/rise-of-trump-harvard/, last accessed 3 October 2017; and Mounk, Yascha (2016). 'The week democracy died', *Slate*, 14 August 2016, http://www.slate.com/articles/news_and_politics/cover_story/2016/08/the_week_democracy_died_how_brexit_nice_turkey_and_trump_are_all_connected.html, last accessed 3 October 2017.

8. Guo, Jeff (2016). 'Income inequality today may be higher today than in any other era', *The Washington Post*, 1 July 2016, https://www.washingtonpost.com/news/wonk/wp/2016/07/01/income-inequality-today-may-be-the-highest-since-the-nations-founding/?utm_term=.223200e16ccf, last accessed 3 October 2017.

9. Tice, DJ. 'The long twilight struggle of the Iron Range', *Minneapolis Star Tribune*, 15 January 2016, http://www.startribune.com/the-long-twilight-struggle-of-the-iron-range/365494171/, last accessed 3 October 2017.

10. Hetherington, M. J., & Weiler, J. D. (2009). *Authoritarianism and polarization in American politics*. Cambridge: Cambridge University Press.

11. Hetherington & Weiler (2009). See also Lavine, H., Burgess, D., Snyder, M., Transue, J., Sullivan, J. L., Haney, B., & Wagner, S. H. (1999). 'Threat, authoritarianism, and voting: An investigation of personality and persuasion', *Personality and Social Psychology Bulletin*, 25(3), 337–47.

12. MacWilliams, M. C. (2016). 'Who decides when the party doesn't? Authoritarian voters and the rise of Donald Trump', *PS: Political Science & Politics*, 49(4), 716–21.

13. Annenberg Public Policy Center (2017). 'Americans are poorly informed about basic constitutional provisions', The Annenberg Public Policy Center of the University of Pennsylvania, 12 September 2017, https://cdn.annenbergpublicpolicycenter.org/wp-content/uploads/2017/09/Civics-survey-Sept-2017-complete.pdf, last accessed 3 October 2017.

14. Grinberg, Emanuella and Elliot C. McLaughlin (2017). 'Travel ban protests stretch into third day from US to UK', CNN, 31 January 2017, http://edition.cnn.com/2017/01/30/politics/travel-ban-protests-immigration/index.html, last accessed 3 October 2017.

15. Dopp, Terrence and Toluse Oluorunnipa (2017). 'Trump Restricts or Bans Travel From Eight Countries', Bloomberg, 25 September 2017, https://www.bloomberg.com/news/articles/2017–09–24/new-trump-ban-restricts-travel-from-eight-countries, last accessed 3 October 2017.

16. Scott, Eugene (2017). 'A day after meeting with Sen. Tim Scott, Trump repeats 'both sides' comments on Charlottesville', The Washington Post, 14 September 2017, https://www.washingtonpost.com/news/the-fix/wp/2017/09/14/a-day-after-meeting-with-sen-tim-scott-trump-repeats-both-sides-comments-on-charlottesville/?utm_term=.168da72aaeeb, last accessed 3 October 2017.

17. McCain, John (2017). 'Statement by Senator John McCain on White Supremacist Attack in Charlottesville', https://www.mccain.senate.gov/public/index.cfm/2017/8/statement-by-senator-john-mccain-on-white-supremacist-attack-in-charlottesville, last accessed 4 October 2017; Samuelson, Kate (2017). 'Read Mitt Romney's Full Message on Donald Trump's Response to Charlottesville', TIME, 18 August 2017, http://time.com/4906768/read-mitt-romneys-trump-charlottesville/, last accessed 4 October 2017.

18. Alcindor, Yamiche and J. David Goodman (2017). 'Trump Family Wedding Planner to Head New York's Federal Housing Office', The New York Times, 16 June 2017, https://www.nytimes.com/2017/06/16/us/politics/trump-family-wedding-planner-to-head-new-yorks-federal-housing-office.html, last accessed 4 October 2017.

19. The New York Times (2016). 'Transcript of Mitt Romney's Speech on Donald Trump', 3 March 2016, https://www.nytimes.com/2016/03/04/us/politics/mitt-romney-speech.html, last accessed 4 October 2017.

20. Rogin, Josh (2017). 'State Department considers scrubbing democracy promotion from its mission', The Washington Post, 1 August 2017, https://www.washingtonpost.com/news/josh-rogin/wp/2017/08/01/state-department-considers-scrubbing-democracy-promotion-from-its-mission/?utm_term=.ec90624cb51f, last accessed 3 October 2017.

21. Reagan, Ronald (1961). 'Encroaching Control', speech before the Phoenix Chamber of Commerce, 30 March 1961, transcript and audio at https://archive.org/details/RonaldReagan-EncroachingControl, last accessed 4 October 2017.

22. Mounk, Yascha and Roberto Stefan Foa (2016). 'The Danger of Deconsolidation: the democratic disconnect', *Journal of Democracy*, 27(3), 5–17.

23. Taylor, Alan (2017). 'American Nazis in the 1930s—The German American Bund', *The Atlantic*, 5 June 2017, https://www.theatlantic.com/photo/2017/06/american-nazis-in-the-1930sthe-german-american-bund/529185/, last accessed 3 October 2017.

24. Sander, Gordon (2017). 'When Nazis Filled Madison Square Garden', *Politico*, 23 August 2017, http://www.politico.com/magazine/story/2017/08/23/nazi-german-american-bund-rally-madison-square-garden-215522, last accessed 3 October 2017; Giles, Matt (n.d.). 'A Look Back at the 1939 Pro-Nazi Rally at Madison Square Garden and the Protesters Who Organized Against It', *Longreads*, n.d., https://longreads.com/2017/08/14/a-look-back-at-the-1939-pro-nazi-rally-at-madison-square-garden-and-the-protestors-who-organized-against-it/, last accessed 3 October 2017.

25. Calamur, Krishnadev (2017). 'A short history of America First', *The Atlantic*, 21 January 2017, https://www.theatlantic.com/politics/archive/2017/01/trump-america-first/514037/, last accessed 3 October 2017.

1. DOUBLETHINK

1. Orwell, George (1949). *1984*. London: Penguin.

2. Chibwedele, Marian (2015). ZNBC broadcaster, held at gunpoint during the 1997 "Captain Solo" coup attempt. Personal interview, 28 August 2012, Lusaka, Zambia. See also Klaas, Brian (2015). 'Bullets over Ballots: How Electoral Exclusion Increases the Risk of Coups and Civil Wars', DPhil dissertation, University of Oxford.

3. Yea, Sanghan (2017). 'Demystifying the Survival of North Korea'. *Journal of Asian Security and International Affairs*, 4(1), 50–68.

4. Hickman, Leo (2011). 'Kim Jong-il: ten things you never knew', *The Guardian*, 19 December 2011, https://www.theguardian.com/world/shortcuts/2011/dec/19/kim-jong-il-things-never-knew, last accessed 2 October 2017.

5. Agence France Presse (2010). 'N. Korea leader sets world fashion trend: Pyongyang,' 7 April 2010, https://web.archive.org/web/20111219011527/http://www.france24.com/en/20100407-nkorea-leader-sets-world-fashion-trend-pyongyang, last accessed 2 October 2017.

6. Spillius, Alex (2011). 'Kim Jong-il dead: the official titles of North Korea's Unique Leader', *The Telegraph*, 20 December 2010, http://www.telegraph.co.uk/news/worldnews/asia/northkorea/8966735/Kim-Jong-il-dead-the-official-titles-of-North-Koreas-Unique-Leader.html, last accessed 2 October 2017; QI, 'North Korea', http://qi.com/infocloud/north-korea, last accessed 2 October 2017.

7. Ryall, Julian (2011). 'Kim Jong-il's greatest "achievements"', *The Telegraph*, 19 December 2011, http://www.telegraph.co.uk/news/worldnews/asia/northkorea/8965150/Kim-Jong-ils-greatest-achievements.html, last accessed 2 October 2017.

8. Phillips, Jake (2011). 'Kim Jong Un: 10 Things You Might Not Know About North Korea's New Leader', *TIME*, 19 December 2011, http://newsfeed.time.com/2011/12/19/kim-jong-un-10-things-you-might-not-know-about-north-koreas-new-leader/, last accessed 2 October 2017.

9. Withnall, Adam (2015). 'Kim Jong-un learned to drive at age three, North Korean children to be taught', *The Independent*, 9 April 2015, http://www.independent.co.uk/news/world/asia/kim-jong-un-learned-to-drive-at-age-three-north-korean-children-to-be-taught-10165694.html, last accessed 2 October 2017.

10. Ryall, Juilian (2015). 'Kim Jong-un was child prodigy who could drive at age of three, claims North Korean school curriculum', *The Telegraph*, 10 April 2015, http://www.telegraph.co.uk/news/worldnews/asia/northkorea/11526831/Kim-Jong-un-was-child-prodigy-who-could-drive-at-age-of-three-claims-North-Korean-school-curriculum.html, last accessed 2 October 2017.

11. Subramanian, Courtney (2013). 'These Are North Korea's 28 State-Approved Hairstyles', *TIME*, 25 February 2013, http://newsfeed.time.com/2013/02/25/these-are-north-koreas-28-state-approved-hairstyles/, last accessed 2 October 2017; Philips (2010).

12. Kwon, KJ and Ben Westcott (2016). 'Kim Jong Un has executed over 300 people since coming to power', CNN, 29 December 2016.

13. Sang-Hun, Choe (2015). 'North Korea Said to Execute a Top Official, With an Antiaircraft Gun', *The New York Times*, 12 May 2015, https://www.nytimes.com/2015/05/13/world/asia/north-korea-said-to-execute-a-top-official.html?mcubz=1&_r=0, last accessed 2 October 2017.

14. Ryall, Julian (2014). 'North Korean official 'executed by flame-thrower'', *The Telegraph*, 7 April 2014, http://www.telegraph.co.uk/news/worldnews/asia/northkorea/10750082/North-Korean-official-executed-by-flame-thrower.html, last accessed 2 October 2017.

15. Elgot, Jessica (2013). 'Kim Jong Un's Uncle Jang Song Thaek 'Executed By Machine Gun Fire' In N Korea', *Huffington Post*, 13 December 2013, http://www.huffingtonpost.co.uk/2013/12/13/north-korea-execute_n_4437788.html, last accessed 2 October 2017.

16. Williams, Martyn (2016). 'How the Internet Works in North Korea', *Slate*, 28 November 2016, http://www.slate.com/articles/technology/future_tense/2016/11/how_the_internet_works_in_north_korea.html, last accessed 2 October 2017.

17. Ford, Matt (2017). 'Trump's Press Secretary Falsely Claims: 'Largest Audience Ever to Witness an Inauguration, Period'', *The Atlantic*, 21 January 2017, https://www.theatlantic.com/politics/archive/2017/01/inauguration-crowd-size/514058/, last accessed 2 October 2017.

18. Qiu, Linda (2017). 'Donald Trump had biggest inaugural crowd ever? Metrics don't show it', *Politifact*, 21 January 2017, http://www.politifact.com/truth-o-meter/statements/2017/jan/21/sean-spicer/trump-had-biggest-inaugural-crowd-ever-metrics-don/, last accessed 2 October 2017.

19. Author's own count. Tweet archives available from the Trump Twitter Archive: http://www.trumptwitterarchive.com/archive, last accessed 2 October 2017.

20. Konnikova, Maria (2017). 'Trump's Lies vs. Your Brain', *Politico*, January/February 2017, http://www.politico.com/magazine/story/2017/01/donald-trump-lies-liar-effect-brain-214658, last accessed 25 September 2017.

21. *The Washington Post* (2017). 'The Fact Checker's ongoing database of

the false and misleading claims made by President Trump during his first 365 days in office', as of 8 September 2017, https://www.washingtonpost.com/graphics/politics/trump-claims-database/?utm_term=.fe6d8ada b6e5, last accessed 2 October 2017.

22. Konnikova (2017).

23. Fazio, Lisa K., Nadia M. Brashier, B. Keith Payne, and Elizabeth J. Marsh (2015). 'Knowledge does not protect against illusory truth', *Journal of Experimental Psychology*, 144(5), 993–1002.

24. Nyhan, Brendan, and Jason Reifler (2010). "When corrections fail: The persistence of political misperceptions." *Political Behavior* 32(2), 303–30.

25. See Stolberg, Sheryl Gay (2017). 'Many Politicians Lie. But Trump Has Elevated the Art of Fabrication.', *The New York Times*, 7 August 2017, https://www.nytimes.com/2017/08/07/us/politics/lies-trump-obama-mislead.html?mcubz=1, last accessed 2 October 2017.

26. Lucas, Edward (2007). 'The Kremlin's useful idiots', *The Economist*, 29 October 2007, available from: http://www.edwardlucas.com/2007/10/29/diary-day-one/, last accessed 2 October 2017.

27. Kurtzleben, Danielle (2017). 'Trump Embraces One Of Russia's Favorite Propaganda Tactics—Whataboutism', National Public Radio, 17 March 2017, http://www.npr.org/2017/03/17/520435073/trump-embraces-one-of-russias-favorite-propaganda-tactics-whataboutism, last accessed 2 October 2017.

28. Sheth, Sonam (2017). 'Kellyanne Conway makes mind-blowing pivot to Benghazi when grilled about Trump Jr.'s Russia meeting', *Business Insider*, 7 August 2017, http://uk.businessinsider.com/kellyanne-conway-benghazi-trump-jr-russia-meeting-2017–8, last accessed 2 October 2017.

29. Morin, Rebecca (2017). 'Trump defends Putin, says US has "a lot of killers"', *Politico*, 5 February 2017, http://www.politico.eu/article/trump-defends-putin-says-us-has-a-lot-of-killers/, last accessed 2 October 2017.

30. Bellafante, Ginia (2007). 'Crazy, He Calls Me (and Terrified, I Agree)', *New York Times Theater Review*, 24 May 2007, http://www.nytimes.

com/2007/05/24/theater/reviews/24gasl.html?mcubz=1, last accessed 2 October 2017.

31. Finnegan, Michael and Noah Bierman (2016). 'Trump's endorsement of violence reaches new level: He may pay legal fees for assault suspect', *Los Angeles Times*, 13 March 2016, http://www.latimes.com/politics/la-na-trump-campaign-protests-20160313-story.html, last accessed 2 October 2017.

32. Hensch, Mark (2016). 'Trump: 'I never said' I'd pay legal fees for alleged sucker-puncher', *The Hill*, 15 March 2016, http://thehill.com/blogs/ballot-box/presidential-races/273016-trump-i-never-said-i-was-going-to-for-fees-for-my, last accessed 2 October 2017.

33. Ghitis, Frida (2017). 'Donald Trump is "gaslighting" all of us', CNN, 16 January 2017, http://edition.cnn.com/2017/01/10/opinions/donald-trump-is-gaslighting-america-ghitis/index.html, last accessed 25 September 2017.

34. Wagner, John (2017). 'Trump's comparison of U.S. intelligence community to Nazi Germany rebuked by Anti-Defamation League', *The Washington Post*, 11 January 2017, https://www.washingtonpost.com/news/post-politics/wp/2017/01/11/trumps-comparison-of-u-s-intelligence-community-to-nazi-germany-rebuked-by-anti-defamation-league/?utm_term=.0429046c248c, last accessed 2 October 2017.

35. Malka, Ariel and Yphtach Lelkes (2017). 'In a new poll, half of Republicans say they would support postponing the 2020 election if Trump proposed it', *The Washington Post* ('Monkey Cage'), 10 August 2017, https://www.washingtonpost.com/news/monkey-cage/wp/2017/08/10/in-a-new-poll-half-of-republicans-say-they-would-support-postponing-the-2020-election-if-trump-proposed-it/?utm_term=.e307baf53d11, last accessed 25 September 2017.

36. Jacobs, Peter (2017). 'Trump blames Obama for 122 "vicious" Guantanamo prisoners returning "to the battlefield"—but 113 of them were released under Bush', *Business Insider*, 7 March 2017, http://uk.businessinsider.com/trump-blames-obama-for-guantanamo-prisoners-returning-to-battlefield-2017-3, last accessed 2 October 2017.

37. Greenberg, Andy (2017). 'The FBI Has Been Investigating Trump's Russia Ties Since July', *Wired*, 20 March 2017, https://www.wired.

com/2017/03/fbi-director-comey-confirms-investigation-trump-campaigns-russia-ties/, last accessed 2 October 2017.

38. Kruzel, John (2017). 'Trump's Pants on Fire claim that CNN ratings are "way down"', *Politifact*, 3 July 2017, http://www.politifact.com/truth-o-meter/statements/2017/jul/03/donald-trump/trumps-pants-fire-claim-cnn-ratings-are-way-down/, last accessed 2 October 2017.

39. Prokop, Andrew (2017). 'Trump promised not to cut Medicaid. His health bill will cut $880 billion from it.', *Vox*, 13 March 2017, https://www.vox.com/2017/3/13/14914812/trump-ahca-medicaid-cuts, last accessed 2 October 2017.

40. Thompson, Alex (2017). 'Trump gets a folder full of positive news about himself twice a day', *Vice News*, 9 August 2017, https://news.vice.com/story/trump-folder-positive-news-white-house, last accessed 2 October 2017.

41. Seipel, Arnie (2016). 'FACT CHECK: Trump Falsely Claims A 'Massive Landslide Victory'', National Public Radio, 11 December 2016, http://www.npr.org/2016/12/11/505182622/fact-check-trump-claims-a-massive-landslide-victory-but-history-differs, last accessed 2 October 2017; for Bill Clinton's votes, see Peters, Gerhard and John Woolley (1999–2017). 'Election of 1992', The American Presidency Project, http://www.presidency.ucsb.edu/showelection.php?year=1992, last accessed 2 October 2017; and Peters, Gerhard and John Woolley (1999–2017). 'Election of 1996', The American Presidency Project, http://www.presidency.ucsb.edu/showelection.php?year=1996, last accessed 2 October 2017.

42. See The White House (2017). 'Signed Legislation', available from https://www.whitehouse.gov/briefing-room/signed-legislation, last accessed 2 October 2017.

43. Sky News (2017). 'Boy Scout leaders did not praise Donald Trump speech, White House admits', 3 August 2017, http://news.sky.com/story/boy-scout-leaders-did-not-praise-donald-trump-speech-white-house-admits-10971583, last accessed 2 October 2017.

44. Lanktree, Graham (2017). 'Alex Jones Refuses To Apologize For Sandy Hook Conspiracy Theory', *Newsweek*, 19 June 2017, http://www.news-

week.com/alex-jones-megyn-kelly-sandy-hook-infowars-627129, last accessed 2 October 2017.

45. Griffing, Alexander (2017). 'Meet Alex Jones, Donald Trump's Favorite Conspiracy Theorist', *Haaretz*, 13 June 2017, https://www.haaretz.com/us-news/1.774690, last accessed 2 October 2017.

46. Horsey, Alexander (2013). 'Alex Jones has a sick theory about the Boston Marathon bombings', *Los Angeles Times*, 19 April 2013, http://articles.latimes.com/2013/apr/19/nation/la-na-tt-alex-jones-20130418, last accessed 2 October 2017.

47. Collins, Ben (2017). 'NASA Denies That It's Running a Child Slave Colony on Mars', *The Daily Beast*, 29 June 2017, http://www.thedailybeast.com/nasa-denies-that-its-running-a-child-slave-colony-on-mars, last accessed 2 October 2017.

2. FAKE NEWS!

1. Major General Weerachon Sukhonthapatipak (2017). Spokesman for Thailand's military government. Personal interviews, 13 February 2017 and 18 December 2014, Bangkok, Thailand.

2. Rojanaphruk, Pravit (2014). Journalist for *The Nation* newspaper. Personal interview, 9 December 2014, Bangkok, Thailand.

3. Rojanaphruk, Pravit (2016). Journalist for *The Nation* newspaper. Personal interview, 12 March 2016, Bangkok, Thailand.

4. Rojanaphruk, Pravit (2017). Journalist for *The Nation* newspaper. Personal interview, 13 February 2017, Bangkok, Thailand.

5. Committee to Protect Journalists (2017). 'Thai columnist Pravit Rojanaphruk charged with two cases of sedition', 8 August 2017, https://cpj.org/2017/08/thai-columnist-pravit-rojanaphruk-charged-with-two.php, last accessed 5 October 2017.

6. Rojanaphruk, Pravit (2017). 'Why sedition charges won't silence me', *Khaosod English*, 19 August 2017, http://www.khaosodenglish.com/opinion/2017/08/19/sedition-charges-wont-silence/, last accessed 5 October 2017

7. CNN (2007). 'Turks grieve over journalist's killing', 19 January 2007,

http://edition.cnn.com/2007/WORLD/europe/01/19/turkey.dink/, last accessed 4 October 2017.

8. *The Washington Post* (2015). 'Turkey's president deepens his attacks on the press', 6 December 2015, https://www.washingtonpost.com/opin-ions/turkeys-president-deepens-his-attacks-on-the-press/2015/12/06/f01f2f9e-97a3–11e5-b499–76cbec161973_story.html?utm_term=.dd50cdb880b1, last accessed 4 October 2017; Committee to Protect Journalists (2012). 'Turkey's Press Freedom Crisis: The Dark Days of Jailing Journalists and Criminalizing Dissent', special report, October 2012, https://cpj.org/reports/Turkey2012.English.pdf, last accessed 26 September 2017.

9. Caryl, Christian (2017). 'With Trump's attack on the press, American democracy approaches a critical moment', *The Washington Post*, 2 June 2017, https://www.washingtonpost.com/news/democracy-post/wp/2017/06/02/the-coming-crackdown-on-the-american-press/?nid&utm_term=.83f02c79d562, last accessed 26 September 2017.

10. Lipman, Masha, and Michael McFaul (2001). '"Managed Democracy" in Russia: Putin and the Press', *Harvard International Journal of Press/Politics*, 6(3), 116–27.

11. Dougherty, Jill (2015). 'How the Media Became One of Putin's Most Powerful Weapons', *The Atlantic*, 21 April 2015, https://www.theatlan-tic.com/international/archive/2015/04/how-the-media-became-putins-most-powerful-weapon/391062/, last accessed 5 October 2017.

12. Streckfuss, David (2010). *Truth on trial in Thailand: Defamation, treason, and lèse-majesté*. London: Routledge.

13. *The Economist*/YouGov (2017). 'Poll, July 23–25, 2017—1500 US Adults', pp. 77–86, https://d25d2506sfb94s.cloudfront.net/cumulus_uploads/document/u4wgpax6ng/econTabReport.pdf, last accessed 26 September 2017.

14. Marist College Institute for Public Opinion (2017). 'NBR/PBS NewsHour/Marist Poll: Partisan Rancor at Fever Pitch in Washington, D.C.', 3 July 2017, http://maristpoll.marist.edu/wp-content/misc/usa-polls/us170621_PBS_NPR/NPR_PBS%20NewsHour_Marist%20Poll_Written%20Summary%20of%20Findings_Democracy_Trust_July%202007.pdf, last accessed 26 September 2017.

15. *The Economist*/You Gov (2017), p. 98.

16. Borchers, Callum (2017). 'Let's try not to freak out about this poll showing Republican support for censoring 'biased' news', *The Washington Post*, 1 August 2017, https://www.washingtonpost.com/news/the-fix/wp/2017/08/01/lets-try-not-to-freak-out-about-this-poll-showing-republican-support-for-censoring-biased-news/?utm_term=.9d34146eeeaf, last accessed 5 October 2017.

17. Gold, Hadas (2016). 'Donald Trump: We're going to "open up" libel laws', *Politico*, 26 February 2016, http://www.politico.com/blogs/on-media/2016/02/donald-trump-libel-laws-219866, last accessed 5 October 2017.

18. In 2014, for example, the Russian government threatened to shut down the *Lenta.ru* news site because it had linked to content that the regime deemed "extremist". The site fired the chief editor, and replaced her with a pro-Kremlin editor instead. Benyumov, Konstantin for Meduza.io (2016). 'How Russia's independent media was dismantled piece by piece', *The Guardian*, 25 May 2016, https://www.theguardian.com/world/2016/may/25/how-russia-independent-media-was-dismantled-piece-by-piece, last accessed 2 October 2017.

19. Grynbaum, Michael M. (2017). 'The Network Against the Leader of the Free World', *The New York Times*, 5 July 2017, https://www.nytimes.com/2017/07/05/business/media/jeffrey-zucker-cnn-trump.html, last accessed 26 September 2017.

20. For instance, H. John Rogers, a Democrat primary candidate to represent West Virginia in the Senate, punched a reporter at his campaign launch in 1981, having already "jumped" a police chief by his own admission. He was unsuccessful—just as he twice failed to become governor of the state. Borchers, Callum (2017). 'A Senate candidate punched a reporter in 1981. He says he would do it again.', *The Washington Post*, 25 May 2017, https://www.washingtonpost.com/news/the-fix/wp/2017/05/25/meet-another-national-candidate-who-assaulted-a-reporter-hes-still-not-sorry-36-years-later/?utm_term=.da235cc9d451, last accessed 2 October 2017.

21. Sullivan, Eileen and Maggie Haberman (2017). 'Trump Shares, Then Deletes, Twitter Post of Train Hitting Cartoon Person Covered by CNN

Logo', *The New York Times*, 15 August 2017, https://www.nytimes.com/2017/08/15/us/politics/trump-shares-then-deletes-twitter-post-of-cnn-cartoon-being-hit-by-train.html?mcubz=1, last accessed 5 October 2017.

22. Gray, Rosie (2017). 'Trump Defends White-Nationalist Protesters: "Some Very Fine People on Both Sides"', *The Atlantic*, 15 August 2017, https://www.theatlantic.com/politics/archive/2017/08/trump-defends-white-nationalist-protesters-some-very-fine-people-on-both-sides/537012/, last accessed 5 October 2017.

23. Carter, Brandon (2017). 'Trump suggests WH "not have press conferences" unless he does them himself', *The Hill*, 12 May 2017, http://thehill.com/homenews/administration/333179-trump-suggests-white-house-not-have-press-conferences-unless-i-do, last accessed 26 September 2017.

24. Lizza, Ryan (2017). 'Anthony Scaramucci Called Me to Unload About White House Leakers, Reince Priebus, and Steve Bannon', *The New Yorker*, 27 July 2017, https://www.newyorker.com/news/ryan-lizza/anthony-scaramucci-called-me-to-unload-about-white-house-leakers-reince-priebus-and-steve-bannon, last accessed 5 October 2017.

25. Peters, Gerhard and John T. Woolley (1999–2017). 'Presidential News Conferences', The American Presidency Project, data through 20 September 2017, http://www.presidency.ucsb.edu/data/newsconferences.php, last accessed 26 September 2017.

26. Vitali, Ali, Abigail Williams, and Halimah Abdullah (2017). 'Trump and Lavrov Meet Amid Scrutiny of Campaign, Russia Ties', NBC News, 10 May 2017, https://www.nbcnews.com/politics/white-house/trump-lavrov-meet-amid-scrutiny-campaign-russia-ties-n757321, last accessed 5 October 2017.

27. Network star Eric Bolling, author of *The Swamp: Washington's Murky Pool of Corruption and Cronyism and How Trump Can Drain It*, has since been fired by Fox News for unrelated reasons.

28. *The Week* (2017). 'Fox News' Jesse Watters pines for Trump the dictator: "Maybe we could repeal ObamaCare"', 28 July 2017, http://theweek.com/speedreads/715060/fox-news-jesse-watters-pines-trump-dictator-maybe-could-repeal-obamacare, last accessed 5 October 2017.

29. Klaas, Brian (2016). *The Despot's Accomplice: How the West is Aiding and Abetting the Decline of Democracy*. London: Hurst.

30. Graphic tweeted by Brendan Nyhan (@brendannyhan), professor at Dartmouth College: https://twitter.com/BrendanNyhan/status/824104 161239269376

31. Pilkington, Ed (2017). 'The strange case of Fox News, Trump and the death of young Democrat Seth Rich', *The Guardian*, 7 August 2017, https://www.theguardian.com/media/2017/aug/07/seth-rich-trump-white-house-fox-news, last accessed 5 October 2017.

32. Bureau of Labor Statistics (2017). 'Current Employment Statistics.' Data available from: https://www.bls.gov/ces/

33. Illing, Sean (2017). 'Media scholar on Trump TV: "This is Orwellian, and it's happening right now, right here"', *Vox*, 9 August 2017, https://www.vox.com/conversations/2017/8/9/16112430/donald-trump-tv-kay-leigh-mcenany-state-propaganda-lara-trump, last accessed 5 October 2017.

34. Siemaszko, Corky (2017). 'George W. Bush: Free Press "Indispensable to Democracy"', NBC News, 27 February 2017, https://www.nbcnews.com/news/us-news/george-w-bush-free-press-indispensable-democracy-n726141, last accessed 5 October 2017.

3. LOCK HER UP!

1. Nyaklyayew, Uladzimir (2015). Former presidential candidate and poet. Personal interview, 16 December 2015. Minsk, Belarus.

2. Statkevich, Mikalai (2015). Former presidential candidate. Personal interview, 17 December 2015, Minsk, Belarus.

3. O'Keefe, Ed (2017). 'Comey repeats that Lynch asked him to describe Clinton investigations as a "matter"', *The Washington Post*, 8 June 2017, https://www.washingtonpost.com/politics/2017/live-updates/trump-white-house/james-comey-testimony-what-we-learn/comey-repeats-that-lynch-asked-him-to-describe-clinton-investigations-as-a-matter/?utm_term=.19388addf6cd, last accessed 5 October 2017.

4. Comey is, of course, accused by supporters of Hillary Clinton of sabotaging her campaign with the letter he wrote in late October, just days

before the presidential election. There is evidence that it drastically affected the election. My point here is not to say that Comey handled the case perfectly, but rather to say that he was clearly aware of how politically sensitive the investigation was, and at least aimed to make clear that the investigation was not affected by political interference.

5. Rhodan, Maya (2016). 'Read FBI Director James Comey's Speech on the Hillary Clinton Email Probe', *TIME*, 5 July 2016, http://time.com/4393372/james-comey-fbi-hillary-clinton-email-speech-transcript/, last accessed 5 October 2017.

6. Smith, David (2017). 'White House begins investigation into use of private email accounts—reports', *The Guardian*, 29 September 2017, https://www.theguardian.com/us-news/2017/sep/29/white-house-investigation-private-email-accounts?utm_source=esp&utm_medium=Email&utm_campaign=GU+Today+main+NEW+H+categories&utm_term=245704&subid=15949854&CMP=EMCNEWEML6619I2, last accessed 5 October 2017.

7. Phelps, Jordyn (2016). 'Chris Christie Stages Raucous Mock Trial of Hillary Clinton at Convention', ABC News, 19 July 2016, http://abcnews.go.com/Politics/chris-christie-stages-raucous-mock-trial-hillary-clinton/story?id=40717891, last accessed 5 October 2017.

8. Kaufman, Ellie, Eric Levenson and Sarah Jorgensen (2017). 'Bridgegate scandal: Ex-Christie allies sentenced to prison time', CNN, 30 March 2017, http://edition.cnn.com/2017/03/29/us/bridgegate-sentencing/index.html, last accessed 5 October 2017.

9. Valencia, Robert (2017). 'Russia Probe: Manafort And Flynn Likely To Face Criminal Charges, Senator Says', *Newsweek*, 26 September 2017, http://www.newsweek.com/russia-probe-manafort-and-flynn-likely-face-criminal-charges-senator-says-672038, last accessed 5 October 2017.

10. Lynch, David J. and Courtney Weaver (2017). 'Sessions distances himself from Trump rhetoric', *Financial Times*, 11 January 2017, https://www.ft.com/content/9dd49cf8-d742-11e6-944b-e7eb37a6aa8e, last accessed 5 October 2017; Swaine, Jon (2017). 'The key points from Jeff Sessions' confirmation hearing', *The Guardian*, 10 January 2017, https://

www.theguardian.com/us-news/2017/jan/10/jeff-sessions-attorney-general-confirmation-hearing-news, last accessed 5 October 2017.

11. YouGov poll (2016). 'Presidential debate poll', 10–12 October 2016, available at https://d25d2506sfb94s.cloudfront.net/cumulus_uploads/document/xoxwe4phmo/tabs_OP_Presidential_Debate_20161012.pdf, last accessed 5 October 2017.

12. Leigh Cowan, Alison (2001). 'Plotting A Pardon; Rich Cashed In A World Of Chits To Win Pardon', *The New York Times*, 11 April 2001, http://www.nytimes.com/2001/04/11/us/plotting-a-pardon-rich-cashed-in-a-world-of-chits-to-win-pardon.html?pagewanted=all&src=pm, last accessed 5 October 2017.

13. Tweet by Joe Arpaio (@realsheriffjoe), 28 June 2013, https://twitter.com/RealSheriffJoe/status/350777000698462208, last accessed 5 October 2017.

14. Fernandez, Valeria (2017). 'Arizona's "concentration camp": why was Tent City kept open for 24 years?', *The Guardian*, 21 August 2017, https://www.theguardian.com/cities/2017/aug/21/arizona-phoenix-concentration-camp-tent-city-jail-joe-arpaio-immigration, last accessed 5 October 2017.

15. Lacey, Michael (2015). 'Prisoners Hang Themselves in Sheriff Joe Arpaio's Jails at a Rate That Dwarfs Other County Lockups', *Phoenix New Times*, 24 November 2015, http://www.phoenixnewtimes.com/news/prisoners-hang-themselves-in-sheriff-joe-arpaios-jails-at-a-rate-that-dwarfs-other-county-lockups-7845679, last accessed 5 October 2017.

16. Ibid.

17. Phippen, J. Weston (2016). 'The Last of the Birthers', *The Atlantic*, 15 December 2016, https://www.theatlantic.com/news/archive/2016/12/sheriff-joe-arpaio-the-birther/510857/, last accessed 5 October 2017.

18. Friedersdorf, Conor (2017). 'The Arpaio Pardon Is a Flagrant Assault on Civil Rights', *The Atlantic*, 26 August 2017, https://www.theatlantic.com/politics/archive/2017/08/a-flagrant-assault-on-latino-civil-rights/538119/, last accessed 5 October 2017.

19. Lacey, Marc (2011). 'U.S. Finds Pervasive Bias Against Latinos by Arizona Sheriff', *The New York Times*, 15 December 2011, http://www.

nytimes.com/2011/12/16/us/arizona-sheriffs-office-unfairly-targeted-latinos-justice-department-says.html?mcubz=1, last accessed 5 October 2017.

20. Peralta, Eyder (2012). 'Sheriff Arpaio Sends Publicly Funded Deputy to Hawaii on "Birther Hunt"', NPR, 22 May 2012, http://www.npr.org/sections/thetwo-way/2012/05/22/153313783/sheriff-arpaio-sends-publicly-funded-deputy-to-hawaii-on-birther-hunt, last accessed 27 September 2017.

21. Reilly, Mollie (2016). 'There's Still No Evidence That Trump Sent Investigators to Hawaii To Dig Up Dirt On Obama', *Huffington Post*, 16 September 2016, http://www.huffingtonpost.com/entry/donald-trump-hawaii-investigators_us_57dc3bffe4b04a1497b46da1, last accessed 27 September 2017.

22. Lemons, Stephen (2010). 'Joe Arpaio: Tent City a "Concentration Camp"', *Phoenix New Times*, 2 August 2010, http://www.phoenixnewtimes.com/news/joe-arpaio-tent-city-a-concentration-camp-6500984, last accessed 5 October 2017.

23. Nazaryan, Alexander (2017). 'Donald Trump and Joe Arpaio: A Bromance Forged in Birtherism and Xenophobia', *Newsweek*, 28 August 2017, http://www.newsweek.com/trump-arpaio-pardon-arizona-maricopa-immigration-655995, last accessed 5 October 2017.

24. Pérez-Peña, Richard (2017). 'Former Arizona Sheriff Joe Arpaio Is Convicted of Criminal Contempt', *The New York Times*, 31 July 2017, https://www.nytimes.com/2017/07/31/us/sheriff-joe-arpaio-convicted-arizona.html?mcubz=1, last accessed 5 October 2017.

25. Haberman, Maggie (2017). 'Trump Asked Top Aides Months Ago if Arpaio Case Could Be Dropped, Officials Say', *The New York Times*, 26 August 2017, https://www.nytimes.com/2017/08/26/us/politics/political-reaction-trump-pardon-arpaio.html?mcubz=1, last accessed 5 October 2017.

26. Fox News (2017). 'Joe Arpaio: If they can go after me, they can go after anyone', 23 August 2017, http://www.foxnews.com/transcript/2017/08/23/joe-arpaio-if-can-go-after-me-can-go-after-anyone.html, last accessed 5 October 2017.

4. FROM RUSSIA WITH LOVE

1. Arango, Tim (2013). 'Corruption Scandal Is Edging Near Turkish Premier', *The New York Times*, 25 December 2013, http://www.nytimes.com/2013/12/26/world/europe/turkish-cabinet-members-resign.html?mcubz=1, last accessed 1 October 2017.

2. Orucoglu, Berivan (2015). 'Why Turkey's Mother of All Corruption Scandals Refuses to Go Away', *Foreign Policy*, 6 January 2015, http://foreignpolicy.com/2015/01/06/why-turkeys-mother-of-all-corruption-scandals-refuses-to-go-away/, last accessed 1 October 2017.

3. Sherlock, Ruth (2014). 'Turkey continues with huge purge of judges and police', *The Telegraph*, 22 January 2014, http://www.telegraph.co.uk/news/worldnews/europe/turkey/10590399/Turkey-continues-with-huge-purge-of-judges-and-police.html, last accessed 1 October 2017.

4. Barkey, Henry J. (2013). 'Icarus and Erdogan's corruption scandal', *Foreign Policy*, 27 December 2013, http://foreignpolicy.com/2013/12/27/icarus-and-erdogans-corruption-scandal/, last accessed 1 October 2017.

5. Nixon, Richard (1973). 'Statement about the Watergate Investigation', 22 May 1973. Available from the University of California Santa Barbara American Presidency Project, http://www.presidency.ucsb.edu/ws/?pid=3855, last accessed 1 October 2017.

6. Woodward, Bob and Carl Bernstein (1973). 'Nixon Sees 'Witch-Hunt,' Insiders Say', *The Washington Post*, 22 July 1973.

7. Olson, K.W., & Holland, M. (2003). *Watergate: the presidential scandal that shook America*. Lawrence, KS: University Press of Kansas.

8. There are hundreds of news stories about these conclusions by the US intelligence community. At the time of writing (October 2017), no US intelligence official has publicly disagreed with this assessment.

9. Berenson, Tessa (2017). 'Was Donald Trump Jr.'s Russia Meeting Illegal? Here's What Experts Say', *TIME*, 12 July 2017, http://time.com/4854592/donald-trump-jr-russia-email-laws/, last accessed 1 October 2017.

10. Bertrand, Natasha (2017). '"Help world peace and make a lot of money": Here's the letter of intent to build a Trump Tower Moscow', *Business*

Insider, 8 September 2017, http://uk.businessinsider.com/trump-tower-moscow-letter-of-intent-2017–9, last accessed 1 October 2017.

11. Borger, Gloria and Marshall Cohen (2017). 'Document details scrapped deal for Trump Tower Moscow', CNN, 9 September 2017, http://edition.cnn.com/2017/09/08/politics/document-trump-tower-moscow/index.html, last accessed 1 October 2017.

12. Apuzzo, Matt and Maggie Haberman (2017). 'Trump Associate Boasted That Moscow Business Deal "Will Get Donald Elected"', *The New York Times*, 28 August 2017, https://www.nytimes.com/2017/08/28/us/politics/trump-tower-putin-felix-sater.html?mcubz=1&_r=0, last accessed 1 October 2017.

13. Graham, David A. (2017). 'Trump's Business Dealings Come Back to Haunt Him', *The Atlantic*, 29 August 2017, https://www.theatlantic.com/politics/archive/2017/08/trumps-business-gets-him-in-trouble/538341/, last accessed 1 October 2017.

14. Dilanian, Ken (2017). 'Russians Paid Mike Flynn $45K for Moscow Speech, Documents Show', NBC News, 16 March 2017, https://www.nbcnews.com/news/us-news/russians-paid-mike-flynn-45k-moscow-speech-documents-show-n734506, last accessed 1 October 2017.

15. Windrem, Robert (2017). 'Guess Who Came to Dinner With Flynn and Putin', NBC News, 18 April 2017, https://www.nbcnews.com/news/world/guess-who-came-dinner-flynn-putin-n742696, last accessed 1 October 2017.

16. Arkin, Daniel (2017). 'Michael Flynn initially failed to disclose payments from Russia-linked firms, documents show', CNBC, 2 April 2017, https://www.cnbc.com/2017/04/02/michael-flynn-initially-failed-to-disclose-payments-from-russia-linked-firms-documents-show.html, last accessed 1 October 2017.

17. Landay, Jonathan and Arshad Mohammed (2017). 'Trump adviser had five calls with Russian envoy on day of sanctions: sources', Reuters, 13 January 2017, https://www.reuters.com/article/us-usa-trump-russia/trump-adviser-had-five-calls-with-russian-envoy-on-day-of-sanctions-sources-idUSKBN14X1YX, last accessed 1 October 2017.

18. 'Team Trump: Flynn called Russia ambassador, no sanction talk "plain and simple"', Fox News, 14 January 2017, http://www.foxnews.com/

politics/2017/01/14/team-trump-flynn-called-russia-ambassador-no-sanction-talk-plain-and-simple.html, last accessed 1 October 2017.

19. Miller, Greg, Adam Entous and Ellen Nakashima (2017). 'National security adviser Flynn discussed sanctions with Russian ambassador, despite denials, officials say', *The Washington Post*, 9 February 2017, https://www.washingtonpost.com/world/national-security/national-security-adviser-flynn-discussed-sanctions-with-russian-ambassador-despite-denials-officials-say/2017/02/09/f85b29d6-ee11–11e6-b4ff-ac2cf509efe5_story.html?utm_term=.8cf22e075ad5, last accessed 1 October 2017; Lizza, Ryan (2017). 'Could Michael Flynn Turn on Trump?', *The New Yorker*, 31 March 2017, https://www.newyorker.com/news/ryan-lizza/could-michael-flynn-turn-on-trump, last accessed 1 October 2017.

20. Sevastopulo, Demetri (2017). 'Trump was warned twice on risk of Russia blackmailing Flynn', *Financial Times*, 9 May 2017, https://www.ft.com/content/8880e674–3433–11e7–99bd-13beb0903fa3, last accessed 1 October 2017.

21. Graham, David (2016). 'The Manafort Dossier', *The Atlantic*, 15 August 2016, https://www.theatlantic.com/politics/archive/2016/08/the-manafort-dossier/495851/, last accessed 1 October 2017.

22. Burns, Alexander and Maggie Haberman (2016). 'Donald Trump Hires Paul Manafort to Lead Delegate Effort', *The New York Times*, 28 March 2016, https://www.nytimes.com/politics/first-draft/2016/03/28/donald-trump-hires-paul-manafort-to-lead-delegate-effort/?mcubz=1, last accessed 1 October 2017.

23. Kramer, Andrew E., Mike McIntire, and Barry Meier (2016). 'Secret Ledger in Ukraine Lists Cash for Donald Trump's Campaign Chief', *The New York Times*, 14 August 2016, https://www.nytimes.com/2016/08/15/us/politics/paul-manafort-ukraine-donald-trump.html?mcubz=1, last accessed 1 October 2017.

24. Horowitz, Jeff and Desmond Butler (2016). 'Manafort tied to undisclosed foreign lobbying', Associated Press, 17 August 2016, https://apnews.com/c01989a47ee5421593ba1b301ec07813, last accessed 1 October 2017.

25. Gillum, Jack and Chad Day (2017). 'Manafort firm received Ukraine

ledger payout', Associated Press, 12 April 2017, https://www.boston-globe.com/news/nation/2017/04/12/exclusive-manafort-firm-received-ukraine-ledger-payout/TK9zH4regQIYkvNY5qZzUJ/story.html, last accessed 1 October 2017.

26. Hennessey, Susan, Shannon Togawa Mercer, Benjamin Wittes (2017). 'The Latest Scoops from CNN and the New York Times', Lawfare, 18 September 2017, https://lawfareblog.com/latest-scoops-cnn-and-new-york-times-quick-and-dirty-analysis, last accessed 1 October 2017.

27. Kirsch, Noah (2017). 'Powerful Russian Partner Boasts Of Ongoing Access To Trump Family', Forbes, 20 March 2017, https://www.forbes.com/sites/noahkirsch/2017/03/20/russian-billionaire-family-trump-ties-ongoing/#7282745969b3, last accessed 1 October 2017.

28. Bertrand, Natasha (2017). 'A cover story and a 'green light': Trump Jr.'s meeting has all the signs of a Russian intelligence operation', Business Insider, 19 July 2017, http://uk.businessinsider.com/was-trump-jr-rus-sia-meeting-an-intelligence-operation-spies-2017–7?r=US&IR=T, last accessed 1 October 2017.

29. Donald Trump Jr. posted the e-mail exchange on Twitter directly. It is available from Alvarez, Priscilla and Elaine Godfrey (2017). 'Donald Trump Jr.'s Email Exchange With Rob Goldstone,' The Atlantic, 11 July 2017, https://www.theatlantic.com/politics/archive/2017/07/donald-trumps-jrs-email-exchange/533244/, last accessed 1 October 2017.

30. Bump, Phillip (2017). 'Why Donald Trump Jr.'s phone calls matter', The Washington Post, 8 September 2017, https://www.washingtonpost.com/news/politics/wp/2017/09/08/why-donald-trump-jr-s-phone-calls-matter/?utm_term=.6eda0f2f0556, last accessed 1 October 2017.

31. Khan, Shehab (2017). 'Donald Trump held press conference promising more dirt on Clinton hours after Donald Trump Jr's Russia emails', The Independent, 12 July 2017, http://www.independent.co.uk/news/world/americas/us-politics/donald-trump-jr-hillary-clinton-russia-email-press-conference-dirt-democratic-us-president-election-a7836826.html, last accessed 1 October 2017.

32. Tsvetkova, Maria and Jack Stubbs (2017). 'Exclusive—Moscow lawyer who met Trump Jr. had Russian spy agency as client', Reuters, 21 July 2017, https://uk.reuters.com/article/uk-usa-trump-russia-lawyer-exclu-

sive/exclusive-moscow-lawyer-who-met-trump-jr-had-russian-spy-agency-as-client-idUKKBN1A61MF, last accessed 2 October 2017.

33. Dilanian, Ken, Natasha Lebedva, and Hallie Jackson (2017). 'Former Soviet Counterintelligence Officer at Meeting With Donald Trump Jr. and Russian Lawyer', NBC News, 14 July 2017, https://www.nbcnews.com/news/us-news/russian-lawyer-brought-ex-soviet-counter-intelligence-officer-trump-team-n782851, last accessed 1 October 2017.

34. Smith, Allan (2017). 'Russian-American lobbyist says Russian lawyer presented documents in Trump Jr. meeting', Business Insider, 14 July 2017, http://uk.businessinsider.com/rinat-akhmetshin-trump-jr-meeting-russia-documents-2017–7, last accessed 1 October 2017.

35. Berenson (2017).

36. Bennett, John (2017). 'Was President at Trump Tower When Son Met Russian Lawyer?', Roll Call, 14 July 2017, https://www.rollcall.com/politics/president-trump-tower-son-met-russian-lawyer, last accessed 1 October 2017.

37. Bertrand (2017).

38. Bump, Phillip (2017). 'What happened and when: The timeline leading up to Donald Trump Jr.'s fateful meeting', The Washington Post, 11 July 2017, https://www.washingtonpost.com/news/politics/wp/2017/07/11/what-happened-and-when-the-timeline-leading-up-to-donald-trump-jr-s-fateful-meeting/?utm_term=.8e5d02e5e5aa, last accessed 1 October 2017.

39. Keneally, Michael (2017). 'Ex-Trump campaign manager Paul Manafort told ABC News in July that alleged Russia ties were 'absurd'', ABC News, 22 March 2017, http://abcnews.go.com/Politics/trump-campaign-manager-paul-manafort-called-questions-alleged/story?id=46298966, last accessed 1 October 2017.

40. Lizza, Ryan (2017). 'Donald Trump Jr.'s e-mails have fundamentally changed the Russia story', The New Yorker, 11 July 2017, https://www.newyorker.com/news/ryan-lizza/the-trump-teams-crumbling-russia-defense, last accessed 1 October 2017.

41. Holpuch, Amanda (2017). 'Timeline: Trump and associates denied Russia involvement at least 20 times', The Guardian, 11 July 2017,

https://www.theguardian.com/us-news/2017/jul/11/donald-trump-russia-timeline-campaign-denials, last accessed 1 October 2017.

42. Lind, Dara (2017). 'Donald Trump Jr.'s ever-shifting excuses on Russia: a clear timeline', *Vox*, 11 July 2017, https://www.vox.com/policy-and-politics/2017/7/11/15954012/trump-jr-emails-russia, last accessed 1 October 2017.

43. Becker, Jo, Matt Apuzzo, and Adam Goldman (2017). 'Trump's Son Met With Russian Lawyer After Being Promised Damaging Information on Clinton', *The New York Times*, 9 July 2017, https://www.nytimes.com/2017/07/09/us/politics/trump-russia-kushner-manafort.html?mcubz=1, last accessed 1 October 2017.

44. Apuzzo, Matt, Jo Becker, Adam Goldman, and Maggie Haberman (2017). 'Trump Jr. Was Told in Email of Russian Effort to Aid Campaign', *The New York Times*, 10 July 2017, https://www.nytimes.com/2017/07/10/us/politics/donald-trump-jr-russia-email-candidacy.html?mcubz=1, last accessed 1 October 2017.

45. Harding, Luke, Stephanie Kirchgaessner, and Nick Hopkins (2017). 'British spies were first to spot Trump team's links with Russia', *The Guardian*, 13 April 2017, https://www.theguardian.com/uk-news/2017/apr/13/british-spies-first-to-spot-trump-team-links-russia, last accessed 1 October 2017.

46. *The Washington Post* (2016). 'A transcript of Donald Trump's meeting with The Washington Post editorial board', 21 March 2016, https://www.washingtonpost.com/blogs/post-partisan/wp/2016/03/21/a-transcript-of-donald-trumps-meeting-with-the-washington-post-editorial-board/?utm_term=.df50caf1c53e, last accessed 1 October 2017.

47. Hamburger, Tom, Carol D. Leonnig, and Rosalind S. Helderman (2017). 'Trump campaign emails show aide's repeated efforts to set up Russia meetings', *The Washington Post*, 14 August 2017, https://www.washingtonpost.com/politics/trump-campaign-emails-show-aides-repeated-efforts-to-set-up-russia-meetings/2017/08/14/54d08da6–7dc2–11e7–83c7–5bd5460f0d7e_story.html?utm_term=.1b1c8236ce40, last accessed 1 October 2017.

48. Green, Mirand and Manu Raju (2017). 'FBI monitored former Trump campaign adviser Carter Page on Russia', CNN, 12 April 2017, http://

edition.cnn.com/2017/04/12/politics/fbi-carter-page-russia/index.html, last accessed 1 October 2017.

49. See Title I of the Foreign Intelligence Surveillance Act (1978).

50. Meyer, Josh and Kenneth P. Vogel (2017). 'Trump campaign approved adviser's trip to Moscow', *Politico*, 7 March 2017, http://www.politico.com/story/2017/03/carter-page-russia-trip-trump-corey-lewandowski-235784, last accessed 1 October 2017; Sherlock, Ruth (2016). 'Donald Trump aide slams America's policy on Russia during speech in Moscow', *The Telegraph*, 8 July 2016, http://www.telegraph.co.uk/news/2016/07/08/donald-trumps-adviser-slams-american-policy-on-russia-during-spe/, last accessed 2 October 2017.

51. Meyer, Josh (2017). 'Former Trump adviser Carter Page also met with Russian envoy', *Politico*, 2 March 2017, http://www.politico.com/story/2017/03/carter-page-russian-ambassador-meeting-235626, last accessed 1 October 2017.

52. Zapotosky, Matt, Sari Horwitz, Devlin Barrett and Adam Entous (2017). 'Jared Kushner now a focus in Russia investigation', *The Washington Post*, 25 May 2017, https://www.washingtonpost.com/world/national-security/jared-kushner-now-a-focus-in-russia-investigation/2017/05/25/f078db74–40c7–11e7–8c25–44d09ff5a4a8_story.html?utm_term=.03dd32fa54fb, last accessed 1 October 2017.

53. Sanger, David E. and Eric Schmitt (2016). 'Spy Agency Consensus Grows That Russia Hacked D.N.C.', *The New York Times*, 26 July 2016, https://www.nytimes.com/2016/07/27/us/politics/spy-agency-consensus-grows-that-russia-hacked-dnc.html, last accessed 2 October 2017.

54. Entous, Adam, Ellen Nakashima and Greg Miller (2017). 'Sessions met with Russian envoy twice last year, encounters he later did not disclose', *The Washington Post*, 1 March 2017, https://www.washingtonpost.com/world/national-security/sessions-spoke-twice-with-russian-ambassador-during-trumps-presidential-campaign-justice-officials-say/2017/03/01/77205eda-feac-11e6–99b4–9e613afeb09f_story.html?utm_term=.4b15a4e5617a, last accessed 1 October 2017; Guccifer 2.0 (2016). 'New DNC Docs', Guccifer 2.0 website, 14 July 2016, https://guccifer2.wordpress.com/2016/07/14/new-dnc-docs/, last accessed 2 October 2017.

55. Bendix, Aria and Adam Serwer (2017). 'Sessions Discussed Campaign Matters With Russian Ambassador', *The Atlantic*, 21 July 2017, https://www.theatlantic.com/politics/archive/2017/07/sessions-discussed-campaign-matters-with-russian-ambassador/534579/, last accessed 1 October 2017.

56. Estepa, Jessica (2017). 'What did Al Franken ask Jeff Sessions during his confirmation hearing?', *USA Today*, 13 June 2017, https://www.usatoday.com/story/news/politics/onpolitics/2017/06/13/what-did-al-franken-ask-jeff-sessions-during-his-confirmation-hearing/102819246/, last accessed 1 October 2017.

57. Entous, Adam (2017). 'House majority leader to colleagues in 2016: "I think Putin pays" Trump', *The Washington Post*, 17 May 2017, https://www.washingtonpost.com/world/national-security/house-majority-leader-to-colleagues-in-2016-i-think-putin-pays-trump/2017/05/17/515f6f8a-3aff-11e7–8854–21f359183e8c_story.html?utm_term=.ab4aff443fa1, last accessed 1 October 2017.

58. Naylor, Brian (2016). 'How The Trump Campaign Weakened The Republican Platform On Aid To Ukraine', National Public Radio, 6 August 2016, http://www.npr.org/2016/08/06/488876597/how-the-trump-campaign-weakened-the-republican-platform-on-aid-to-ukraine, last accessed 1 October 2017.

59. Parker, Ashley and David E. Sanger (2016). 'Donald Trump Calls on Russia to Find Hillary Clinton's Missing Emails', *The New York Times*, 27 July 2016, https://www.nytimes.com/2016/07/28/us/politics/donald-trump-russia-clinton-emails.html?mcubz=1, last accessed 1 October 2017.

60. Henton, George (2015). 'Thailand's Prime Minister Wants to Shut Down Media Outlets That Don't Praise the Government', *Vice News*, 6 April 2015, https://news.vice.com/article/thailands-prime-minister-wants-to-shut-down-media-outlets-that-dont-praise-the-government, last accessed 2 October 2017.

61. Kaczynski, Andrew, Nathan McDermott, and Chris Massie (2017). 'Trump adviser Roger Stone repeatedly claimed to know of forthcoming WikiLeaks dumps', CNN, 21 March 2017, http://edition.cnn.

com/2017/03/20/politics/kfile-roger-stone-wikileaks-claims/index. html, last accessed 1 October 2017.

62. Fahrenthold, David (2016). 'Trump recorded having extremely lewd conversation about women in 2005', *The Washington Post*, 8 October 2016, https://www.washingtonpost.com/politics/trump-recorded-having-extremely-lewd-conversation-about-women-in-2005/2016/10/07/3b9ce776–8cb4–11e6-bf8a-3d26847eeed4_story.html?utm_term=.10dec5f49711, last accessed 1 October 2017.

63. Marshall, Josh (2017). 'Look at the Timeline', *Talking Points Memo*, 11 July 2017, http://talkingpointsmemo.com/edblog/look-at-the-time-line, last accessed 1 October 2017.

64. Kaczynski, Andrew, Nathan McDermott, and Chris Massie (2017). 'Trump adviser Roger Stone repeatedly claimed to know of forthcoming WikiLeaks dumps', CNN, 21 March 2017, http://edition.cnn. com/2017/03/20/politics/kfile-roger-stone-wikileaks-claims/index. html, last accessed 2 October 2017.

65. Legum, Judd (2017). 'Trump mentioned Wikileaks 164 times in last month of election, now claims it didn't impact one voter', *ThinkProgress*, 8 January 2017, https://thinkprogress.org/trump-mentioned-wikileaks-164-times-in-last-month-of-election-now-claims-it-didnt-impact-one-40aa62ea5002/, last accessed 1 October 2017.

66. Bertrand, Natasha (2017). 'Jared Kushner gave a confusing explanation for his alleged 'back channel' plan with Russia', *Business Insider*, 24 July 2017, http://uk.businessinsider.com/jared-kushner-russia-back-channel-testimony-2017–7, last accessed 1 October 2017.

67. Winter, Tom and Robert Windrem (2017). 'Kushner Met With Russian Banker Who Is Putin Crony, Spy School Grad', NBC News, 27 May 2017, https://www.nbcnews.com/news/us-news/kushner-met-russian-banker-who-putin-crony-spy-school-grad-n765311, last accessed 1 October 2017.

68. Filipov, David, Amy Brittain, Rosalind S. Helderman and Tom Hamburger (2017). 'Explanations for Kushner's meeting with head of Kremlin-linked bank don't match up', *The Washington Post*, 1 June 2017, https://www.washingtonpost.com/politics/explanations-for-kushners-meeting-with-head-of-kremlin-linked-bank-dont-

match-up/2017/06/01/dd1bdbb0–460a-11e7-bcde-624ad94170ab_
story.html?utm_term=.90b6424dbf61, last accessed 1 October 2017.

69. Savransky, Rebecca (2017). 'Kushner updated disclosure to add more
than 100 foreign contacts: report', *The Hill*, 13 July 2017, http://the-
hill.com/homenews/administration/341844-kushner-updated-disclo-
sure-to-add-more-than-100-foreign-contacts, last accessed 1 October
2017.

70. Sitrin, Carly (2017). 'Kushner's lawyers say he mistakenly left meetings
with the Russians off his security forms twice', *Vox*, 14 July 2017,
https://www.vox.com/policy-and-politics/2017/7/14/15971508/kush-
ner-lawyers-russian-meetings-security-clearance-forms, last accessed
1 October 2017.

71. Reuters (2017). 'Comey says Trump told him, 'I need loyalty. I expect
loyalty', 7 June 2017, https://www.reuters.com/article/us-usa-trump-
russia-comey-loyalty/comey-says-trump-told-him-i-need-loyalty-i-
expect-loyalty-idUSKBN18Y2QJ, last accessed 1 October 2017.

72. Schmidt, Michael (2017). 'Comey Memo Says Trump Asked Him to
End Flynn Investigation', *The New York Times*, 16 May 2017, https://
www.nytimes.com/2017/05/16/us/politics/james-comey-trump-flynn-
russia-investigation.html?mcubz=1, last accessed 1 October 2017.

73. Chong, Jane (2017). 'The Bogus Memos of the Trump Administration',
The New Yorker, 20 May 2017, https://www.newyorker.com/news/
news-desk/the-bogus-memos-of-the-trump-administration, last
accessed 1 October 2017.

74. CNN (2017). 'Partial transcript: NBC News interview with Donald
Trump', 11 May 2017, http://edition.cnn.com/2017/05/11/politics/tran-
script-donald-trump-nbc-news/index.html, last accessed 4 October
2017.

75. Baker, Peter (2017). 'Trump Was Involved in Drafting Son's Statement,
Aide Confirms', *The New York Times*, 1 August 2017, https://www.
nytimes.com/2017/08/01/us/politics/trump-was-involved-in-drafting-
sons-statement-aide-confirms.html?mcubz=1, last accessed 1 October
2017.

76. See Phillips, Amber (2017). 'Why is Trump surprised Jeff Sessions
recused himself from the Russia investigation?', *The Washington Post*,

19 July 2017, https://www.washingtonpost.com/news/the-fix/wp/2017/07/19/wait-why-is-trump-surprised-jeff-sessions-recused-himself-from-the-russia-investigation/?utm_term=.b991219bbf64, last accessed 1 October 2017.

77. Baker, Peter, Michael Schmidt, and Maggie Haberman (2017). 'Citing Recusal, Trump Says He Wouldn't Have Hired Sessions', *The New York Times*, 19 July 2017, https://www.nytimes.com/2017/07/19/us/politics/trump-interview-sessions-russia.html?mcubz=1, last accessed 1 October 2017.

78. Parker, Ashley (2017). 'Trump claims to be victim of 'witch hunt' following appointment of special counsel in Russia case', *The Washington Post*, 18 May 2017, https://www.washingtonpost.com/news/post-politics/wp/2017/05/18/trump-claims-to-be-victim-of-witch-hunt-following-appointment-of-special-counsel-in-russia-case/?utm_term=.4ea8f397ae8a, last accessed 1 October 2017.

5. HOW TO RIG AN ELECTION

1. Gallup (2017). 'Presidential job approval center.' Data available from: http://news.gallup.com/interactives/185273/presidential-job-approval-center.aspx, last accessed 5 October 2017.

2. Fisher, Max (2013). 'Oops: Azerbaijan Released Election Results Before Voting Had Even Started', *The Washington Post*, 5 March 2010, https://www.washingtonpost.com/news/worldviews/wp/2013/10/09/oops-azerbaijan-released-election-results-before-voting-had-even-started/?utm_term=.07771cf02ba8, last accessed 27 September 2017.

3. Associated Press (2004). 'Invisible ink: how they rigged the vote', republished in *The Sydney Morning Herald*, 2 December 2004, http://www.smh.com.au/news/World/Invisible-ink-how-they-rigged-the-vote/2004/12/02/1101923247133.html, last accessed 5 October 2017.

4. Whitmore, Brian (1998). 'St. Pete Poll Plays Double Jeopardy', *The Moscow Times*, 6 October 1998, http://old.themoscowtimes.com/sitemap/free/1998/10/article/st-pete-poll-plays-double-jeopardy/284395.html/, last accessed 5 October 2017.

5. Onion, Rebecca (2013). 'Take the Impossible "Literacy" Test Louisiana

Gave Black Voters in the 1960s', *Slate*, 28 June 2013, http://www.slate.com/blogs/the_vault/2013/06/28/voting_rights_and_the_supreme_court_the_impossible_literacy_test_louisiana.html, last accessed 5 October 2017.

6. Crozier, Michel, Samuel P. Huntington, and Joji Watanuki (1975). *The crisis of democracy. Vol. 70.* New York: New York University Press, 1975.

7. Koranda, Jeannine (2010). 'Dead folks voting? At least one's still alive', *The Wichita Eagle*, 29 October 2010, http://www.kansas.com/news/politics-government/election/article1046914.html, last accessed 5 October 2017.

8. Office of the Governor of Kansas (2011). 'Governor Signs Voter ID Bill', press release, 18 April 2011, available from https://governor.kansas.gov/04–18–11-governor-signs-voter-id-bill/, last accessed 5 October 2017.

9. Berman, Ari (2017). 'The Man Behind Trump's Voter-Fraud Obsession', *The New York Times Magazine*, 13 June 2017, https://www.nytimes.com/2017/06/13/magazine/the-man-behind-trumps-voter-fraud-obsession.html?mcubz=1, last accessed 5 October 2017.

10. Ibid.

11. Goel, Sharad et al (2016). 'One Person, One Vote: Estimating the Prevalence of Double Voting in U.S. Presidential Elections', working paper, available from: https://5harad.com/papers/1person-1vote.pdf, last accessed 5 October 2017.

12. Hegeman, Roxana (2017). 'Uncounted Kansas ballots fuel fears about Kobach's proposals', *Kiro7*, 23 August 2017, http://www.kiro7.com/news/uncounted-kansas-ballots-fuel-fears-about-kobachs-proposals/596788663, last accessed 5 October 2017.

13. Ryan, Josiah (2017). 'Trump-cited study author (still) refuses to show proof of voter fraud', CNN, 28 January 2017, http://edition.cnn.com/2017/01/27/politics/gregg-phillips-voter-fraud-donald-trump-cnntv/index.html, last accessed 5 October 2017.

14. Burke, Garance (2017). 'Trump's voter fraud expert registered in 3 states', Associated Press, 31 January 2017, https://apnews.com/80497cfb5f054c9b8c9e0f8f5ca30a62, last accessed 5 October 2017.

15. Richman, Jesse and David Earnest (2014). 'Could non-citizens decide

the November election?', *The Washington Post*, Monkey Cage blog, 24 October 2014, https://www.washingtonpost.com/news/monkey-cage/wp/2014/10/24/could-non-citizens-decide-the-november-election/?utm_term=.f69ba3ad1017, last accessed 5 October 2017.

16. See Tesler, Michael (2014). 'Methodological challenges affect study of non-citizens' voting', *The Washington Post*, Monkey Cage blog, 27 October 2014, https://www.washingtonpost.com/news/monkey-cage/wp/2014/10/27/methodological-challenges-affect-study-of-non-citizens-voting/?utm_term=.ea92b932951a, last accessed 5 October 2017. Petition is discussed in Eaton, Joshua (2017). 'The "farcical" stats Republicans use to claim millions voted illegally', *ThinkProgress*, 7 April 2017, https://thinkprogress.org/exclusive-the-farcical-stats-republicans-use-to-claim-millions-voted-illegally-f7866eda9f0c/, last accessed 5 October 2017.

17. A full summary of all major studies on voter fraud is available from Brennan Center for Justice (2017). 'Debunking the Voter Fraud Myth', 31 January 2017, https://www.brennancenter.org/analysis/debunking-voter-fraud-myth, last accessed 5 October 2017.

18. Bump, Phillip (2016). 'There have been just four documented cases of voter fraud in the 2016 election', *The Washington Post*, 1 December 2016, https://www.washingtonpost.com/news/the-fix/wp/2016/12/01/0-000002-percent-of-all-the-ballots-cast-in-the-2016-election-were-fraudulent/?utm_term=.90cf2df64879, last accessed 5 October 2017.

19. North Carolina State Board of Elections (2017). 'Post-Election Audit Report', 21 April 2017, https://s3.amazonaws.com/dl.ncsbe.gov/sboe/Post-Election%20Audit%20Report_2016%20General%20Election/Post-Election_Audit_Report.pdf, last accessed 5 October 2017.

20. Levitt, Justin (2014). 'A comprehensive investigation of voter impersonation finds 31 credible incidents out of one billion ballots cast', *The Washington Post*, 6 August 2014, https://www.washingtonpost.com/news/wonk/wp/2014/08/06/a-comprehensive-investigation-of-voter-impersonation-finds-31-credible-incidents-out-of-one-billion-ballots-cast/?utm_term=.c8a1a8351528, last accessed 5 October 2017.

21. Brennan Center for Justice (2017); Lipton, Eric and Ian Urbina (2007).

'In 5-Year Effort, Scant Evidence of Voter Fraud', *The New York Times*, 12 April 2007, http://www.nytimes.com/2007/04/12/washington/12fraud.html?mcubz=1, last accessed 5 October 2017.

22. Strauss, Daniel (2016). 'Trump camp moves to block Michigan recount', *Politico*, 1 December 2016, http://www.politico.com/story/2016/12/donald-trump-michigan-recount-blocked-232076, last accessed 5 October 2017.

23. May, Patrick (2017). 'Trump says illegal votes cost him California. Here's why that's preposterous', *The Mercury News*, 26 January 2017, http://www.mercurynews.com/2017/01/26/trump-says-illegal-votes-cost-him-california-heres-why-thats-preposterous/, last accessed 5 October 2017.

24. Savransky, Rebecca (2017). 'Klobuchar To Commission On Election Integrity: Go Jump in a Lake', *The Hill*, 3 July 2017, http://thehill.com/homenews/senate/340540-klobuchar-to-commission-on-election-integrity-go-jump-in-a-lake, last accessed 5 October 2017.

25. Brennan Center for Justice at New York University School of Law (2017). 'Voting Laws Roundup 2017', 10 May 2017, https://www.brennancenter.org/analysis/voting-laws-roundup-2017, last accessed 28 September 2017.

26. Shephard, Steven (2017). 'Poll: Half of Trump voters say Trump won popular vote', *Politico*, 26 July 2017, http://www.politico.com/story/2017/07/26/trump-clinton-popular-vote-240966, last accessed 5 October 2017.

27. Morning Consult/*Politico* (2017). 'National Tracking Poll', 26–28 January 2017, http://www.politico.com/f/?id=00000159-f6e7-da98-a77d-f6f7cba90001, last accessed 5 October 2017.

28. Shackelford, Scott et al. (2016). 'Making Democracy Harder to Hack', *U. Mich. Journal of Law Reform*, 50(3).

29. Ward, Alex (2017). 'Russia hacked voting systems in 39 states before the 2016 presidential election', *Vox*, 13 June 2017, https://www.vox.com/world/2017/6/13/15791744/russia-election-39-states-hack-putin-trump-sessions, last accessed 28 September 2017.

30. Gambino, Laren and Sabrina Siddiqui (2016). 'Obama expels 35 Russian diplomats in retaliation for US election hacking', *The Guardian*,

30 December 2016, https://www.theguardian.com/us-news/2016/dec/29/barack-obama-sanctions-russia-election-hack, last accessed 5 October 2017.

31. Isikoff, Michael (2017). 'How the Trump administration's secret efforts to ease Russia sanctions fell short', Yahoo News, 2 June 2017, https://www.yahoo.com/news/trump-administrations-secret-efforts-ease-russia-sanctions-fell-short-231301145.html, last accessed 5 October 2017.

32. Blake, Andrews (2017). 'White House considers returning diplomatic compounds to Russia', *The Washington Times*, 1 June 2017, http://www.washingtontimes.com/news/2017/jun/1/white-house-considers-returning-diplomatic-compoun/, last accessed 5 October 2017.

33. Little, Becky (2017). 'America and Russia Have Been Expelling One Another's Diplomats Since 1986', The History Channel, 31 July 2017, http://www.history.com/news/america-and-russia-have-been-expelling-one-anothers-diplomats-since-1986, last accessed 5 October 2017; and Risen, James and Jane Perlez (2001). 'Russian Diplomats Ordered Expelled In A Countermove', *The New York Times*, 22 March 2001, http://www.nytimes.com/2001/03/22/world/russian-diplomats-ordered-expelled-in-a-countermove.html?mcubz=1, last accessed 5 October 2017.

6. DIVIDE AND RULE

1. Associated Press (2003). 'Idi Amin, a Brutal Dictator Of Uganda, Is Dead at 80', *The New York Times*, 16 August 2003, http://www.nytimes.com/2003/08/16/world/idi-amin-a-brutal-dictator-of-uganda-is-dead-at-80.html?mcubz=1, last accessed 5 October 2017. last accessed 5 October 2017. "launchede of private email accounts—reports'the Internet

2. Post, Jerrold M (2014). 'Dreams of glory: Narcissism and politics', *Psychoanalytic Inquiry* 34(5), 475–85; O'Regan, Colm (2012). 'The rise of inflated job titles', BBC News, 17 July 2012, http://www.bbc.co.uk/news/magazine-18855099, last accessed 5 October 2017.

3. Keatley, Patrick (2003). 'Obituary: Idi Amin', *The Guardian*, 18 August 2003, https://www.theguardian.com/news/2003/aug/18/guardianobituaries, last accessed 5 October 2017.

4. Avirgan, T., & Honey, M. (1983). *War in Uganda: the legacy of Idi Amin*. Dar es Salaam: Tanzania Publishing House.

5. Griffin-Angus, Mariah (2012). 'The Torture Chambers That Spoil Uganda's 50th Birthday', *The Huffington Post*, 5 November 2012, http://www.huffingtonpost.ca/mariah-griffinangus/uganda_b_1857574.html, last accessed 5 October 2017.

6. World Bank (2017). 'GDP per capita (current US$)', https://data.worldbank.org/indicator/NY.GDP.PCAP.CD, last accessed 5 October 2017.

7. Dowden, Richard (1992). 'Short-sighted demagogue who played the race card: Idi Amin', *The Independent*, 4 August 1992, http://www.independent.co.uk/news/world/short-sighted-demagogue-who-played-the-race-card-idi-amin-expelled-the-asians-20-years-ago-richard-1538196.html, last accessed 5 October 2017.

8. Otunnu, Ogenga (2016). *Crisis of Legitimacy and Political Violence in Uganda, 1890 to 1979*. Cham, Switzerland: Springer International Publishing.

9. Kaplan, Morris (1973). 'Major Landlord Accused Of Antiblack Bias in City', *The New York Times*, 16 October 1973, http://www.nytimes.com/1973/10/16/archives/major-landlord-accused-of-antiblack-bias-in-city-us-accuses-major.html?mcubz=1&_r=0, last accessed 5 October 2017.

10. Laughland, Oliver (2016). 'Donald Trump and the Central Park Five: the racially charged rise of a demagogue', *The Guardian*, 17 February 2016, https://www.theguardian.com/us-news/2016/feb/17/central-park-five-donald-trump-jogger-rape-case-new-york, last accessed 5 October 2017.

11. Filipovic, Jill (2012). 'The painful lessons of the Central Park Five and the jogger rape case', *The Guardian*, 5 October 2012, https://www.theguardian.com/commentisfree/2012/oct/05/central-park-five-rape-case, last accessed 5 October 2017.

12. Burns, Sarah (2016). 'Why Trump Doubled Down on the Central Park Five', *The New York Times*, 17 October 2016, https://www.nytimes.com/2016/10/18/opinion/why-trump-doubled-down-on-the-central-park-five.html?mcubz=1&_r=0, last accessed 2 October 2017.

13. UPI (1992). 'Trump Plaza loses appeal of discrimination penalty', 19 October 1992.

14. Rayne, Naja (2016). 'Donald Trump Once Wanted to Make a Black Versus White Season of *The Apprentice*', *People*, 19 May 2016, http://people.com/celebrity/donald-trump-wanted-to-make-season-5-of-the-apprentice-fairly-controversial/, last accessed 5 October 2017.

15. Elliott, Justin (2011). 'Right-wing publisher: We run "some misinformation"', *Salon*, 11 April 2011, https://www.salon.com/2011/04/11/joseph_farah_wnd_misinformation/, last accessed 5 October 2017.

16. Rutz, Jim (2006). 'Soy is making kids "gay"', WorldNetDaily.com, 12 December 2006, http://www.wnd.com/2006/12/39253/, last accessed 5 October 2017.

17. Elliott (2011).

18. Parker, Ashley and Steve Eder (2016). 'Inside the Six Weeks Donald Trump was a Nonstop "Birther"', *The New York Times*, 2 July 2016, https://www.nytimes.com/2016/07/03/us/politics/donald-trump-birther-obama.html?mcubz=1, last accessed 5 October 2017.

19. Morales, Lymari (2011). 'Obama's Birth Certificate Convinces Some, but Not All, Skeptics', Gallup, 13 May 2011, http://news.gallup.com/poll/147530/obama-birth-certificate-convinces-not-skeptics.aspx, last accessed 5 October 2017.

20. Wheaton, Sarah (2008). 'Anti-Obama Author on 9/11 Conspiracy', *The New York Times*, 14 August 2008, https://thecaucus.blogs.nytimes.com/2008/08/14/anti-obama-author-on-911-conspiracy/?mcubz=1, last accessed 5 October 2017.

21. Corsi, Jerome R and Craig Smith (2005), *Black Gold Stranglehold*, Long Beach, California: WND Books.

22. Kludt, Tom (2017). 'Infowars taps Trump-friendly birther to lead Washington coverage', CNN, 31 January 2017, http://money.cnn.com/2017/01/31/media/infowars-jerome-corsi-washington-bureau-chief/index.html, last accessed 5 October 2017.

23. Krieg, Gregory (2016). '14 of Trump's most outrageous "birther" claims—half from after 2011', CNN, 16 September 2016, http://edition.cnn.com/2016/09/09/politics/donald-trump-birther/index.html, last accessed 5 October 2017.

24. Parker and Eder (2016).

25. Clinton, Josh and Carrie Roush (2016). 'Poll: Persistent Partisan Divide Over "Birther" Question', NBC News, 10 August 2016, https://www.nbcnews.com/politics/2016-election/poll-persistent-partisan-divide-over-birther-question-n627446, last accessed 5 October 2017.

26. Fahrenthold, David (2016). 'Trump recorded having extremely lewd conversation about women in 2005', *The Washington Post*, 8 October 2016, https://www.washingtonpost.com/politics/trump-recorded-having-extremely-lewd-conversation-about-women-in-2005/2016/10/07/3b9ce776–8cb4–11e6-bf8a-3d26847eeed4_story.html?utm_term=.ccf088a83eee, last accessed 5 October 2017.

27. Zong, Jie and Jeanne Batalova (2016). 'Mexican Immigrants in the United States', Migration Policy Institute, 17 March 2016, http://www.migrationpolicy.org/article/mexican-immigrants-united-states, last accessed 5 October 2017.

28. *The Washington Post* (2015). 'Full text: Donald Trump announces a presidential bid', 16 June 2015, https://www.washingtonpost.com/news/post-politics/wp/2015/06/16/full-text-donald-trump-announces-a-presidential-bid/?utm_term=.f6813a024dcb, last accessed 5 October 2017.

29. Johnson, Jenna (2015). 'Trump calls for "total and complete shutdown of Muslims entering the United States"', *The Washington Post*, 7 December 2015, https://www.washingtonpost.com/news/post-politics/wp/2015/12/07/donald-trump-calls-for-total-and-complete-shutdown-of-muslims-entering-the-united-states/?utm_term=.e4e78a2e9913, last accessed 5 October 2017.

30. Jake Tapper, 'State of the Union' show transcript, CNN, 28 February 2016, http://transcripts.cnn.com/TRANSCRIPTS/1602/28/sotu.01.html, last accessed 5 October 2017.

31. Qiu, Linda (2016). 'Donald Trump's absurd claim that he knows nothing about former KKK leader David Duke', *Politifact*, 2 March 2016, http://www.politifact.com/truth-o-meter/statements/2016/mar/02/donald-trump/trumps-absurd-claim-he-knows-nothing-about-former-mer-/, last accessed 5 October 2017.

32. *The Week* (2016). 'White nationalists praise Trump for going "full wink-

wink-wink'", 13 July 2016, http://theweek.com/speedreads/635678/white-nationalists-praise-trump-going-full-winkwinkwink, last accessed 5 October 2017.

33. Kopan, Tal (2016). 'Donald Trump retweets "White Genocide" Twitter user', CNN, 22 January 2016, http://edition.cnn.com/2016/01/22/politics/donald-trump-retweet-white-genocide/index.html, last accessed 5 October 2017.

34. Berger, JM (2016). 'How white nationalists learned to love Donald Trump', *Politico*, 26 October 2016, http://www.politico.eu/article/how-white-nationalists-learned-to-love-donald-trump/, last accessed 5 October 2017.

35. Ibid.; Holley, Peter (2016). 'Hear a white nationalist's robocall urging Iowa voters to back Trump', *The Washington Post*, 12 January 2016, https://www.washingtonpost.com/news/post-politics/wp/2016/01/12/why-this-leading-white-nationalist-is-urging-iowa-voters-to-back-donald-trump/?utm_term=.4d56747de23c, last accessed 5 October 2017.

36. Nguyen, Tina (2017). 'Steve Bannon has a Nazi problem', *Vanity Fair*, 12 September 2017, https://www.vanityfair.com/news/2017/09/steve-bannon-has-a-nazi-problem, last accessed 5 October 2017.

37. Silver, Nate (2016). 'The Mythology Of Trump's "Working Class" Support', *FiveThirtyEight*, 3 May 2016, https://fivethirtyeight.com/features/the-mythology-of-trumps-working-class-support/, last accessed 5 October 2017.

38. Ingraham, Christopher (2017). 'The entire coal industry employs fewer people than Arby's', *The Washington Post*, 31 March 2017, https://www.washingtonpost.com/news/wonk/wp/2017/03/31/8-surprisingly-small-industries-that-employ-more-people-than-coal/?utm_term=.0e1e838e0cd2, last accessed 5 October 2017.

39. Edison Research (2016). 'Exit Polls', available on CNN, 23 November 2016, http://edition.cnn.com/election/results/exit-polls, last accessed 5 October 2017.

40. Cox, Daniel, Rachel Lienesch and Robert P. Jones (2017). 'Beyond Economics: Fears of Cultural Displacement Pushed the White Working Class to Trump', PRRI/*The Atlantic* Report, 9 May 2017, https://www.prri.org/research/white-working-class-attitudes-economy-trade-immi-

gration-election-donald-trump/, last accessed 4 October 2017; Wood, Thomas (2017). 'Racism motivated Trump voters more than authoritarianism', *The Washington Post*, Monkey Cage blog, 17 April 2017, https://www.washingtonpost.com/news/monkey-cage/wp/2017/04/17/racism-motivated-trump-voters-more-than-authoritarianism-or-income-inequality/?utm_term=.03a2fcb8e4fa, last accessed 4 October 2017.

41. Fossett, Katelyn (2017). 'The Trouble with Trump's Immigrant Crimes List', *Politico*, 7 March 2017, http://www.politico.com/magazine/story/2017/03/donald-trump-immigrant-crimes-list-214878, last accessed 5 October 2017.

42. Pérez-Peña, Richard (2017). 'Contrary to Trump's Claims, Immigrants Are Less Likely to Commit Crimes', *The New York Times*, 26 January 2017, https://www.nytimes.com/2017/01/26/us/trump-illegal-immigrants-crime.html?mcubz=1, last accessed 5 October 2017.

43. Department of Homeland Security (2017). 'DHS Announces Launch of New Office for Victims of Illegal Immigrant Crime', press release, 26 April 2017, https://www.dhs.gov/news/2017/04/26/dhs-announces-launch-new-office-victims-illegal-immigrant-crime, last accessed 5 October 2017.

44. Sweeney, Don (2017). 'Trump critics troll his "criminal alien" crime hotline with reports of UFOs and aliens', *The Miami Herald*, 27 April 2017, http://www.miamiherald.com/news/nation-world/national/article147295794.html, last accessed 5 October 2017.

45. Wilts, Alexandra (2017). 'Donald Trump seemingly endorses police brutality', *The Independent*, 28 July 2017, http://www.independent.co.uk/news/world/americas/us-politics/donald-trump-long-island-brutality-police-suffolk-a7866071.html, last accessed 5 October 2017.

46. Ibid.

47. Fernandez, Manny (2015). 'Freddie Gray's Injury and the Police "Rough Ride"', *The New York Times*, 30 April 2015, https://www.nytimes.com/2015/05/01/us/freddie-grays-injury-and-the-police-rough-ride.html?mcubz=1, last accessed 5 October 2017.

48. Merica, Dan (2017). 'Trump condemns "hatred, bigotry and violence on many sides" in Charlottesville', CNN, 13 August 2017, http://edi-

tion.cnn.com/2017/08/12/politics/trump-statement-alt-right-protests/index.html, last accessed 5 October 2017.

49. Gray, Rosie (2017). 'Trump Defends White-Nationalist Protesters: "Some Very Fine People on Both Sides"', *The Atlantic*, 15 August 2017, https://www.theatlantic.com/politics/archive/2017/08/trump-defends-white-nationalist-protesters-some-very-fine-people-on-both-sides/537012/, last accessed 5 October 2017.

50. Lopez, German (2017). 'We need to stop acting like Trump isn't pandering to white supremacists', *Vox*, 14 August 2017, https://www.vox.com/policy-and-politics/2017/8/13/16140504/trump-charlottesville-white-supremacists, last accessed 5 October 2017.

51. Yilek, Caitlin (2017). 'Man who tweeted Trump eclipse meme said "we have enough of these jews where I live"', *The Washington Examiner*, 24 August 2017, http://www.washingtonexaminer.com/man-who-tweeted-trump-eclipse-meme-said-we-have-enough-of-these-jews-where-i-live/article/2632486, last accessed 5 October 2017.

52. Lee, Jasmine and Kevin Quealy (2017). 'The 372 People, Places and Things Donald Trump Has Insulted on Twitter: A Complete List', *The New York Times*, 25 September 2017, https://www.nytimes.com/interactive/2016/01/28/upshot/donald-trump-twitter-insults.html?mcubz=1, last accessed 5 October 2017.

53. Brinson, Will (2016). 'Here's how Nate Boyer got Colin Kaepernick to go from sitting to kneeling', CBS News, 27 September 2016, https://www.cbssports.com/nfl/news/heres-how-nate-boyer-got-colin-kaepernick-to-go-from-sitting-to-kneeling/, last accessed 5 October 2017.

54. Berkowitz, Steve (2017). 'How much money NFL owners have donated to Donald Trump', *USA Today*, 24 September 2017, https://www.usatoday.com/story/sports/nfl/2017/09/24/how-much-money-nfl-owners-have-donated-donald-trump/698256001/, last accessed 5 October 2017.

55. Fox, Nick (2017). 'The President Demands Silence From Colin Kaepernick', *The New York Times*, 23 September 2017, https://www.nytimes.com/2017/09/23/opinion/trump-curry-kaepernick-lebron.html?mcubz=1, last accessed 5 October 2017.

7. FLOOD THE SWAMP

1. Smith, David (2015). 'Where Concorde once flew: the story of President Mobutu's "African Versailles"', *The Guardian*, 10 February 2015, https://www.theguardian.com/cities/2015/feb/10/where-concorde-once-flew-the-story-of-president-mobutus-african-versailles, last accessed 5 October 2017. last accessed 5 October 2017. "rts that he requested government jet for his European honeymoon'

2. McCoy, Kevin and David Jackson (2016). 'IRS: Trump can release tax returns, regardless of audit', *USA Today*, 26 February 2016, https://www.usatoday.com/story/news/politics/onpolitics/2016/02/26/donald-trump-internal-revenue-service-audits/80996086/, last accessed 5 October 2017.

3. Ibid.

4. Silverstein, Jason (2017). 'The many times Donald Trump promised he was going to release his tax returns', *New York Daily News*, 16 April 2017, http://www.nydailynews.com/news/politics/times-donald-trump-release-tax-returns-article-1.3061868, last accessed 5 October 2017.

5. Durando, Jessica (2017). 'Trump says "I have nothing to do with Russia." That's not exactly true', *USA Today*, 11 January 2017, https://www.usatoday.com/story/news/world/2017/01/11/donald-trump-russia-vladimir-putin/96444482/, last accessed 5 October 2017.

6. Apuzzo, Matt and Maggie Haberman (2016). 'Trump Associate Boasted That Moscow Business Deal "Will Get Donald Elected"', *The New York Times*, 28 August 2017, https://www.nytimes.com/2017/08/28/us/politics/trump-tower-putin-felix-sater.html?mcubz=1, last accessed 5 October 2017.

7. Rice, Andrew (2017). 'The Original Russia Connection', *New York* magazine, 3 August 2017, http://nymag.com/daily/intelligencer/2017/08/felix-sater-donald-trump-russia-investigation.html, last accessed 5 October 2017.

8. Bowen, Andrew S. (2013). 'How Putin Uses Money Laundering Charges to Control His Opponents', *The Atlantic*, 17 July 2013, https://www.theatlantic.com/international/archive/2013/07/how-putin-uses-money-laundering-charges-to-control-his-opponents/277903/, last accessed 4 October 2017; Cohen, Marshall and Cristina Alesci (2017). 'Experts: Trump

Tower deal risked compromising Trump', CNN, 6 September 2017, http://edition.cnn.com/2017/09/06/politics/trump-tower-moscow-michael-cohen-risked-russian-leverage/index.html, last accessed 4 October 2017.

9. Sanger, David and Maggie Haberman (2017). 'Trump Praises Duterte for Philippine Drug Crackdown in Call Transcript', *The New York Times*, 23 May 2017, https://www.nytimes.com/2017/05/23/us/politics/trump-duterte-phone-transcript-philippine-drug-crackdown.html?mcubz=1, last accessed 5 October 2017.

10. Human Rights Watch (2017). 'Philippines: Police Deceit in 'Drug War' Killings', 2 March 2017, https://www.hrw.org/news/2017/03/02/philippines-police-deceit-drug-war-killings, last accessed 5 October 2017.

11. Reuters (2017). 'Philippine leader says once threw man from helicopter, would do it again', 29 December 2016, https://www.reuters.com/article/us-philippines-duterte-helicopter/philippine-leader-says-once-threw-man-from-helicopter-would-do-it-again-idUSKBN14I0DH, last accessed 5 October 2017; Landler, Mark (2017). 'Trump Invites Rodrigo Duterte to the White House', *The New York Times*, 30 April 2017, https://www.nytimes.com/2017/04/30/us/politics/trump-invites-rodrigo-duterte-to-the-white-house.html?mcubz=1, last accessed 5 October 2017.

12. Lema, Karen and Manuel Mogato (2016). 'Philippines' Duterte likens himself to Hitler, wants to kill millions of drug users', Reuters, 30 September 2016, https://www.reuters.com/article/us-philippines-duterte-hitler/philippines-duterte-likens-himself-to-hitler-wants-to-kill-millions-of-drug-users-idUSKCN1200B9, last accessed 5 October 2017.

13. Eichenwald, Kurt (2016). 'How Donald Trump's Business Ties Are Already Jeopardizing U.S. Interests', *Newsweek*, 13 December 2016, http://www.newsweek.com/2016/12/23/donald-trump-foreign-business-deals-jeopardize-us-531140.html, last accessed 5 October 2017.

14. Joseph, Cameron (2017). 'How Trump could boost fortune by making nice to brutal Filipino strongman: the value of White House invitation', *New York Daily News*, 2 May 2017, http://www.nydailynews.com/news/

politics/philippines-tower-raises-ethics-issues-trump-family-article-1.3126521, last accessed 5 October 2017.

15. Filkins, Dexter (2017). 'Turkey's Vote Makes Erdogan Effectively a Dictator', *The New Yorker*, 17 April 2017, https://www.newyorker.com/news/news-desk/turkeys-vote-makes-erdogan-effectively-a-dictator, last accessed 5 October 2017.

16. Segarra, Lisa Marie (2017). 'President Trump Said in 2015 That He Has a "Little Conflict of Interest" in Turkey', *TIME*, 19 April 2017, http://time.com/4746348/donald-trump-turkey-conflict-interest/, last accessed 5 October 2017.

17. Harwell, Drew and Anu Narayanswamy (2016). 'A scramble to assess the dangers of President-elect Donald Trump's global business empire', *The Washington Post*, 20 November 2016, https://www.washingtonpost.com/business/economy/a-scramble-to-assess-the-dangers-of-president-elects-global-business-empire/2016/11/20/1bbdc2a2-ad18–11e6-a31b-4b6397e625d0_story.html?utm_term=.1a32da68cc6f, last accessed 5 October 2017.

18. Cassidy, John (2016). 'A Saudi Prince Burns Donald Trump', *The New Yorker*, 28 January 2016, https://www.newyorker.com/news/john-cassidy/a-saudi-prince-burns-donald-trump, last accessed 5 October 2017.

19. Kirkpatrick, David (2017). 'Trump's Business Ties in the Gulf Raise Questions About His Allegiances', *The New York Times*, 17 June 2017, https://www.nytimes.com/2017/06/17/world/middleeast/trumps-business-ties-in-persian-gulf-raise-questions-about-his-allegiances.html?mcubz=1, last accessed 5 October 2017.

20. Kocieniewski, David and Caleb Melby (2017). 'Kushners' China Deal Flop Was Part of Much Bigger Hunt for Cash', Bloomberg, 31 August 2017, https://www.bloomberg.com/graphics/2017-kushners-china-deal-flop-was-part-of-much-bigger-hunt-for-cash/, last accessed 5 October 2017.

21. Swan, Jonathan (2017). 'Trump considering ending South Korea trade pact', *Axios*, 2 September 2017, https://www.axios.com/trump-seriously-considering-ending-south-korea-trade-pact-2480777456.html, last accessed 4 October 2017; Borger, Julian (2017). 'Trump's push to

quit South Korea trade pact would mark latest swerve in region on edge', *The Guardian*, 3 September 2017, https://www.theguardian.com/us-news/2017/sep/03/trump-south-korea-trade-north-nuclear-missile-crisis, last accessed 4 October 2017.

22. Frank, Robert (2017). 'Mar-a-Lago membership fee doubles to $200,000', CNBC, 25 January 2017, https://www.cnbc.com/2017/01/25/mar-a-lago-membership-fee-doubles-to-200000.html, last accessed 5 October 2017.

23. Heath, Brad, Fredreka Schouten, Steve Reilly, Nick Penzenstadler and Aamer Madhani (2017). 'Trump gets millions from golf members. CEOs and lobbyists get access to president', *USA Today*, 6 September 2017, https://www.usatoday.com/story/news/2017/09/06/trump-gets-millions-golf-members-ceos-and-lobbyists-get-access-president/632505001/, last accessed 5 October 2017.

24. Ibid.

25. Petulla, Sam (2017). 'Tracking President Trump's Visits to Trump Properties', NBC News, 1 October 2017, https://www.nbcnews.com/politics/donald-trump/how-much-time-trump-spending-trump-properties-n753366, last accessed 5 October 2017.

26. Firozi, Paulina (2016). 'Report: Embassy of Kuwait moves major event to Trump's DC hotel', *The Hill*, 19 December 2016, http://thehill.com/homenews/news/311118-kuwait-embassy-cancels-major-event-at-four-seasons-to-switch-to-trumps-dc-hotel, last accessed 5 October 2017.

27. Bykowicz, Julie, Stephen Braun and The Associated Press(2017). 'Trump's Washington Hotel Saw Almost $20 Million in Revenue', *Fortune*, 17 June 2017, http://fortune.com/2017/06/17/trump-washington-hotel-revenue/, last accessed 5 October 2017.

28. Bagli, Charles (2017). 'Sale of Brooklyn Housing Complex Would Benefit Trump', *The New York Times*, 6 September 2017, https://www.nytimes.com/2017/09/06/nyregion/starrett-city-housing-complex-trump-sale.html?mcubz=1, last accessed 5 October 2017.

29. Gold, Matea (2017). 'Donald Trump Jr. is getting $100,000 for university speech sponsored by GOP donor's company', *The Washington Post*, 1 September 2017, https://www.washingtonpost.com/politics/donald-trump-jr-is-getting-100000-for-university-speech-sponsored-

by-gop-donors-company/2017/09/01/d2f0493a-8f22–11e7–8df5-c2e5cf46c1e2_story.html?utm_term=.fd7997ad7933, last accessed 5 October 2017.

30. Lipton, Eric, Ben Protess, and Andrew Lehren (2017). 'With Trump Appointees, a Raft of Potential Conflicts and "No Transparency"', *The New York Times*, 15 April 2017, https://www.nytimes.com/2017/04/15/us/politics/trump-appointees-potential-conflicts.html?mcubz=1, last accessed 5 October 2017.

31. Ibid.

32. Fears, Darryl (2017). 'National parks put a ban on bottled water to ease pollution. Trump just sided with the lobby that fought it.', *The Washington Post*, 17 August 2017, https://www.washingtonpost.com/news/energy-environment/wp/2017/08/17/national-parks-banned-bottled-water-to-ease-pollution-trump-just-sided-with-the-lobby-that-fought-it/?utm_term=.78081151d5af, last accessed 5 October 2017.

33. Yglesias, Matthew (2017). 'Trump has granted more lobbyist waivers in 4 months than Obama did in 8 years', *Vox*, 1 June 2017, https://www.vox.com/2017/6/1/15723994/trump-ethics-waivers, last accessed 5 October 2017.

34. Baker, Peter and Matthew Rosenberg (2017). 'Michael Flynn Was Paid to Represent Turkey's Interests During Trump Campaign', *The New York Times*, 10 March 2017, https://www.nytimes.com/2017/03/10/us/politics/michael-flynn-turkey.html?mcubz=1, last accessed 5 October 2017.

35. Pramuk, Jacob and Dan Mangan (2017). 'Tom Price resigns as Trump administration health chief after outrage over private jet flights', CNBC, 29 September 2017, https://www.cnbc.com/2017/09/29/price-out-as-trump-health-chief-after-outrage-over-private-jet-flights.html, last accessed 5 October 2017.

36. Horton, Alex and Damian Paletta (2017). 'Mnuchin pushes back against reports that he requested government jet for his European honeymoon', *The Washington Post*, 14 September 2017, https://www.washingtonpost.com/news/wonk/wp/2017/09/14/mnuchin-eclipses-past-travel-backlash-with-pricey-request-european-honeymoon-by-military-jet/?utm_term=.8645335018be, last accessed 5 October 2017.

37. Lipton, Eric (2017). 'White House Official's Political Tweet Was Illegal, Agency Says', *The New York Times*, 9 June 2017, https://www.nytimes.com/2017/06/09/us/politics/dan-scavino-hatch-act-amash.html?mcubz=1, last accessed 5 October 2017.

38. Phillips, Kristine (2017). '"Go buy Ivanka's stuff," Kellyanne Conway said. Then the first daughter's fashion sales exploded.', *The Washington Post*, 10 March 2017, https://www.washingtonpost.com/news/business/wp/2017/03/10/go-buy-ivankas-stuff-kellyanne-conway-said-then-the-first-daughters-fashion-sales-exploded/?utm_term=.91767355c141, last accessed 5 October 2017.

39. Overby, Peter and Marilyn Geewax (2017). 'Ethics Office Director Walter Shaub Resigns, Saying Rules Need To Be Tougher', National Public Radio, 6 July 2017, http://www.npr.org/2017/07/06/535781749/ethics-office-director-walter-shaub-resigns-saying-rules-need-to-be-tougher, last accessed 5 October 2017.

8. THE DEEP STATE?

1. CNN (2007). 'Bhutto said she'd blame Musharraf if killed', 28 December 2007, http://edition.cnn.com/2007/WORLD/asiapcf/12/27/bhutto.security/, last accessed 5 October 2017.

2. Schmidle, Nicholas (2010). *To live or to perish forever: two tumultuous years in Pakistan.* New York: Henry Holt and Company.

3. Masood, Salman and Carlotta Gall (2007). 'Bhutto Assassination Ignites Disarray', *The New York Times*, 28 December 2007, http://www.nytimes.com/2007/12/28/world/asia/28pakistan.html?mcubz=1, last accessed 5 October 2017.

4. O'Neil, Patrick H (2013). 'The Deep State: An Emerging Concept in Comparative Politics', SSRN Working Paper Series. Rochester, NY: SSRN.

5. Filkins, Dexter (2012). 'The Deep State', *The New Yorker*, 12 March 2012, https://www.newyorker.com/magazine/2012/03/12/the-deep-state, last accessed 5 October 2017; Filiu, Jean-Pierre (2015). *From Deep State to Islamic State: The Arab counter-revolution and its jihadi legacy.* New York: Oxford University Press.

6. *Media Matters* (2017). 'Newt Gingrich: The Congressional Budget Office is "part of the deep state"', 29 June 2017, https://www.mediamatters.org/video/2017/06/29/newt-gingrich-congressional-budget-office-part-deep-state/217111, last accessed 5 October 2017.

7. Greenwood, Max (2017). 'White House pre-buts CBO healthcare score: "Little more than fake news"', *The Hill*, 15 July 2017, http://thehill.com/policy/healthcare/342183-white-house-aides-prebut-cbo-healthcare-score-little-more-than-fake-news, last accessed 2 October 2017.

8. Tankersley, Jim (2015). 'GOP leaders tap Keith Hall to lead CBO', *The Washington Post*, 27 February 2015, https://www.washingtonpost.com/business/economy/gop-leaders-tap-keith-hall-to-lead-cbo/2015/02/27/f17321d8-beba-11e4-b274-e5209a3bc9a9_story.html?utm_term=.a1e212979045, last accessed 5 October 2017.

9. Savransky, Rebecca (2017). 'Gingrich: Mueller tip of "deep state spear"', *The Hill*, 15 June 2017, http://thehill.com/homenews/house/337912-gingrich-mueller-tip-of-the-deep-state-spear, last accessed 5 October 2017.

10. Manchester, Julia (2017). 'Trump promotes Hannity's "deep state" monologue', *The Hill*, 16 June 2017, http://thehill.com/media/338241-trump-shares-hannity-tweet-on-monologue-calling-for-leakers-to-be-jailed, last accessed 5 October 2017.

11. Pew Research (2017). 'Public Trust in Government Remains Near Historic Lows as Partisan Attitudes Shift', 3 May 2017, http://www.people-press.org/2017/05/03/public-trust-in-government-remains-near-historic-lows-as-partisan-attitudes-shift/, last accessed 5 October 2017.

12. Eilperin, Juliet and Chris Mooney (2016). 'Over 2,000 scientists urge Trump to respect "scientific integrity and independence"', *The Washington Post*, 30 November 2016, https://www.washingtonpost.com/news/energy-environment/wp/2016/11/30/22-nobel-prize-winners-urge-trump-to-respect-scientific-integrity-and-independence/?utm_term=.c356ea2b296b, last accessed 5 October 2017.

13. Matthews, Dylan (2017). 'Donald Trump has tweeted climate change scepticism 115 times. Here's all of it.', *Vox*, 1 June 2017, https://www.

vox.com/policy-and-politics/2017/6/1/15726472/trump-tweets-global-warming-paris-climate-agreement, last accessed 1 October 2017.

14. Friedman, Lisa (2017). 'Scientists Fear Trump Will Dismiss Blunt Climate Report', *The New York Times*, 7 August 2017, https://www.nytimes.com/2017/08/07/climate/climate-change-drastic-warming-trump.html?mcubz=1&_r=0, last accessed 5 October 2017.

15. NASA (2017). 'Astronaut Biography: Charles F. Bolden', January 2017, https://www.jsc.nasa.gov/Bios/htmlbios/bolden-cf.pdf

16. Voosen, Paul (2017). 'Trump has picked a politician to lead NASA. Is that a good thing?', *Science*, 1 September 2017, http://www.sciencemag.org/news/2017/09/trump-has-picked-politician-lead-nasa-good-thing, last accessed 5 October 2017.

17. Green, Miranda (2017). 'Senators oppose Trump's pick to head NASA', CNN, 15 September 2017, http://edition.cnn.com/2017/09/14/politics/jim-bridenstine-nasa-opposition/index.html, last accessed 5 October 2017.

18. Lanktree, Graham (2017). 'Who Is Jim Bridenstine, The Climate Change Denier Trump Picked To Head Nasa?', *Newsweek*, 7 September 2017, http://www.newsweek.com/who-jim-bridenstine-climate-change-denier-trump-picked-head-nasa-660926, last accessed 5 October 2017.

19. Goldenberg, Suzanne and Helena Bengtsson (2016). 'Biggest US coal company funded dozens of groups questioning climate change', *The Guardian*, 13 June 2016, https://www.theguardian.com/environment/2016/jun/13/peabody-energy-coal-mining-climate-change-denial-funding, last accessed 2 October 2017; Cook, John (2016). 'A brief history of fossil-fuelled climate denial', *The Conversation*, 21 June 2016, https://theconversation.com/a-brief-history-of-fossil-fuelled-climate-denial-61273, last accessed 2 October 2017.

20. Green, Miranda (2017). 'The battle over science in the Trump administration', CNN, 9 August 2017, http://edition.cnn.com/2017/08/05/politics/trump-battle-science-epa-energy-climate/index.html, last accessed 5 October 2017.

21. Koebler, Jason (2017). 'All References to Climate Change Have Been

Deleted From the White House Website', *Motherboard*, 20 January 2017, https://motherboard.vice.com/en_us/article/d7yeej/all-references-to-climate-change-have-been-deleted-from-the-white-house-website-5886b75d0b367c453f87dd14, last accessed 2 October 2017; Jones, Rhett (2017). 'The White House Science Division Officially Has Zero Staff Members', *Gizmodo*, 1 July 2017, https://gizmodo.com/the-white-house-science-division-officially-has-no-one-1796575648, last accessed 2 October 2017.

22. Tuttle, Ian (2016). 'Yes, Trump University was a Massive Scam', *The National Review*, 26 February 2016, http://www.nationalreview.com/corner/432010/trump-university-was-massive-scam, last accessed 5 October 2017.

23. Eder, Steve and Jennifer Medina (2017). 'Trump University Suit Settlement Approved by Judge', *The New York Times*, 31 March 2017, https://www.nytimes.com/2017/03/31/us/trump-university-settlement.html?mcubz=1, last accessed 5 October 2017.

24. Daly, Michael (2016). 'The Mexican Judge Trump Slimed Is Really Making America Great Again', *The Daily Beast*, 2 June 2016, http://www.thedailybeast.com/the-mexican-judge-trump-slimed-is-really-making-america-great-again, last accessed 5 October 2017; Krieg, Gregory (2016). '5 things to know about Judge Gonzalo Curiel', CNN, 7 June 2016, http://edition.cnn.com/2016/06/06/politics/judge-gonzalo-curiel-donald-trump-university/index.html, last accessed 5 October 2017.

25. Wolf, Z. Byron (2017). 'Read this: How Trump defended criticism of judge for being "Mexican"', CNN, 20 April 2017, http://edition.cnn.com/2017/04/20/politics/donald-trump-gonzalo-curiel-jake-tapper-transcript/index.html, last accessed 5 October 2017.

26. Caygle, Heather (2016). 'Ryan: Trump's comments "textbook definition" of racism', *Politico*, 7 June 2016, http://www.politico.com/story/2016/06/paul-ryan-trump-judge-223991, last accessed 5 October 2017.

27. Healy, Patrick and Michael Barbaro (2015). 'Donald Trump Calls for Barring Muslims From Entering U.S.', *The New York Times*, 7 December 2015, https://www.nytimes.com/politics/first-draft/2015/12/07/don-

ald-trump-calls-for-banning-muslims-from-entering-u-s/?mcubz=1, last accessed 5 October 2017.

28. Phillips, Kristine (2017). 'All the times Trump personally attacked judges—and why his tirades are "worse than wrong"', *The Washington Post*, 26 April 2017, https://www.washingtonpost.com/news/the-fix/wp/2017/04/26/all-the-times-trump-personally-attacked-judges-and-why-his-tirades-are-worse-than-wrong/?utm_term=.2859c0df08d6, last accessed 5 October 2017.

29. Bump, Philip (2017). 'The travel ban going into effect would have saved zero lives from terrorist attacks in the last 20 years', *The Washington Post*, 29 June 2017, https://www.washingtonpost.com/news/politics/wp/2017/06/29/the-travel-ban-going-into-effect-would-have-saved-zero-lives-from-terrorist-attacks-in-the-last-20-years/?utm_term=.3a2a43a4f30d, last accessed 2 October 2017.

30. Lynch, David J. (2017). 'Trump loyalists lash out at "deep state gone rogue"', *Financial Times*, 10 August 2017, https://www.ft.com/content/64b8f8d2-7d47-11e7-9108-edda0bcbc928, last accessed 5 October 2017.

31. Quigley, Aidan (2017). 'Deep State Is "Going To Kill The President," Alex Jones Claims', *Newsweek*, 4 August 2017, http://www.newsweek.com/alex-jones-says-deep-state-going-kill-president-646802, last accessed 5 October 2017.

32. Collins, Ben (2017). 'NASA Denies That It's Running a Child Slave Colony on Mars', *The Daily Beast*, 29 June 2017, http://www.thedailybeast.com/nasa-denies-that-its-running-a-child-slave-colony-on-mars, last accessed 5 October 2017.

33. Bradner, Eric (2015). 'Trump praises 9/11 truther's "amazing" reputation', CNN, 2 December 2015, http://edition.cnn.com/2015/12/02/politics/donald-trump-praises-9-11-truther-alex-jones/index.html, last accessed 5 October 2017.

34. Herb, Jeremy and Zachary Cohen (2017). 'Trump still doesn't seem to believe his intelligence agencies on Russia', CNN, 7 July 2017, http://edition.cnn.com/2017/07/06/politics/trump-intelligence-agencies-russia/index.html, last accessed 5 October 2017.

35. Betts, Richard K. (2009). *Enemies of Intelligence: Knowledge and power in American national security*. New York: Columbia University Press.

36. Pillar, Paul (2006). 'Intelligence, Policy, and the War in Iraq', *Foreign Affairs*, March/April 2006, https://www.foreignaffairs.com/articles/iraq/2006–03–01/intelligence-policy-and-war-iraq, last accessed 5 October 2017; Heer, Jeet (2016). 'The Danger of Politicizing Intelligence', *The New Republic*, 12 December 2016, https://newrepublic.com/article/139275/danger-politicizing-intelligence, last accessed 5 October 2017.

37. Wagner, John (2017). 'Trump's comparison of U.S. intelligence community to Nazi Germany rebuked by Anti-Defamation League', *The Washington Post*, 11 January 2017, https://www.washingtonpost.com/news/post-politics/wp/2017/01/11/trumps-comparison-of-u-s-intelligence-community-to-nazi-germany-rebuked-by-anti-defamation-league/?utm_term=.0932ef1c93ab, last accessed 2 October 2017.

38. Osnos, Evan (2017). 'The Trump Campaign Has Been Under Investigation Since July', *The New Yorker*, 20 March 2017, https://www.newyorker.com/news/news-desk/the-trump-campaign-has-been-under-investigation-since-july, last accessed 5 October 2017.

39. Murray, Mark (2017). 'Poll: More Americans Believe Comey Over Trump', NBC News, 23 June 2017, https://www.nbcnews.com/politics/first-read/poll-more-americans-believe-comey-over-trump-n776006, last accessed 5 October 2017.

40. Cohen, David S. (2017). 'Trump is trying to politicize intelligence to support his Iran policy. That's dangerous.', *The Washington Post*, 4 August 2017, https://www.washingtonpost.com/opinions/trump-is-trying-to-politicize-intelligence-to-support-his-iran-policy-thats-dangerous/2017/08/04/ffb192e0–77b6–11e7–8f39–eeb7d3a2d304_story.html?utm_term=.1c009e91e3df, last accessed 5 October 2017.

41. Ibid.

42. Gallup (2017). 'Confidence in Institutions', http://news.gallup.com/poll/1597/confidence-institutions.aspx, last accessed 2 October 2017,

43. Kheel, Rebecca (2017). 'Senate panel easily approves waiver for Mattis', *The Hill*, 12 January 2017, http://thehill.com/policy/defense/313996-

armed-services-committee-easily-passes-mattis-waiver, last accessed 5 October 2017.

44. Baker, Peter and Michael R. Gordon (2017). 'Trump Chooses H.R. McMaster as National Security Adviser', *The New York Times*, https://www.nytimes.com/2017/02/20/us/politics/mcmaster-national-security-adviser-trump.html?mcubz=1, last accessed 5 October 2017.

45. Bump, Philip (2017). 'Most Americans still want Trump to stop tweeting—and think he's unfit for office', *The Washington Post*, 27 September 2017, https://www.washingtonpost.com/news/politics/wp/2017/09/27/most-americans-still-want-trump-to-stop-tweeting-and-think-hes-unfit-for-office/?utm_term=.8a6200e784d9, last accessed 2 October 2017.

46. Naughton, James (1974). 'Nixon Slide From Power: Backers Gave Final Push', *The New York Times*, 12 August 1974, http://www.nytimes.com/1974/08/12/archives/nixon-slide-from-power-backers-gave-final-push-former-defenders.html?mcubz=1, last accessed 5 October 2017.

9. TAKE YOUR KIDS TO WORK DAY

1. Uzbek-German Forum (2015). 'The Government's Riches, the People's Burden: Human Rights Violations in Uzbekistan's 2014 Cotton Harvest', 13 April 2015, http://uzbekgermanforum.org/the-governments-riches-the-peoples-burden-human-rights-violations-in-uzbekistans-2014-cotton-harvest-2/, last accessed 5 October 2017. last accessed 5 October 2017. ".ts that he requested government jet for his European honeymoon'

2. Paton Walsh, Nick (2003). 'US looks away as new ally tortures Islamists', *The Guardian*, 26 May 2003, https://www.theguardian.com/world/2003/may/26/nickpatonwalsh, last accessed 5 October 2017.

3. Najibullah, Farangis (2012). 'Uzbekistan's "House Of Torture"', RFERL, 5 August 2012, https://www.rferl.org/a/uzbekistans-house-of-torture/24667200.html, last accessed 5 October 2017.

4. OCCRP (2015). 'The Prodigal Daughter', May 2015, https://www.occrp.org/en/corruptistan/uzbekistan/gulnarakarimova/index.html, last accessed 5 October 2017.

5. Merkelson, Suzanne (2011). 'The Zoolander Effect', *Foreign Policy*, 1 March 2011, http://foreignpolicy.com/2011/03/01/the-zoolander-effect/, last accessed 5 October 2017; Orange, Richard (2010). 'Daughter of Uzbek president unveils her fashion collection', *The Telegraph*, 12 September 2010, http://www.telegraph.co.uk/news/worldnews/asia/uzbekistan/7998056/Daughter-of-Uzbek-president-unveils-her-fashion-collection.html, last accessed 5 October 2017.

6. Carbone, Nick (2011). 'Dictator's Daughter Dropped from Fashion Week Show Lineup', *TIME*, 10 September 2011, http://newsfeed.time.com/2011/09/10/dictator%E2%80%99s-daughter-dropped-from-fashion-week-show-lineup/, last accessed 5 October 2017.

7. Kendzior, Sarah (2017). 'The tale of the dictator's daughter and her prince', The Correspondent, May 2017, https://thecorrespondent.com/6591/the-tale-of-the-dictators-daughter-and-her-prince/186426 5121147–43ede0f9, last accessed 5 October 2017.

8. Fortin, Jacey (2017). 'Ivanka Trump Briefly Takes Her Father's Seat at the Table. Outrage Follows', *The New York Times*, 8 July 2017, https://www.nytimes.com/2017/07/08/world/europe/ivanka-trump-seat-table-group-of-20-summit.html?mcubz=1, last accessed 5 October 2017.

9. Bomboy, Scott (2016). 'Presidential nepotism debate goes back to the Founders' time', National Constitution Center, 21 November 2016, https://constitutioncenter.org/blog/presidential-nepotism-debate-goes-back-to-the-founders-time/, last accessed 5 October 2017.

10. Salinger, Lawrence M. (2005). *Encyclopedia of White-collar & Corporate Crime*. Thousand Oaks, California: Sage Publications

11. Rubino, Rich (2017). 'Nepotism In The White House: It's All Relative', *Huffington Post*, 11 April 2017, http://www.huffingtonpost.com/entry/nepotism-in-the-white-house-its-all-relative_us_58eb5edce4b0acd784ca5a11, last accessed 5 October 2017.

12. Joseph, Cameron (2016). 'Donald Trump says if he wasn't caught cheating on his "beautiful wife" Ivana with girlfriend Marla Maples, life would've stayed "a bowl of cherries" in 1994', *New York Daily News*, 8 October 2016, http://www.nydailynews.com/news/politics/trump-cheating-ivana-marla-beautiful-1994-article-1.2822695, last accessed 5 October 2017.

13. Withnall, Adam (2016). 'Donald Trump's unsettling record of comments about his daughter Ivanka', *The Independent*, 10 October 2016, http://www.independent.co.uk/news/world/americas/us-elections/donald-trump-ivanka-trump-creepiest-most-unsettling-comments-a-roundup-a7353876.html, last accessed 5 October 2017.

14. Kaczynski, Andrew, Chris Massie, and Nate McDermott (2016). 'Donald Trump to Howard Stern: It's okay to call my daughter a "piece of ass"', CNN, 9 October 2016, http://edition.cnn.com/2016/10/08/politics/trump-on-howard-stern/index.html, last accessed 5 October 2017.

15. Ibid.

16. Withnall (2016).

17. *New York* magazine (2004). 'Did Their Father Really Know Best?', 14 December 2004, http://nymag.com/nymetro/news/people/features/10610/index4.html, last accessed 5 October 2017.

18. Withnall (2016).

19. Barbaro, Michael and Jonathan Mahler (2016). 'Quiet Fixer in Donald Trump's Campaign: His Son-in-Law, Jared Kushner', *The New York Times*, 4 July 2016, https://www.nytimes.com/2016/07/05/us/politics/jared-kushner-donald-trump.html?mcubz=1, last accessed 5 October 2017.

20. Blake, Aaron (2017). 'Henry Kissinger's lukewarm non-endorsement of Jared Kushner is even more damning than it seems', *The Washington Post*, 20 April 2017, https://www.washingtonpost.com/news/the-fix/wp/2017/04/20/henry-kissingers-lukewarm-non-endorsement-of-jared-kushner/, last accessed 5 October 2017.; Hensch, Mark (2017). 'Ryan, Kushner met for dinner: report', *The Hill*, 2 February 2017, http://thehill.com/homenews/administration/317505-ryan-kushner-met-for-dinner-report, last accessed 4 October 2017; Graves, Lucia (2017). 'Donald Trump and Rupert Murdoch: inside the billionaire bromance', *The Guardian*, 16 June 2017, https://www.theguardian.com/us-news/2017/jun/16/donald-trump-rupert-murdoch-friendship-fox-news, last accessed 4 October 2017.

21. Diamond, Jeremy (2016). 'Donald Trump's "Star of David" tweet controversy, explained', CNN, 5 July 2016, http://edition.cnn.com/2016/

07/04/politics/donald-trump-star-of-david-tweet-explained/index.html, last accessed 5 October 2017.

22. Kushner, Jared (2016). 'Jared Kushner: The Donald Trump I Know', *Observer* (New York), 6 July 2016, http://observer.com/2016/07/jared-kushner-the-donald-trump-i-know/, last accessed 5 October 2017.

23. Kruse, Michael (2015). 'The 199 Most Donald Trump Things Donald Trump Has Ever Said', *Politico*, 14 August 2015, http://www.politico.com/magazine/story/2015/08/the-absolute-trumpest-121328,   last accessed 5 October 2017.

24. Zimmerman, Neetzan (2015). 'Trump mocks Fiorina's physical appearance: "Look at that face!"', *The Hill*, 9 September 2015, http://thehill.com/blogs/blog-briefing-room/253178-trump-insults-fiorinas-physical-appearance-look-at-that-face, last accessed 5 October 2017.

25. CBS News (2016). 'Ivanka Trump responds to "disturbing" accusations about her father', 18 May 2016, https://www.cbsnews.com/news/ivanka-trump-defends-donald-new-york-times-article-attacks-against-women-business-working-woman/, last accessed 5 October 2017.

26. Fahrenthold, David (2016). 'Trump recorded having extremely lewd conversation about women in 2005', *The Washington Post*, 8 October 2016, https://www.washingtonpost.com/politics/trump-recorded-having-extremely-lewd-conversation-about-women-in-2005/2016/10/07/3b9ce776–8cb4–11e6-bf8a-3d26847eeed4_story.html?utm_term=.1266aee2155e, last accessed 5 October 2017.

27. Relman, Eliza (2017). 'Here's how Ivanka Trump reacted behind closed doors after seeing the Access Hollywood tape', *Business Insider*, 2 May 2017, http://uk.businessinsider.com/ivanka-trump-access-hollywood-tape-reaction-2017–5, last accessed 4 October 2017.

28. Reuters (2016). 'Trump denies trying to get security clearance for his children', 16 November 2016, http://www.reuters.com/article/us-usa-trump-clearances/trump-denies-trying-to-get-security-clearance-for-his-children-idUSKBN13B1GB, last accessed 5 October 2017.

29. Haberman, Maggie, J. David Goodman, Coral Davenport and Michael D. Shear, 'Ivanka Trump and Jared Kushner Will Not Seek Security Clearances, Sources Say', *The New York Times*, 16 November 2016,

https://www.nytimes.com/2016/11/16/us/politics/donald-trump-transition.html, last accessed 5 October 2017.

30. Yuhas, Alan (2017). 'Trump names son-in-law Jared Kushner as senior adviser, testing anti-nepotism law', *The Guardian*, 10 January 2017, https://www.theguardian.com/us-news/2017/jan/09/jared-kushner-senior-adviser-donald-trump, last accessed 5 October 2017.

31. Liptak, Kevin (2017). 'Trump's Secretary of Everything: Jared Kushner', CNN, 4 April 2017, http://edition.cnn.com/2017/04/03/politics/jared-kushner-donald-trump-foreign-policy/index.html, last accessed 5 October 2017.

32. *The Onion* (2017). 'Jared Kushner Quietly Transfers "Solve Middle East Crisis" to Next Week's To-Do List', 28 March 2017, http://www.the-onion.com/article/jared-kushner-quietly-transfers-solve-middle-east—55639, last accessed 5 October 2017.

33. Associated Press (2017). 'Ivanka will have access to classified info in new White House role', *New York Post*, 20 March 2017, http://nypost.com/2017/03/20/ivanka-trump-to-join-white-house-staff/, last accessed 5 October 2017.

34. Jackson, David (2017). 'Ivanka Trump gets new White House title', *USA Today*, 29 March 2017, https://www.usatoday.com/story/news/politics/2017/03/29/donald-trump-ivanka-trump/99795232/, last accessed 5 October 2017.

35. Li, David K. (2016). 'Guess who isn't voting for Donald Trump? His kids', *The New York Post*, 11 April 2016, http://nypost.com/2016/04/11/eric-and-ivanka-trump-cant-vote-for-their-dad-in-ny-primary/, last accessed 5 October 2017.

36. Italiano, Laura (2016). 'Ivanka Trump markets her fashion label with RNC dresses', *New York Post*, 23 July 2016, http://nypost.com/2016/07/23/ivanka-trump-markets-her-fashion-label-with-rnc-dresses/, last accessed 5 October 2017.

37. Frieman, Vanessa (2016). 'Ivanka Trump Blurs the Line Between Professional and Political', *The New York Times*, 15 November 2016, https://www.nytimes.com/2016/11/15/fashion/ivanka-trump-bracelet-60-minutes-conflict-of-interest.html?mcubz=1, last accessed 5 October 2017.

38. Lipton, Eric and Maggie Haberman (2016). 'Available to the Highest Bidder: Coffee With Ivanka Trump', *The New York Times*, 15 December 2016, https://www.nytimes.com/2016/12/15/us/politics/ivanka-trump-charity-auction.html, last accessed 5 October 2017.

39. Close, Kerry (2016). 'Ivanka Trump Was Auctioning Off a Charity Coffee Date. Then It Disappeared From the Internet', *TIME*, 16 December 2016, http://time.com/4604992/ivanka-trump-coffee-date-auction/, last accessed 5 October 2017.

40. Northam, Jackie (2017). 'China Defends Trademark Grants For Ivanka Trump Products', NPR, 19 April 2017, http://www.npr.org/sections/thetwo-way/2017/04/19/524765086/china-defends-trademark-grants-for-ivanka-trump-products, last accessed 5 October 2017.

41. Ibid.

42. McCoy, Kevin (2017). 'China factory for Ivanka Trump brand shoes criticized for labor violations', *USA Today*, 21 June 2017, https://www.usatoday.com/story/money/2017/06/21/china-factory-ivanka-trump-brand-shoes-criticized-labor-violations/103071256/, last accessed 5 October 2017.

43. PBS News (2017). 'Kushner family's real estate dealings land foreign-investor visa back in the spotlight', PBS Newshour, 15 June 2017, http://www.pbs.org/newshour/bb/kushner-familys-real-estate-dealings-land-foreign-investor-visa-back-spotlight/, last accessed 5 October 2017.

44. Greenwood, Max (2017). 'Kushner Companies subpoenaed over use of visa program: report', *The Hill*, 2 August 2017, http://thehill.com/blogs/blog-briefing-room/news/345086-kushner-companies-subpoenaed-over-use-of-the-eb-5-visa-program, last accessed 5 October 2017.

45. Abrams, Rachel and Jesse Drucker (2017). 'Ivanka Trump Received at Least $12.6 Million Since 2016, Disclosure Shows', *The New York Times*, 21 July 2017, https://www.nytimes.com/2017/07/21/business/ivanka-trump-jared-kushner-ethics-filing.html?mcubz=1, last accessed 5 October 2017.

46. Eustachewich, Lia (2017). 'Jared Kushner left a lot off his financial disclosure', *New York Post*, 2 May 2017, http://nypost.com/2017/05/02/jared-kushner-didnt-disclose-stake-in-real-estate-startup/, last accessed 5 October 2017; O'Connell, Jonathan, Matea Gold, Drew Harwell and

Steven Rich (2017). 'In revised filing, Kushner reveals dozens of previously undisclosed assets', *The Washington Post*, 21 July 2017, http://nypost.com/2017/05/02/jared-kushner-didnt-disclose-stake-in-real-estate-startup/, last accessed 5 October 2017.

47. Allison, Bill and Caleb Melby (2017). 'Kushner Adds $10 Million in "Omitted" Assets to Disclosure Form', Bloomberg, 22 July 2017, https://www.bloomberg.com/news/articles/2017–07–21/kushner-s-amended-financial-disclosure-shows-sprawling-assets-j5egyvpg, last accessed 5 October 2017.

48. Abrams, Rachel (2017). 'Despite a Trust, Ivanka Trump Still Wields Power Over Her Brand', *The New York Times*, 20 March 2017, https://www.nytimes.com/2017/03/20/business/despite-trust-ivanka-trump-still-wields-power-over-her-brand.html?mcubz=1, last accessed 5 October 2017.

49. Applebaum, Anne (2017). 'Ivanka Trump's White House role is a symbol of democratic decline', *The Washington Post*, 27 April 2017, https://www.washingtonpost.com/opinions/global-opinions/ivanka-trumps-white-house-role-is-a-symbol-of-democratic-decline/2017/04/27/a060980c-2b64-11e7-a616-d7c8a68c1a66_story.html?utm_term=.14f18874d859, last accessed 5 October 2017.

50. Weaver, Courtney (2017). 'John Kelly confronts an outsized family presence in White House', *Financial Times*, 1 August 2017, https://www.ft.com/content/dfb056c6-76d4-11e7-90c0-90a9d1bc9691, last accessed 5 October 2017.

51. Goodwin, Doris Kearns (2009). *Team of Rivals: The political genius of Abraham Lincoln*, London: Penguin.

52. BBC News (2017). 'Gulnara Karimova, Uzbekistan ex-leader's daughter, "detained"', 28 July 2017, http://www.bbc.co.uk/news/world-asia-40751461, last accessed 5 October 2017.

10. THE DESPOT'S CHEERLEADER

1. Mezzofiore, Gianluca (2013). 'Kurdish Genocide in Iraq: Survivors Recount Saddam Terror of Chemical Attacks', IB Times, 18 January 2013,

http://www.ibtimes.co.uk/kurdish-genocide-iraq-saddam-hussein-recognition-chemical-425502

2. BBC News (1988). 'Thousands die in Halabja gas attack', 16 March 1988, http://news.bbc.co.uk/onthisday/hi/dates/stories/march/16/newsid_4304000/4304853.stm. See also: Gosden, Christine, and Derek Gardener (2005). 'ABC of conflict and disaster: Weapons of mass destruction—threats and responses', *BMJ: British Medical Journal* 331(7513), 397.

3. Simpson, John (2012). 'Halabja chemical weapons: A chance to find the men who armed Saddam', BBC News, http://www.bbc.co.uk/news/magazine-20553826

4. *The Telegraph* (2003). 'Chemical and biological weapons explained', The Telegraph, 27 January 2003, http://www.telegraph.co.uk/news/1399850/Chemical-and-biological-weapons-explained.html

5. BBC News (2002). 'Iraqi Kurds recall chemical attack', 17 March 2002, http://news.bbc.co.uk/1/hi/world/middle_east/1877161.stm

6. Vitali, Ali (2016). 'Donald Trump Praises Saddam Hussein's Approach to Terrorism—Again', NBC News, https://www.nbcnews.com/politics/2016-election/donald-trump-praises-saddam-hussein-s-approach-terrorism-again-n604411

7. Johnson, Jenna (2016). 'Donald Trump praises Saddam Hussein for killing terrorists "so good"', The Washington Post, 5 July 2016, https://www.washingtonpost.com/news/post-politics/wp/2016/07/05/donald-trump-praises-saddam-hussein-for-killing-terrorists-so-good/?utm_term=.bf311ae1f619

8. Risen, James and Sheri Fink (2017). 'Trump Said "Torture Works." An Echo Is Feared Worldwide.', 5 January 2017, https://www.nytimes.com/2017/01/05/us/politics/trump-torture-guantanamo.html?mcubz=1&_r=0

9. Masters, James (2017). 'Donald Trump says torture "absolutely works"—but does it?', CNN, 26 January 2017, http://edition.cnn.com/2017/01/26/politics/donald-trump-torture-waterboarding/index.html, last accessed 4 October 2017.

10. Swan, Jonathan (2016). 'Trump calls for "hell of a lot worse than waterboarding"', The Hill, 6 February 2016, http://thehill.com/blogs/ballot-

box/gop-primaries/268530-trump-calls-for-hell-of-a-lot-worse-than-waterboarding

11. Holland, Steve and Jeff Mason (2017). 'Trump tells Middle East to "drive out" Islamist extremists', Reuters, 21 May 2017, https://www.reuters.com/article/us-usa-trump-saudi/trump-tells-middle-east-to-drive-out-islamist-extremists-idUSKCN18H00U

12. Berehulak, Daniel (2016). '"They Are Slaughtering Us Like Animals"', The New York Times, 7 December 2016, https://www.nytimes.com/interactive/2016/12/07/world/asia/rodrigo-duterte-philippines-drugs-killings.html?mcubz=1

13. Berehulak, Daniel (2016); Human Rights Watch (2017). 'License to Kill: Philippine Police Killings in Duterte's "War on Drugs"', 2 March 2017, https://www.hrw.org/report/2017/03/02/license-kill/philippine-police-killings-dutertes-war-drugs

14. Amnesty International (2017). 'Philippines: 32 Killed In A Day As Duterte's "War On Drugs" Hits New Levels Of Barbarity', 16 August 2017, https://www.amnesty.org/en/press-releases/2017/08/philippines-32-killed-in-a-day-as-dutertes-war-on-drugs-hits-new-levels-of-barbarity/; Amnesty International (2017). 'Philippines: "If You Are Poor, You Are Killed": Extrajudicial Killings in the Philippines' "War on Drugs"', report, 31 January 2017, https://www.amnesty.org/en/press-releases/2017/08/philippines-32-killed-in-a-day-as-dutertes-war-on-drugs-hits-new-levels-of-barbarity/, last accessed 4 October 2017.

15. Whaley, Floyd (2016). 'Rodrigo Duterte's Talk of Killing Criminals Raises Fears in Philippines', The New York Times, 17 May 2016, https://www.nytimes.com/2016/05/18/world/asia/rodrigo-duterte-philippines.html?mcubz=1

16. Agence France Presse (2016). 'Philippine president-elect says "corrupt" journalists will be killed', 31 May 2016, https://www.theguardian.com/world/2016/may/31/philippine-president-elect-says-corrupt-journalists-will-be-killed

17. Andrews, Travis (2016). 'Leading Philippine presidential contender: Gang rape victim "so beautiful" he wishes he had "been first"', The Washington Post, 18 April 2016, https://www.washingtonpost.com/news/morning-mix/wp/2016/04/18/leading-philippines-presidential-

contender-gang-rape-victim-so-beautiful-he-wishes-he-had-been-first/?utm_term=.7075eb097cc3

18. Petty, Martin and Karen Lema (2016). 'Expecting policy speech, Filipino businessmen hear Duterte's war talk', Reuters, 27 April 2016, http://www.reuters.com/article/us-philippines-election-duterte/expecting-policy-speech-filipino-businessmen-hear-dutertes-war-talk-idUSKC-N0XO13B

19. Iyengar, Rishi (2016). 'Philippine Presidential Front-Runner Duterte Says He Will Pardon Himself for Mass Murder', 28 April 2016, http://time.com/4310651/duterte-philippines-murder-pardon-himself/

20. BBC News (2016). 'Philippines: Duterte confirms he personally killed three men', 16 December 2016, http://www.bbc.co.uk/news/world-asia-38337746, last accessed 5 October 2017. last accessed 5 October 2017. ".ts that he requested government jet for his European honeymoon'

21. Al-Jazeera (2016). 'Rodrigo Duterte: I once threw a man from a helicopter', 29 December 2016, http://www.aljazeera.com/news/2016/12/rodrigo-duterte-helicopter-161229062349259.html, last accessed 5 October 2017.

22. Holmes, Oliver (2016). 'Rodrigo Duterte vows to kill 3 million drug addicts and likens himself to Hitler', *The Guardian*, 1 October 2016, https://www.theguardian.com/world/2016/sep/30/rodrigo-duterte-vows-to-kill-3-million-drug-addicts-and-likens-himself-to-hitler, last accessed 5 October 2017.

23. Ross, Eleanor (2017). 'Philippines President Duterte's Drug War One Year On: At Least 7,000 Are Dead, But It's Been "Successful"', *Newsweek*, 30 June 2017, http://www.newsweek.com/dutertes-drug-war-7000-success-630392, last accessed 5 October 2017.

24. Reuters (2017). 'Philippines tells EU lawmakers to butt out after criticism of drugs war', 17 March 2017, http://www.reuters.com/article/us-philippines-drugs-eu/philippines-tells-eu-lawmakers-to-butt-out-after-criticism-of-drugs-war-idUSKBN16O17S, last accessed 5 October 2017.

25. Holmes, Ronald and Mark R. Thompson (2017). 'Duterte's Year of Sound and Fury', The Diplomat, 30 June 2017, https://thediplomat.com/2017/06/dutertes-year-of-sound-and-fury/, last accessed 5 October

2017; Gershman, John (2016). 'Human Rights and Duterte's War on Drugs', Council on Foreign Relations, 16 December 2016, https://www.cfr.org/interview/human-rights-and-dutertes-war-drugs, last accessed 5 October 2017.

26. ABC News (2016). 'Barack Obama scraps planned talks with Rodrigo Duterte over "son of a whore" slur', 6 September 2016, http://www.abc.net.au/news/2016–09–06/obama-calls-off-planned-talks-with-duterte/7817454, last accessed 5 October 2017.

27. Krieg, Gregory (2017). 'Trump sounds exactly how you'd expect in his chat with strongman Duterte', CNN, 24 May 2017, http://edition.cnn.com/2017/05/24/politics/trump-duterte-phone-call-annotated/index.html, last accessed 4 October 2017.

28. Klaas, Brian (2016). *The Despot's Accomplice: How the West is Aiding and Abetting the Decline of Democracy.* London: Hurst.

29. Roser, Max (2017). 'Democracy'. Published online at OurWorldInData.org. Retrieved from: https://ourworldindata.org/democracy/, last accessed 5 October 2017; Freedom House (2017). 'Freedom in the World: 2017', https://freedomhouse.org/report/freedom-world/freedom-world-2017, last accessed 5 October 2017.

30. Fukuyama, Francis (2006). *The End of History and the Last Man.* New York: Simon and Schuster.

31. Freedom House (2017).

32. Barkin, Noah and Elizabeth Piper (2017). 'In Davos, Xi makes case for Chinese leadership role', Reuters, 17 January 2017, https://www.reuters.com/article/us-davos-meeting-china/in-davos-xi-makes-case-for-chinese-leadership-role-idUSKBN15118V, last accessed 4 October 2017.

33. Wang, Christine (2017). 'Trump praises Xi soon after death of Chinese dissident', CNBC, 13 July 2017, https://www.cnbc.com/2017/07/13/trump-praises-xi-soon-after-death-of-chinese-dissident.html, last accessed 5 October 2017.

34. Reuters (2017). 'Merkel hails China's Liu as a courageous civil rights fighter', 13 July 2017, https://www.reuters.com/article/us-china-rights-merkel/merkel-hails-chinas-liu-as-a-courageous-civil-rights-fighter-idUSKBN19Y1Z1, last accessed 5 October 2017.

35. Office of US Senator John McCain (2017). 'Statement By Senator John

McCain On Death Of Liu Xiaobo In Chinese Prison', 13 July 2017, https://www.mccain.senate.gov/public/index.cfm/press-releases?ID=EE2C10B4–5659–46CE-9741–390E604FA2FA, last accessed 5 October 2017.

36. US Department of State (2017). 'On the Passing of Liu Xiaobo', 13 July 2017, https://www.state.gov/secretary/remarks/2017/07/272579.htm, last accessed 5 October 2017.

37. The White House (2017). 'Statement from the Press Secretary on the Death of Liu Xiaobo', 13 July 2017, https://www.whitehouse.gov/the-press-office/2017/07/13/statement-press-secretary-death-liu-xiaobo, last accessed 5 October 2017.

38. Kaczynski, Andrew Chris Massie, and Nathan McDermott (2017). '80 times Trump talked about Putin', CNN, http://edition.cnn.com/inter-active/2017/03/politics/trump-putin-russia-timeline/, last accessed 5 October 2017.

39. Warren, Michael (2015). 'Trump: "Our Country Does Plenty of Killing"', *The Weekly Standard*, 18 December 2015, http://www.weeklystandard.com/trump-our-country-does-plenty-of-killing/article/2000295, last accessed 5 October 2017.

40. Filipov, David (2017). 'Here are 10 critics of Vladimir Putin who died violently or in suspicious ways', *The Washington Post*, 23 March 2017, https://www.washingtonpost.com/news/worldviews/wp/2017/03/23/here-are-ten-critics-of-vladimir-putin-who-died-violently-or-in-sus-picious-ways/?utm_term=.8726c7ddc0b7, last accessed 4 October 2017; Committee to Protect Journalists (n.d.). '58 Journalists Killed in Russia/Motive Confirmed', https://cpj.org/killed/europe/russia/, last accessed 4 October 2017; Roazen, Ben (2017). 'The Great Cost of Journalism in Vladimir Putin's Russia', *GQ*, 13 January 2017, https://www.gq.com/story/journalism-in-vladimir-putins-russia, last accessed 4 October 2017.

41. ABC News (2015). '"This Week" Transcript: Gov. Chris Christie, Sen. Bernie Sanders and Donald Trump', 20 December 2015, http://abc-news.go.com/Politics/week-transcript-gov-chris-christie-sen-bernie-sanders/story?id=35854734, last accessed 5 October 2017.

42. UK Home Office (2016). 'The Litvinenko inquiry: report into the death

of Alexander Litvinenko', report from the public inquiry chaired by Sir Robert Owen, 21 January 2016, https://www.gov.uk/government/publications/the-litvinenko-inquiry-report-into-the-death-of-alexander-litvinenko, last accessed 4 October 2017.

43. Campbell, Colin (2016). 'Donald Trump shrugs off allegation that Vladimir Putin "probably approved" assassination of ex-KGB agent', *Business Insider*, 27 January 2016, https://www.businessinsider.com.au/donald-trump-vladmir-putin-alexander-litvinenko-russia-2016–1, last accessed 5 October 2017.

44. Kaczynski and McDermott (2017).

45. Chan, Melissa (2016). 'Donald Trump Says Vladimir Putin Won't "Go Into Ukraine"', *TIME*, 31 July 2016, http://time.com/4432282/donald-trump-vladmir-putin-ukraine/, last accessed 5 October 2017.

46. BBC News (2017). 'Donald Trump: N Korea's Kim Jong-un a "smart cookie"', 30 April 2017, http://www.bbc.co.uk/news/world-asia-39764834, last accessed 5 October 2017.

47. Fredericks, Bob (2017). 'Donald Trump would be "honored" to meet Kim Jong Un', *New York Post*, 1 May 2017, http://nypost.com/2017/05/01/donald-trump-would-be-honored-to-meet-kim-jong-un/, last accessed 5 October 2017.

48. Casert, Raf, Geir Moulson and Associated Press (2017). 'EU, Germany criticize Poland in worsening rule of law spat', Associated Press, 29 August 2017, *Chicago Tribune*, http://www.chicagotribune.com/sns-bc-eu—europe-poland-20170829-story.html, last accessed 5 October 2017.

49. Davies, Christian and Daniel Boffey (2017). 'Donald Trump's Poland visit sparks fears of widening divisions in Europe', *The Guardian*, 4 July 2017, https://www.theguardian.com/us-news/2017/jul/04/donald-trump-poland-visit-fears-widening-europe-warsaw, last accessed 5 October 2017.

50. For instance, Trump's proposed state visit to the UK—an invitation extended by Prime Minister Theresa May, the first foreign leader to visit the newly elected Trump in January 2017—has been postponed indefinitely. It is widely believed that this is due to fears over massive protests. Plucinska, Joanna (2017). 'Donald Trump's UK state visit post-

poned', *Politico*, 11 June 2017, http://www.politico.eu/article/donald-trumps-uk-state-visit-postponed/, last accessed 4 October 2017.

51. Morris, Scott and Isaac Shapiro (2017). 'US Already $26 Billion Short of "Faire Share" Standard for Development Aid', Center for Global Development, 19 May 2017, https://www.cgdev.org/blog/us-already-26-billion-short-fair-share-standard-development-aid, last accessed 4 October 2017.

52. Rogin, Josh (2017). 'State Department considers scrubbing democracy promotion from its mission', *The Washington Post*, 1 August 2017, https://www.washingtonpost.com/news/josh-rogin/wp/2017/08/01/state-department-considers-scrubbing-democracy-promotion-from-its-mission/?utm_term=.f8e937b5b640, last accessed 5 October 2017.

53. Ibid.

54. Reagan, Ronald (1989). 'Farewell Address to the Nation', 11 January 1989, available from The American Presidency Project, http://www.presidency.ucsb.edu/ws/?pid=29650, last accessed 2 October 2017.

55. Pew Research (2017). 'U.S. Image Suffers as Publics Around World Question Trump's Leadership', 26 June 2017, http://www.pewglobal.org/2017/06/26/u-s-image-suffers-as-publics-around-world-question-trumps-leadership/, last accessed 5 October 2017.

56. Pew Research (2017). 'Globally, More Name U.S. Than China as World's Leading Economic Power', 13 July 2017, http://www.pewglobal.org/2017/07/13/more-name-u-s-than-china-as-worlds-leading-economic-power/, last accessed 5 October 2017.

11. THE GHOST OF DESPOTISM YET TO COME: A WARNING IN FOUR ACTS

1. Montanaro, Domenico, Rachel Wellford and Simone Pathe (2014). '2014 midterm election turnout lowest in 70 years', PBS, 10 November 2014, http://www.pbs.org/newshour/updates/2014-midterm-election-turn-out-lowest-in-70-years/, last accessed 4 October 2017.

2. Reuters (2016). 'Georgia detains six it says were trying to sell uranium', 18 April 2016, https://www.reuters.com/article/us-georgia-uranium/

georgia-detains-six-it-says-were-trying-to-sell-uranium-idUSKCN0XF-1HM, last accessed 4 October 2017.

3. *Korematsu v. United States* (1944). Supreme Court decision, 18 December 1944, available at https://www.law.cornell.edu/supremecourt/text/323/214, last accessed 4 October 2017.

4. Abramson, Alana (2016). 'What Trump Has Said About a Muslim Registry', ABC News, 18 November 2016, http://abcnews.go.com/Politics/trump-muslim-registry/story?id=43639946, last accessed 4 October 2017.

5. BBC News (2017). 'Trump: Stop terrorism by "whatever means" necessary', 18 August 2017, http://www.bbc.co.uk/news/world-us-canada-40977702, last accessed 4 October 2017.

6. Gallup (2017). 'Presidential Job Approval Center', data available at http://news.gallup.com/interactives/185273/presidential-job-approval-center.aspx, last accessed 4 October 2017.

CONCLUSION: HOW TO SAVE DEMOCRACY

1. Mackie, Chris (2016). 'Can we learn from Thucydides' writings on the Trump of ancient Athens?', *The Conversation*, 7 August 2016, https://theconversation.com/can-we-learn-from-thucydides-writings-on-the-trump-of-ancient-athens-63391, last accessed 2 October 2017. See also: Dorey, T. A. (1956). 'Aristophanes and Cleon', *Greece & Rome*, 3(2), 132–9.

2. Aristophanes, 'The Knights', *The Complete Greek Drama*, vol. 2 (trans. Eugene O'Neill Jr), lines 190–4. New York: Random House, 1938, available from the Perseus Project: http://www.perseus.tufts.edu/hopper/text?doc=urn:cts:greekLit:tlg0019.tlg002.perseus-eng1:175–212, last accessed 4 October 2017.

3. Hair, William Ivy (1996). *The Kingfish and his Realm: The life and times of Huey P. Long*. Baton Rouge, Louisiana: LSU Press.

4. Hargrave, W. Lee (2004). *LSU Law: The Louisiana State University Law School from 1906 to 1977*. Baton Rouge, Louisiana: LSU Press.

5. Kazin, Michael (2006). 'The Man Who Would Be King', *The Washington Post*, 11 June 2016, http://www.washingtonpost.com/wp-dyn/content/

article/2006/06/08/AR2006060801109.html, last accessed 4 October 2017.

6. Signer, Michael (2009). *Demagogue: the fight to save democracy from its worst enemies.* New York: St. Martin's Press.

7. Ibid, p. 113.

8. Milson, Andrew J., Chara Haeussler Bohan, Perry L. Glanzer, and J. Wesley Null, eds (2004). *Readings in American educational thought: From Puritanism to progressivism.* Charlotte, North Carolina: IAP, p. 184.

9. Montanaro, Domenico, Rachel Wellford, and Simon Pathe (2014). '2014 midterm election turnout lowest in 70 years', PBS Newshour, 10 November 2014, http://www.pbs.org/newshour/updates/2014-midterm-election-turnout-lowest-in-70-years/, last accessed 4 October 2017.

10. The Annenberg Public Policy Center (2017). 'Americans are poorly informed about basic constitutional provisions', 12 September 2017, https://cdn.annenbergpublicpolicycenter.org/wp-content/uploads/2017/09/Civics-survey-Sept-2017-complete.pdf, last accessed 4 October 2017.

11. United States Census Bureau (2017). 'Voting and Registration in the Election of November 2016', May 2017, https://www.census.gov/data/tables/time-series/demo/voting-and-registration/p20–580.html, last accessed 4 October 2017.

12. Begley, Sarah (2016). 'Hillary Clinton Leads by 2.8 Million in Final Popular Vote Count', *TIME*, 20 December 2016, http://time.com/4608555/hillary-clinton-popular-vote-final/, last accessed 4 October 2017.

13. Author's calculation based on publicly available data. For example, see ibid. combined with Real Clear Politics (2016). '2016 Republican Popular Vote', available from: https://www.realclearpolitics.com/epolls/2016/president/republican_vote_count.html, last accessed 4 October 2017.

14. Kaiser Family Foundation (2016). 'Medicaid Expansion Enrollment', https://www.kff.org/health-reform/state-indicator/medicaid-expansion-enrollment/?currentTimeframe=0&sortModel=%7B%22colId%22:%22Location%22,%22sort%22:%22asc%22%7D, last accessed 4 October 2017.

15. Mark Twain, *Notebook*, entry for February–March 1898.

16. Reagan, Ronald (1961). 'Encroaching Control', speech before the Phoenix Chamber of Commerce, 30 March 1961, transcript and audio available at https://archive.org/details/RonaldReagan-Encroaching Control, last accessed 4 October 2017.

17. Chicago Democracy Project. 'Election results for 1996 primary election, Illinois Senate, District 13', available from: http://chicagodemocracy.org/ElectionResults.jsp?election=crdd_primary,gis_entity_crdd_1996_Primary_Election,il_sen_13_dem, last accessed 4 October 2017; Peters, Gerhard and John Woolley (1999–2017). 'Election of 2008', The American Presidency Project, http://www.presidency.ucsb.edu/showelection.php?year=2008, last accessed 4 October 2017.

18. Ferjani, Said (2013). Senior official in the Ennahda political party. Personal interview, 21 October 2013, Tunis, Tunisia.

19. Ibid.

20. Fisher, Marc (2017). 'Who did Trump borrow his press tactics from? Joe McCarthy.', *The Washington Post*, 11 August 2017, https://www.washingtonpost.com/outlook/trumps-approach-to-the-press-mirrors-another-politicians-joe-mccarthy/2017/08/11/80186b0e-7c6f-11e7-a669-b400c5c7e1cc_story.html?utm_term=.26fef7b1fa52, last accessed 4 October 2017.

21. Bayley, Edwin R. (1981). *Joe McCarthy and the Press*. Madison, Wisconsin: University of Wisconsin Press.

22. Murrow, Edward R. (1954). 'A Report on Senator Joseph McCarthy', *See it Now*, CBS, 9 March 1954, video available from: https://www.youtube.com/watch?v=kgejIbN9UYA, last accessed 4 October 2017.